The Bassoon King

The

BASSOON KING

—

MY LIFE IN ART, FAITH, AND IDIOCY

—

Rainn Wilson

DUTTON
— est. 1852 —

DUTTON
—• est. 1852 •—

An imprint of Penguin Random House LLC
375 Hudson Street
New York, New York 10014

Copyright © 2015 by Rainn Wilson
Penguin supports copyright. Copyright fuels creativity, encourages diverse voices, promotes free speech, and creates a vibrant culture. Thank you for buying an authorized edition of this book and for complying with copyright laws by not reproducing, scanning, or distributing any part of it in any form without permission. You are supporting writers and allowing Penguin to continue to publish books for every reader.

DUTTON—EST. 1852 and DUTTON are registered trademarks of
Penguin Random House LLC

All photos courtesy of the author, except for page 28 © Shutterstock and
page 98 © The Science Picture Company.

LIBRARY OF CONGRESS CATALOGING-IN-PUBLICATION DATA
has been applied for.

ISBN 978-0-525-95453-8

Printed in the United States of America
1   3   5   7   9   10   8   6   4   2

Set in Mercury Text G1
Designed by Daniel Lagin

While the author has made every effort to provide accurate telephone numbers, Internet addresses, and other contact information at the time of publication, neither the publisher nor the author assumes any responsibility for errors or for changes that occur after publication. Further, the publisher does not have any control over and does not assume any responsibility for author or third-party websites or their content.

Penguin is committed to publishing works of quality and integrity. In that spirit, we are proud to offer this book to our readers; however, the story, the experiences, and the words are the author's alone. Some names and identifying characteristics have been changed to protect the privacy of the individuals involved.

For Holiday and Walter, my blue skies

SPECIAL THANKS

———

I want to thank the publishers of this book for allowing me to have a special thanks section in which to thank them. I want to also thank Greg Daniels, Paul Lieberstein, and B. J. Novak for their help on the foreword. I also want to thank Mindy Kaling for being so yucky. I want to thank Aaron Lee for being a true friend and one of the funniest people alive. I want to thank the stars of our galaxy for reminding us of how small and significant we are. Matthew McConaughey, thank you for that loan. I want to thank the Germans for all the good times. Hummus. Thanks to Jill Schwartzman for being a terrific editor. Oprah, thanks for the loan. I'll pay you back once I get my next residual check. Call me. Mark Schulman and Richard Abate, thanks. I want to thank my various parents for their patience and understanding. I imagine it must be hard to have your story be written by a minor-TV-celebrity son without having a chance to respond. Also, my dad taught me about art and faith, and for that I'll always be grateful. Phil Pardi, *gracias*. Thanks, *Office* cast. Miss you guys! Rhett Diessner, Ken Bowers. Mark Bamford. Thank you, everyone who bought this book, and double thanks to you if you actually finish it. Thanks, Matt Hoyle.

Thank you, divine spirit mystery of the universe, for letting there be music and children and language and hummus. Kevin O'Neill and Holly and Dylan Reid. Thank you, television and Nick Offerman. Thanks, Mose. Thanks, NBC. I want to thank George R. R. Martin and Marshawn Lynch and Thom Yorke for their awesomeness. Editors, please cut this sentence. If it's still in the final version of the "Special Thanks" section I'll know you didn't actually read the book. Thank you, Arnold Palmer, for the most delightful of beverages.

Most of all I want to thank my wife and soul mate, Holiday Reinhorn, the best writer and person I know, for her expert notes, incredible heart, and, as in all things, her invaluable support. Also, thank you for lending me that money, honey. I'll pay you back. Later, though. I gotta pay Oprah and Matthew back first.

CONTENTS

———

CONTENTS

FOREWORD

──────

By Dwight Kurt Schrute

I AM THE REGIONAL MANAGER OF THE DUNDER MIFFLIN PAPER Company in Scranton, Pennsylvania. I have been chosen at random to write a foreword for this book. The request came in a letter that my cousin Mose first mistook for a sweepstakes win. He ran around our farm, waving the letter for the better part of an afternoon. But I am not gullible like my cousin, who is more book smart than worldly smart.

When someone asks me to do a task, the first thing I do is determine whether the request is some sort of trick. If the request is a trick, then I do not do that thing. If the request is not a trick, then I do the best version of that thing that man or beast has ever undertaken. (You would be surprised how often it turns out to be a trick. If Michael Scott asks me, I do it anyway, though.)

I cannot adequately determine if this request is a trick, so I'm just going to do the thing in a regular, normal way.

I have never written anything like a book foreword before. In fact, I mostly write requisition forms, harvest inventories, and performance reviews. I am very good at these. An example:

Harvest Inventory

Potatoes: 60 lbs

Onions: 51 lbs

Beets: 1,240,567 lbs

I think the above work speaks for itself. It needs to, otherwise it is a useless list.

Once, I wrote a term paper on why there should be no taxes, using examples from post–World War I Germany and pre–World War III Germany.

Once, I wrote a letter to a girl in my high school named Ilona Staller. She never wrote me back. Her loss. Ilona, if you are reading this, you made a tremendous error as you could have gotten with THIS (I am pointing to my genitalia).

Let me be perfectly clear: I don't like this book. I don't care about "funny stories" regarding some stupid actor. Other than Charles Bronson and anyone from the cast of *Game of Thrones*. And Bruce Lee. And Lackawanna County Honorary Deputy Sheriffs Paul and Mira Sorvino. And Alexander Godunov from the movie *Witness*. And I love Sam Neill from *Jurassic Park* and *Omen III: The Final Conflict*. How come he's not in more stuff? He's got such a long, thin mouth. I'd definitely read his book.

Also, I once read *The Dolph Lundgren Handbook: Everything You Need to Know About Dolph Lundgren* when I was nineteen. But there were no funny stories. Just FACTS about perhaps the greatest Swedish actor of the 1980s. Did you know that Dolph Lundgren as Ivan Drago punched Sylvester Stallone so hard during the filming of *Rocky IV* that he put him in the hospital for nine days? NINE DAYS!!! I would love to be put in the hospital by Dolph Lundgren.

I do not read books for funny stories or whimsical insights. *Ever.* If I am reading a book, it is for the purpose of absorbing factual information about what is happening on Planet Earth, Middle Earth, Westeros, *Galactica*, Asgard, Mount Olympus, or Lackawanna County.

This writer, "Rainn Wilson," is a laughable idiot. He thinks he's funny, but he's merely pathetic. Unless you think stories about weird religions, nerd-loving parents, bassoons, and acting are fascinating. I sure don't.

Ooooh, you did live plays in the theater. Big deal. So did the cast of *Glee* and nobody cares about them anymore.

Oooooh, so you were an actor on TV shows. Well so was Jack Bauer. You don't see Jack Bauer writing a book about his life. (He's got serious work to do, plus his life is classified. And when the hell would he write, anyway? I've seen every minute of his day, the guy doesn't even have time to urinate!) Actually, maybe he has written a book about his life. I wouldn't know. The last time I was in that section of the bookstore was a long time ago, and I stormed out in anger because they did not have a book by Sam Neill that I had gotten my heart set on during the long drive to the Wilkes-Barre Borders (now defunct) from my farm (still in business, thank you very much).

OOOOH, YOU'RE A MEMBER OF AN OBSCURE, STRANGE-SOUNDING RELIGIOUS MINORITY. WELL, WHY DON'T YOU RENT *WITNESS* AND WATCH THOSE TEENAGE PUNKS DAB ICE CREAM ON ALEXANDER GODUNOV AND LET'S SEE WHO'S BEEN PERSECUTED WORSE!

Also, why is this privileged Hollywood windbag writing a *memoir* when he's in his forties? It doesn't make any sense. He's not even close to death. (Although, after reading this pile of steaming goat feces, I wish he was.)

Fact: NO. ONE. CARES.

So why am I writing the foreword at all?

Easy. The money. The publisher agreed to pay me three hundred dollars ($300!!!) for the first 1,000 words of this foreword and 33 cents a word thereafter.

Take a word like "at." Watch this: *AT*—boom! Thirty-three cents! (And another 33 cents for the *boom*!) This whole diversion is about $7.59. (But enough about the math, I'm not paid for numbers.)

Suck on this, publisher:

Oafidjf;aksdj; vkjna sd;kjvn;kasdjnvkjansdlk vjnalskdjnvlkasjndv kajnsdkjn adkvjna klsdjn laksdjnvkajs ndvkjnas djknvdkj n;ad ksjnvakvjnkasdjnvk anvddsvd siufhlauk hclkruhvl kvavhkrjclakrjh znlkrj.nkjnr.kjn>KJ N>KEJN.kJN>KjN>KJNiu4f hliaeuhae rufo a84oiufahhi 4uakh43h iufaosdfao ijdf;lasdj;cijaei jejksck jh.zu ekh.ku hsj.jndc 123456789 asdf asdf asdf

Well, who's the sucker now, Dutton? (A division of Penguin, which is a division of Penguin Random House, which is co-owned by Bertelsmann, a German media conglomerate that was the single biggest publisher of Nazi war propaganda in the '30s, which many of your readers would conclude is a very, very bad thing.)

Need a few more words . . .

The quick brown fox jumped over the lazy dogs.

That sentence uses every single letter in the alphabet, FYI.

So does this one I just came up with:

Zachary's X-ray is very jubilant, wanting pom fokd q.

Actually, let me use this opportunity to discuss books that I want to write. Or read.

There is a definite lack of cookbooks that focus on venison and woodland game. Let's say you have a freezer full of skunk steaks and the back half of a bear and you want to make a delicious meal in twenty minutes armed with only an acetylene torch and an ax. What do you do?

The answer will be available in my new bestseller, *Meat Me in the Freezer,* a novel by Dwight Kurt Schrute.

Other book ideas:

Mennonite Ghost Stories

Some of the scariest ghosts don't use any technology and have big round hats.

Conspiracy Theories: Who's Really Behind Them?

The book they didn't want you to read and will probably kill you if they ever find out that you have read.

Seeds for Idiots

Soy, corn, wheat, sorghum, rice, barley, beet, etc. . . .

Short-Sleeve Shirts

Effortless style in a world gone long-sleeve bananas!

Hold This Book over a Candle

Fun games for kids written entirely with my own secret invisible ink. Ink that comes from a special pen I keep in my pants.

How to Make Love Like the Kaiser

Sex tips from pre–World War I Germany and pre–World War III Germany. With a foreword by Angela Martin!

Rolling in the Bones of Oxen:
A New Generation of Schrutes

A pictorial history of my son, Philip. Over four thousand photos!

Ultimately, I wanted to be a part of this project because as a lifelong employee of a paper company, and this being a book, tens of thousands of trees will have been chopped down and processed in the making and binding of it. You are reading this waste of a book on one of the most practical, renewable, and flat substances known to man. I hope you'll buy it, have a book-burning party because of how terrible it is, and then buy another one just for the hell of it. This may not be economical or convenient, but it's good for the paper business, which in turn is good for me.

And if you want to write angry letters to the publishers I hope you'll choose Dunder Mifflin's twenty-weight bond. Treat yourself right with DM's smooth-writing, high-rag-content bond in cream, white, and ecru!

Oh, and if you are reading this on a computerized reading machine, *F@*& YOU*!!!

*Note for the editor: That was 1,400 words. Now 1,408. 1,410 total. 1,412. You owe me $300 plus .33¢ x 419.

I'll give you this last sentence for free as a bonus.

Chapter 1

WHAT SHALL WE NAME BABY FATHEAD?

———

I HAD THE BIGGEST, FATTEST HEAD OF ANY BABY THAT WAS ever born into the human species. My head was—and remains—a combination of the head from the alien in *Alien* and a prize-winning albino casaba melon from the Iowa State Fair.

I feel truly sorry for my parents, Patricia (Shay) Whitman and Robert (Bob) Wilson, when I imagine them cradling my doughy giganticness in the rain-soaked winter of 1966 on their houseboat in Seattle. I was one of those tots that you see and gasp under your breath in quizzical horror. I wasn't one of those babies that made it easy for viewers to hide their surprised revulsion. I'm sure no one knew what to say when they saw my white, bloated, Macy's Thanksgiving Day Parade head lolling about on my snowy, damp, potato-sack body. I was like some kind of larva. I was the color of grubworms that have never seen the sun. Picture an ashen manatee with a tiny human face. Now picture this creature screaming to have its diaper changed.

You get the idea.

No, you don't. I need to keep going.

I'm not sure if you fully understand the large-headed, pale horror of baby Rainn. If there were a maggot with vaguely human features, wrapped in swaddling clothes, that would have been me. The University of Washington hospital probably bleached the entire pediatric ward after I left due to my resemblance to a life-size white blood corpuscle. I was like Louie Anderson with the head of E.T. (Note: I wanted to include a baby photo here, but the publisher refused, citing research that 80 percent of people read celebrity biographies while eating lunch.) If the nurse at the hospital had swapped me with a big-eyed albino hippo baby, that would have explained everything. Instead, my parents were handed a lumpy, Jabba the Hutt–like infant that made sounds like a calf being strangled by an octopus. Me.

Okay, *now* you get the idea. Moving on.

Obviously I don't know much about my infancy and early childhood. Just weird little details I've gleaned from my curiously uncommunicative, bohemian, proto-hippie parents.

From what I understand, after I was born a furious debate raged between Bob and Shay over what to name me. You see, in case you didn't manage to gather it from the cover of this book, or from the title credits of *The Office* or *Backstrom*, my name is Rainn. R-A-I-N-N. Two *n*s. How did I come to have this moniker? How did my parents arrive at it? It's quite simple actually.

Weird name + weird kid = weird parents.

To call my parents odd is perhaps the biggest understatement any person could ever make. Kind of like calling Hitler mean or Warren Buffett well-off. There will be much written about my parents. All of them.

My mom, Patricia, changed her name to Shay in 1965. She was raised on a farm in Weyauwega, Wisconsin, and spent a year living with chickens. I'm not exaggerating. Her brothers and sister were all older.

Her mom died when she was two (appendicitis) and her dad didn't have the ability to watch her and farm the farm at the same time.

(Note: I don't actually know what Grampa Rollie Whitman did on that farm other than what I've gleaned from TV shows like *Little House on the Prairie* and books like *Charlotte's Web* and the Bible. He probably "sowed seed" and drove a tractor around with a floppy hat. Actually, it was probably a baseball cap because he was pretty macho and it was Wisconsin. I imagine there were animals to "slop" and various things that needed trimming, etc. I know there's a time for planting a time for harvesting and for *everything there is a season, turn turn turn*. This I know from the Byrds.)

So Rollie Whitman would leave my three- or four-year-old eventual mommy, Patty (soon to be Shay), in with the chickens and pigs for a good part of the day. She would play with the chicks and the worms and the corn kernels and piglets and pebbles and mud balls in said coop and wait for her older siblings to come back from the one-room schoolhouse several miles away. That experience alone is enough to drive any person nuttier than Björk or Cher. Throw in a lot of rampant alcoholism and a family that was only capable of expressing one emotion, *anger*, and you've got a recipe for weird.

My dad, Robert George Wilson, also had a pretty miserable childhood. His dad, Chester Wilson, was an alcoholic who looked like Gollum's fat Midwestern uncle and allegedly stole his lightning rod company, Wilcor Grounding Systems, from his very own brother and made millions off of it while his brother moved back to Minnesota and had to run Wilson Brothers Auto Parts in Thief River Falls.

(True actual story: I'm a little resentful of ol' Chester, as we were always very poor while I was growing up and he was super rich, a millionaire member of the Seattle Yacht Club who lived in the wealthiest part of the city. Also, the only present I ever got from ol' Chester was when I was ten—a plaid thermos, which had obviously been regifted. I once tried to use the thermos and put hot chocolate in it. The glass interior of said thermos exploded and shot up toward my face, narrowly missing my eyeballs. RIP, Chester. I hope you're sipping champagne out of that big plaid thermos in the sky, looking down at us Wilsons with mercy and the teeniest bit of remorse.)

When my dad was about eight, his mother was staying at a sanatorium in Chicago, where she was being treated for tuberculosis. Sanatoriums, it should be noted, were used to treat almost all women's health issues of the era. One day he and his sister, my aunt Wendy, got all dressed up to visit their mom when she was very close to being released and there was a commotion. From a bathroom window she had seen her children in the courtyard below, run to greet them, slipped, and hit her head on a sink and died.

When I finally got the full story out of my father only a few years ago, he told it with such grace and sadness it broke my heart. He told me about going home in his little suit and tie, sitting at the kitchen table, and saying to his (probably drunk and angry) dad and relatives: "But who is going to take care of me?"

And that really is the question, folks. Isn't it?

My grandfather promptly hired a nanny from Minnesota who had a daughter from being knocked up by a traveling salesman of the northern reaches. Chester immediately re-impregnated said nanny and was forced by cultural pressures to marry her. She was quite resentful of my dad and my aunt Wendy, Chester's original children, and was terribly abusive to them. To this day, Bob refers to her as "Evil of Doom" and tells stories of abuse that would curl your spine.

One of my favorites from his childhood was how Chester bought a little "one-armed bandit" slot machine and would give my dad his weekly allowance in change and make him put it in the coin slot. If it "hit," he'd do great and make several dollars. If not, my dad had no allowance for the week. Of course, it never hit and my dad went money-free for most of his childhood. This was a lesson in "hard knocks" and "how the world works," I suppose. Dick move, Grampa.

My dad had the soul of an artist. For a middle-class boy from Downers Grove, Illinois, there could be nothing stranger than an early interest in Tchaikovsky, Lord Byron, and abstract expressionism. Chester probably thought he had fathered an alien. And in some ways he had.

At any rate, these two "interesting" people, products of their peculiar childhood traumas, lived in an artsy abode and had a peculiar conundrum: find a name for the imminent advent of their very own baby Stewie.

Apparently, my mom fought for months to name me Thucydides. Yes, *that* Thucydides. You know, the ancient Greek historian, author of the international bestseller *The History of the Peloponnesian War*.

I truly don't know what she could have been thinking. Was there any thought or follow-through to that idea? Rainn is bad enough. What parent in their right mind would want to name their child after someone ancient, Greek, and unpronounceable?

What would it have been like to have been named Thucydides and be playing on a third-grade playground? With Rainn as my name I was frequently tortured at recess. With Thucydides, I would have been eviscerated and excoriated in contemptuous teasing until, like Carrie, I would have needed to seek my revenge with psychic dark magic.

So why Rainn?

My dad was way into Rainer Maria Rilke, the mystical Austrian poet. He was the guy who famously and perceptively wrote:

> Have patience with everything that remains unsolved in your heart. Try to love the questions themselves, like locked rooms and like books written in a foreign language. Do not now look

for the answers. They cannot now be given to you because you could not live them. It is a question of experiencing everything. At present you need to live the question. Perhaps you will gradually, without even noticing it, find yourself experiencing the answer, some distant day.

Living the questions. That's the key.

So, my dad wanted to call me Rainer. The only problem? There's a giant mountain that hovers over the skyline of Seattle, which is perilously close to the name: Mount Rainier.

I picture weird chicken-coop Mommy and slot-machine Daddy having a conversation about my name on the deck of their rainy houseboat on Lake Union in Seattle.

Shay: I want to name our baby Geebothrax.

Bob: Why?

Shay: Because I like the sound of it.

Bob: I'm not sure. . . .

Shay: Well, what would you name him?

Bob: I want to name him Lord Byron Tchaikovsky Pollock.

Shay: You can't just name him after your favorite artists! That's not how this works, Bob!

Bob: Well, you can't just name him after a made-up alien warlord.

Shay: Geebothrax has a nice ring to it. Besides, he kind of looks like an alien warlord with the way his head looks in the ultrasound.

Bob: Ultrasounds haven't been invented yet.

Shay: Oh. Well, how about Thucydides?

Bob: Who?

Shay: You know, the ancient Greek historian, author of *The History of the Peloponnesian War*?

[pause]

Bob: Maybe Geebothrax isn't that bad after all.

Shay: We could combine them. How about Thucydithrax?

Bob: What about Rainer?

Shay: After the Austrian mystic poet?

Bob: Exactly—

Shay: Or that enormous mountain right over there.

Bob: [gulps] We could switch it up so people don't get him confused with the mountain.

Shay: Like Rain?

Bob: Too hippie-ish.

Shay: Hippies haven't been invented yet. It's 1965.

Bob: Oh, right. Well, then, let's stick an extra letter in there for no apparent reason whatsoever.

Shay: Rrain! I love it!

They shake hands and gaze out at the mist over Lake Union, wondering about their ability to ever truly master that most difficult of tasks, for which all else is but preparation: *love.*

(Note: Feel free to perform this conversation as a scene in your acting class. Post the video online and I'll give you acting notes, gratis.)

So "Rainn" was decided upon and my proto-hippie ne'er-do-wells (nerd-do-wells) continued with their midsixties lives in the rainy seaport of Seattle.

The city of Seattle was a mossy, shambly town with a dubious history.

It was created in the late 1800s by Chief Sealth, who invented salmon and wisdom. White men settled there because they loved coffee and kayaking and wanted a place to wear their new jerkins of "flannel." The world's first "indie" group was a jug band called Pearl Jam-boree that refused representation and would only play late nights at a waterfront bar called Cobain's Pub. Chief Sealth was noted as saying, "I saw them before they sold out and made all those lame gramophone recordings of 1882. Now *everybody* likes them" (rolls eyes, puffs on enormous pipe).

None of that is remotely true, but it would be a way cooler history than the boring lumber-and-pioneer-filled one we were all taught in seventh-grade Washington State history class.

We Seattle-ites always wanted the city to be where it eventually ended up, which is not such a good thing in retrospect. Be careful what you wish for. It was a backwater in the 1970s, famous only for the film *It Happened at the World's Fair* with Elvis Presley as a crop-dusting pilot dancing under the Space Needle with a little Chinese girl and wooing a forgettable, pretty young nurse with his guitar. As a city, we couldn't get any respect back then, even with the 1979 world champion SuperSonics.

We just wanted people to like us! We wanted to be San Francisco! How come everyone in the world loved San Francisco and knew every morsel of Frisco history when our little mossy burg was such a forgotten cultural backwater?! San Francisco had the 49ers and the Golden

Gate Bridge and Chinatown and Rice-A-Roni and cable cars. We had Boeing. San Francisco had redwoods and Berkeley and Steinbeck and Alcatraz. We had . . . Boeing.

Okay, now I get why.

Seattle was a moody little town, nestled under mountains and fir trees and drizzly, low, maritime clouds. There were lumberjacks around. At least there must have been with all the trucks of trees proceeding down from the mountains filled with "Washington toothpicks." There were fishermen and airplane assemblers and surly, wool-clad Scandinavian laborers drinking Rainier Beer by the gallon.

Eventually we got a baseball and a football team, but that still didn't help us too much. It wasn't until the advent of Microsoft, grunge rock, *Sleepless in Seattle,* and Starbucks in the early nineties that Seattle became a bit of a cultural force and got finally put on the map. And what did that get us? A bunch of annoying Californians moving to the Pacific Northwest and driving up the GD real estate market! Just ask any Seattle-ite.

But I'm a little ahead of myself. Back to the midsixties. It was somewhere around this time of maritime child-naming that my parents both became members of the Baha'i Faith.

The Baha'i Faith is a lovely, peaceful religion that believes all religions are actually one faith and all people are worshipping the same God. This all-loving God sends down special teachers every thousand years or so to impart the next chapter in humanity's ongoing, inevitable spiritual education. Besides believing that Krishna, the Buddha, Abraham, Moses, Jesus, and Muhammad were all divine spokesmen, Baha'is are followers of the most recent of these "manifestations of God," a man named Baha'u'llah (whose name means "the Glory of God") who lived in Persia in the mid-1800s and brought a modern message of peace for today's disunited world.

There's a lot more to it than this, but I just don't want to get all "religion-y" on you so soon in the story. Please refer to the addendum at the end of the book, "The Baha'i Faith: An Introduction," to find out more.

Just do me a favor. Don't Wikipedia it. That drives me crazy. You'll end up a "wikipediot."™*

So my parents, as oddball as they already were (and I think I've painted a pretty clear portrait of their oddball-ishness to this point), decided to become members of an obscure religious faith, which removed them even further from the mainstream.

Bob had found out about the Baha'i Faith from some bohemian dude he met on the not-so-mean streets of Seattle and had a profound, mystical experience in which he was inspired to embrace what the Baha'i Faith professed was indeed true. After looking them up in the phone book, he got an appointment with the Local Spiritual Assembly of the Baha'is of Seattle (as there are no clergy in the religion, democratically elected bodies serve as administrative heads on the local, national, and international level) and told them he wanted to become a Baha'i. The group of nine members incredulously told him, essentially, "Well, you can't just walk in off the street and become a Baha'i—you have to at least read some books first." They handed him a big stack of Baha'i books and told him to come back when he had finished them. He read them all and came back the next week, and after quizzing him a bit, they somewhat reluctantly allowed him to join. Things were a bit different back then.

My dad was a clerk at several of Seattle's best bookstores at the

---

* Wikipediots are message board dwellers who, while living in their parents' basement or working in IT departments, read the Wikipedia entry on, say, "chaos theory" and then hold forth as if they're an expert to all their friends.

A global religion with over five million followers that is rich in history, writings, ideas, and mystical, mysterious beauty simply cannot be encapsulated by a couple pages of dry, disjointed facts collectively written by unwashed Wiki-nerds.

time, Hartman's and Shorey's. He spent his time painting abstract oil paintings, listening to Dave Brubeck and Mahler, and, now, reading mystical texts from nineteenth-century Persia.

In 1968 a strange and dramatic thing happened that resulted in my mom and dad getting a divorce. I'm not going to tell you what this event was. I'm saving it for later because for me it's pretty darned profound and has to do with the course of my life's journey. (And, frankly, I'm saving the juicy details for special dramatic effect in chapter 7.)

My folks got a divorce. My mom took off and I remained with my dad.

He was heartbroken and devastated and did what any recently divorced bohemian Baha'i dad with a tumescent tot would do in his situation: He moved to Central America and got remarried.

Chapter 2

THE WORMS OF NICARAGUA

—

APPARENTLY, BOB'S BLOATED, IVORY PUPA MADE MY DAD somewhat of a chick magnet, and he remarried as soon as he possibly could to my stepmom, Kristin, also a Seattle-ite and a Baha'i.

Kristin Harris (now Wilson), a recent graduate of Seattle University, had come down to Central America at the same time as my father. She babysat me a lot and was very sweet and kind and pretty, and so my dad married her in a trice.

They had no idea what they were getting into.

After a brief stint in Mexico City, where the wedding occurred, we ended up for some reason in the town of Bluefields on the remote Caribbean coast of Nicaragua. Bluefields is a loco place.

There still are no roads in or out of Bluefields, just a dirt landing strip cut out of the thick jungle. Or you can drive from Managua to the mountain town of Rama and then take a five-hour ferry ride down the Rio Escondido. The city was founded by Dutch pirates on the lam from the Spanish, and the Mosquito Coast was claimed by the English soon thereafter. This remote, jungle-y swamp became a haven for escaped slaves from throughout the Caribbean, and many locals can claim ancestry from the slaves who got down with the now essentially extinct Arawak Indians of the Caribbean.

Many races and cultures mix into a giant, swampy jambalaya in Bluefields. You would, on the docks of the seaport, hear Jamaican patois, various versions of Creole, Spanish, and Miskito (the local native dialect), as well as many variations of English. The music was a mash-up of reggae and dancehall from Jamaica, calypso and soca from Trinidad, son from Cuba, salsa, and even country and western, which was brought to the area by the American employees of the venal United Fruit Company (which raped and pillaged the land for cheap bananas as well as staged multiple coups and invasions all over the hemisphere! Hence the name "banana republic." An amazing history. Check it out. *But not on Wikipedia*.). Many of the popular songs of all genres were then re-recorded in Bluefields with Miskito lyrics!

(In fact my dad later had a radio show on Sunday afternoons on the local Catholic-owned Bluefields radio station, where he played his classical music records and talked about the composers and their syphilitic lives.)

And now? One of the poorest sections of the Caribbean is also one of the principal havens for drug runners moving cocaine from Colombia to Mexico. The narco-traffickers control the politics and the local economy on every level. Fishermen can make a great deal of pesos when they find "white lobsters," the bales of cocaine that float up to shore, having been thrown off cigarette boats during occasional drug raids. It's also one of the most dangerous places in Central America, with a ridiculous murder and kidnapping rate. Throw in malaria, dysentery, sharks, parasites, quicksand, and jellyfish, and you've got yourself a party!

———

The good and loco people of Bluefields probably didn't know what hit them when our weird, white family showed up: my dad; my naïve, curly-haired stepmom, Kristin; and a blond, thunder-egg-headed, wide-eyed, three-year-old gringo potato boy. For seventy-five dollars a month we rented this giant, haunted Victorian house on top of a hill, overlooking the rickety seaside town.

Everyone there probably hoped that the ghosts would eat us like in the movie *Poltergeist*. The local rumors about our haunted house involved a crazy American shrimp boat captain who had kept the body of his dead wife up in the attic and whose corpse was eventually discovered there. Neighbors swore that there was an occasional late-night light in the attic window, and that was the lamp of the ship captain waiting for his wife.

My dad swears that there were real, actual ghosts in that rickety old house. Every night he would hear this mysterious *screeeeeeee* sound. Like something scraping on the floor. And every morning he would come downstairs and notice that the furniture was arranged a bit different. So he got some chalk and put little circles around the chair and table legs to mark their locations on the floor. In the morning, after once again hearing the scraping noises, he noticed that literally every single piece of furniture had been slid several inches or several feet outside of the chalk circles. Freaky.

So my dad did what any good Baha'i living in a haunted Victorian house in Central America would do. He said some Baha'i prayers for the dead. And you know what? It worked. Those pesky Nicaraguan poltergeists stopped their shenanigans forevermore. Take that, Nicaraguan poltergeists! Take that, ghoulish shrimp boat captain! Baha'i power, yeah!

I was pretty young in Nicaragua, but I have some very distinct and fond memories of the insanity of that place. I remember seeing several movies, including *The Sound of Music*, at the movie theater downtown. The theater experience was a little different down there. The place would be PACKED, no matter what the film. You would bring in food and beer and babies, and there were rats and stray dogs begging for food everywhere. People talked through the entire movie, which blared at full volume on the cheap, tinny sound system. And the strangest thing of all was that because Nicaragua was so Catholic, anything deemed "disrespectful" to the nuns had been edited from the movie. So every time a nun started to sing or dance or joke, there was a hard, abrupt edit and the film would skip jerkily ahead to the next scene, making the film about half as long and far more fun.

My dad took many trips out in the jungles to visit the Miskito Indians. He tells some amazing stories from his time there. Once, in the remotest possible village, he was asked to teach them baseball. He got these hard round fruits from the trees and had them carve a bat out of a branch with a machete. They cleared out a little field from the jungle and the entire village lined up to play—men, women, children, and even grandparents. The fruit-baseballs would take about three at bats before finally exploding into mush, at which the entire village would applaud. They played all day long, day after day, from sunup to sundown, and who knows, maybe they're still playing to this day.

He tells of listening to one of the moon landings on the radio, and how when they translated to the tribesmen that there were men actually walking on the moon, the men started pointing at the moon and laughing at the ridiculousness of that concept.

Once, my dad tells me, a Miskito man came up to him and said to him with confused disbelief, "Mr. Bob. Is it true that in America there is actually a man who *doesn't believe in GOD*?!"

My dad responded that there was indeed a person like that and the man walked away shaking his head incredulously.

Because I was so young, my memories pop like Technicolor acid-dream postcards, spliced and pasted together, flickering in a mental strobe light.

- I remember Kristin getting caught in quicksand on the muddy beach and being pulled out of the sinkhole by a guy with a tree branch.
- I remember a friend of ours emerging from the ocean after a swim. He was screaming and falling to his knees, covered in jellyfish stings.
- I remember running and flying kites on the hilltop with the local kids, all of them barefoot, me in giant rubber boots that cheese-grated my ankle bones.
- I remember "Devil Day," the local equivalent of Halloween, when terrifying men dressed as devils in outfits adorned with wings ran around with fireworks. They would chase kids, pick them up, and scare the holy bejeezus out of them by tickling them and screaming in their faces. I was so horrified that this would happen to me that I refused to go outside. (I'm pretty sure this was the work of the Catholic Church, turning a fun pagan festival into a helpful, traumatic reminder of the evils of Satan.)
- I remember bulls being driven and herded up and down the mud streets by Nicaraguan cowboys who lived in the jungle.
- I remember the best oatmeal ever made, served up by our cook, Antonia, and the taste of fresh shrimp and fried plantains.

But what I remember most about Nicaragua is the critters. Creatures abound in the muddy tropics. We had a tremendous variety of pets and animals and pests sprawling every which way around our tropical compound.

Here's a compendium of my history with the varmints of Nicaragua:

Mosquito

I remember awakening every morning to a fog of whining mosquitoes clamoring around the mosquito netting that surrounded my bed. I'm talking hundreds of the things. And they were quick too. Not the fat, lazy, drolling mosquito DC-10s of North America. No, these were the malaria-bearing, dive-bombing, demon-hummingbird mosquitoes of the Caribbean swamps. Fierce, bloodlust-filled insect TIE fighters. I would spend about an hour after waking trying to kill each one of them by slapping them through the netting and watching them fall, curled and dry, to their tiny deaths. Who needed video games?

My dad actually caught malaria from one of the buggers and almost died after recurring bouts of 103-degree tropical fevers and shaking and cold sweats and delusions. I remember him on his sickbed and remember trying to piece together in my four- or five-year-old brain that he had gotten this terrible illness from one of those little annoying insects that I slapped silly every morning. It just didn't add up. He's fine, by the way. He didn't die. In fact, he's probably reading this right now. Hi, Dad!

Dog

We had a stray dog named Hieronymus Bosch. You know, the insane, postapocalyptic fifteenth-century Flemish painter obsessed with the nine circles of hell? He looked exactly like you'd think a stray mutt eating garbage off the streets of an impoverished port city would look like. I'm betting that to this day we are the only people in the history of Central America who have ever or will ever own a dog named Hieronymus Bosch.

Parrot

Besides the flocks of actual jungle parrots that would cackle and zoom about the swampy, jungle-y trees, we had a "pet" parrot named Jose who would only say one word: *Jose*. Over and over and over again. "Jose!" "Jose!" It got pretty annoying. Even for a four-year-old. "Rrrawk! Jose!" He spent most of his time with a sheet over his cage, as that would effectively shut him up. I would feed him bananas that grew on the giant green banana trees in our backyard and would try to get him to say *"Hola"* or *"Rainn"* or *"Buenos días."* Anything other than "Jose." To no avail. Now that I think about it, maybe his name wasn't Jose, but his previous owner might have been named Jose. Or maybe he was a racist parrot and just called everybody Jose in a kind of contempt for all things Latin.

Sloth

We had a pet sloth named Andrew. Sloths are bizarre. They are SUPER slow and nocturnal. (Like a lot of my Midwestern relatives, now that I come to think of it.) Andrew was kept in a cage on our front porch. Sloths, if you don't know this, are ridiculously strong, and EVERY night, Andrew would slowly, slowly, slowly bend the bars of his cage, make his way out, and seek food or whatever the hell he would seek on his lugubrious nightly escape. Every morning we would gaze at the bent bars on the top of the cage and scout around for our lethargic escapee. They are so incredibly slow that he would only get about thirty feet away, max. We would find him in a banana bush or a palm tree or a tropical shrub, having fallen asleep with a twig or a leaf in his mouth. We would then return him to his cage, bend the bars back into place, and start the whole nightly Sartre-ian exercise over again.

Oyster

My dad didn't really know what he'd do for work when he got to Nicaragua, but when he saw the endless oyster beds lying off the coast he got a brilliant idea: Put those suckers into jars and send 'em up to the big city for cash, baby, yeah! He employed several dozen Miskito workers and even had a profit-sharing program for them. This worked out well for several years, but he got tired of bribing all the corrupt Nicaraguan officials, and his enterprise shut down after about a billion oysters and a couple thousand dollars.

Amoeba

Amoebas are the jellyfish-like microscopic creatures you study in seventh-grade biology. They blurb around, sucking up and surrounding things like in the fifties horror movie *The Blob*. Apparently they sometimes lodge in your gut and make you *crazy* sick. This is called amoebic dysentery. Apparently it comes with jet-stream diarrhea. And I got it. I get heartsick just thinking about how hard that must have been for little Rainn, lying limp in his humid mosquito-encrusted bed, shooting an occasional fire-hose spray of diarrhea out of his little ass-trumpet with amoebas gurgling around in his innards, devouring things.

Monkey

The neighbors had a monkey named Chacho. He rode on their dog's back. He would swing over to our house all the time and eat our sugar cubes, beg for food, and poop in our kitchen. He was pesky and my parents hated him and would shoo him out the window by banging saucepans.

Outhouse Vermin

We didn't have indoor plumbing. We had a rickety outhouse. And the poo-and-pee hole was filled with ridiculous amounts of creatures that would scatter when you flashed your flashlight down there: lizards, spiders, roaches, and albino frogs. Yes, that's right. White, cave-dwelling frogs that had never seen the light of day and habitated in our poop. Where the hell did those things come from? How did they find our outhouse? Were they in every outhouse in Nicaragua? Unknown. White poo frogs. Think about it. Sketch one in the margin of this book!

Boar

There were many Indian members of the Baha'i Faith up the Mosquito Coast in a place called Monkey Point, and we would often visit them in boats. You could take a little motorboat up the coastline, close to shore, which was very long and grueling, or a big fishing boat, which was less long and grueling. Kristin and I took the fishing boat and got terrifically seasick. If you've ever gotten seasick before, you'll know it's like an inescapable torture of constant nausea where you can't move without puking and your head throbs mercilessly. Like watching *Dancing with the Stars*.

On one of these visits the Indians shot a boar with a .22 rifle for a big feast. They were very friendly and had a fascinating culture. Except for the .22, they were extremely primitive, and the children loved the gifts we would bring them of balloons and little toys and sparklers. They would gather around these miraculous objects and their brains would explode in delight. I remember there were these giant glowing beetles that would light up and fly around like lightning bugs. The Miskito children would tie a string around their necks, and the beetles would float aloft, being held by the strings, buzzing and leaving a trail of light in the air. Us gringos would gather around these miraculous objects and our brains would explode in delight.

We all got our thing.

I remember that the banana-leaf-and-plank huts had dirt floors, but the women of the village would spend a lot of time sweeping them with a straw broom. This brought me no end of amusement as I thought it ridiculous to sweep dirt since there was only more dirt underneath. It still doesn't completely make sense to me.

I've only had boar meat once in my life and it was when I was four or five, that feast night on the Mosquito Coast. I remember eating the roasted boar steak and it had a gross metallic taste to it. Turns out I had been given the piece with the bullet lodged in it. I think after crying I was given some oatmeal or something, and I went to bed in a hammock watching the giant, luminous beetles arc across the night sky.

Worm

My most vivid memory of my life in Nicaragua involves worms coming out of my butthole. If you'd had worms come out of your butthole, I'm sure that'd be a vivid memory for you too. I'm not exactly sure how I got the worms that eventually came out of my anuscus, but their exit couldn't have been more memorable.

Apparently, at some point in time, my parents must have caught on to the fact that I had worms and had me take some medicine. The kind of intestinal parasite that I had was called the large roundworm. That's an excellent description by whoever named said worm. It was large (like ten inches long), round, and definitely a worm.

(All animals should be named that way, now that I think about it. The elephant should be called the HUGE GRAY BIG-EARED TRUNK MAMMAL, for instance. The cougar could be called BIG TAN MOUNTAIN FELINE and the alligator the LONG SNAP-MOUTHED RIVER REPTILE.)

My parents did not warn me that I had taken deworming medication and what would happen once I did. So one day, Kristin and I were walking down the muddy street in Bluefields when I felt a curious sensation down around my little fart chimney.

All of a sudden, it felt like a snake was in my undies. I yelped and reached into my pants to pull out a ten-inch, white (round) worm, which thrashed around in the air quite violently. I threw the grotesque parasite onto the ground and a bunch of neighborhood kids witnessed this act and crowded around accordingly. My stepmom shouted, "¡Matalo!" or "Kill it!" and a kid brought out a shovel and Kristin stabbed the offending large roundworm over and over, slicing it into still-wiggling sections, which she buried in the ground.

The neighborhood kids looked at me like I was possessed by Satan and spitting demon worms from my pants. And in a way they were right.

This whole event happened all over again when we were living back in the States. This time I was fortunate enough to be sitting on a toilet, and as quickly as it emerged from its moist, dark kingdom it was flushed away into the mysterious sewer system of Olympia, Washington.

I often wonder how my identity was defined by my time in Central America. I suppose that underneath my white, suburban, gawky exterior there is a closet of hidden memories that includes monkeys and jungles and worms and glowing beetles. When I was in college and read *One Hundred Years of Solitude* by Gabriel García Márquez (truly one of the greatest books ever written), a flood of memories came back to me and I felt an odd kinship with the Buendía family. I spoke fluent Spanish as a child that I forgot as soon as I had spent some time in the States and had watched umpteen episodes of *The Munsters* and eaten enough cheeseburgers and Slurpees to have Nicaragua recede like a distant fever dream. But throughout the course of growing up, I always identified with the people of Central America and have a deep heart-connection to that language and culture. As difficult as I'm sure it was, I'm grateful for the experience and will treasure the mystery, danger, and romance of living in such a remote, forgotten, loco place.

We left Nicaragua in 1971, when I was five years old. There were no decent schools there and my parents wanted to get me back to America for my education. Plus they were beyond broke and miserable.

The colorful, brief bursts of jungle-y memories that I have from that time truly entice me. Someday soon I want to go back to those swampy tropics with my dad and tromp around the old neighborhood, sample some oysters and plantains, visit the monkeys and sloths, and take a good look down a random outhouse toilet at night with a flashlight.

Chapter 3

MY SEVENTIES SHOW

WE WERE POOR, BUT WE WERE UNHAPPY.
I'm not exactly sure why, but my family moved to Olympia, Washington, when I was five years old. I looked a bit more normal by then, as my torso had stretched to better align with *mi cabeza grande*. While attending Garfield Elementary School on the west side of Olympia, I pretended to have a normal childhood.

My parents were not very good or very happy together, you see. Nice people both, they just didn't click. For their entire fifteen-year marriage. I suppose, when you look back at my dad's story, you see a man who was bereft and heartbroken, tending to an unfortunate-looking child in Central America. Here was an attractive fellow Baha'i, my stepmom, looking for love and seemingly finding it in the arms of a sweet, bespectacled bohemian with a giant, white son.

Not too long ago, I asked both Bob and Kristin when they knew it was a mistake for them to have gotten married. They both replied: "One year." One year in, they knew their marriage was a terrible mistake and that they were a misfit match that would never really connect and know love. I think of their prolonged misery as they suffered it out until their inevitable divorce in 1984.

I think of the sadness of their souls, as my stepmom swept the porch of our house in Bluefields and as my dad oversaw his oyster harvest, both of them sighing and looking out onto the dramatic Nicaraguan sky in a separate shared moment, knowing in their heart of hearts that they did not belong together.

There was also a very strange issue at the center of this "lack of love" in their marriage and in our family. We were members of the Baha'i Faith, which professes *love* as the defining power of the universe, a force that can heal all wounds and is needed to unify and mend our ailing planet. And yet there was not a whole lot of that *actual* love to be found under our roof. This created a kind of crazy-making dichotomy in our household, where "love" was given a tremendous amount of lip service but wasn't put into much tangible practice. For a child, it's a peculiar kind of quandary to grow up in the midst of such desolate spiritual hypocrisy.

I remember awkward spaghetti dinners with halting conversations and that lonely longing in my chest to have a loving, laughing family. The kind of family we watched on all our favorite shows while eating Swanson TV dinners on folding trays. I remember feeling that something was just not right in this familial picture but being unable to put my finger on what exactly it was. Perhaps that's why I've always been drawn to the "sad clown" roles, as it often became my task to liven things up in our dour house with jokes and goofing off. I was loved growing up—stories were read, fevers were tended to, art was made, prayers were said—but there was a bereft, alienated cloud over the three of us that's palpable to me to this day.

So why did they stay together until I left for college in 1984? For me? For the "stick-it-out-ive-ness" surrounding marriage that they inherited from their parents' generation? For their faith, which allows but greatly discourages divorce? For the tiny spark of real love that did exist between them that they hoped, through the fog of denial, would grow eventually into the fire of true companionship?

Who knows? All I can say, from personal experience, is that staying together "for the children" is a terrible idea. Don't get me wrong, jettisoning one's marriage because times are tough or you're too selfish or lazy to do some hard-ass work on your relationship is an even more grotesque idea, *especially* if there are children, but the kids of the world deserve parents who are living vital, connected, passionate lives, in partnership with a supportive mate.

Perhaps we should go back to my namesake, Rainer Maria Rilke, for some insights?

> For one human being to love another; that is perhaps the most difficult of all our tasks, the ultimate, the last test and proof, the work for which all other work is but preparation.

That's the kicker, isn't it? I have great empathy for anyone who struggles with this, this "love," the most difficult of all tasks.

M. Scott Peck wrote the most beautiful definition of marriage I've ever read. His book *The Road Less Traveled* is known as "self-help" but it really is a spiritual/psychological treasure chest, and I highly recommend it.

> Love is the will to extend one's self for the purpose of nurturing one's own or another's spiritual growth.... Love is as love does. Love is an act of will—namely, both an intention and an action. Will also implies choice. We do not have to love. We choose to love.

I'm inspired by the idea of a couple that choose to extend themselves for the spiritual growth of the other person. We CHOOSE to love, and I'm floored by the concept that love is both intention and action. Our challenge then is to do specific actions on a daily basis to nurture our partner's spiritual growth.

For instance, today I told my wife I'd take care of something that needed taking care of and then I sent her this text:

If that's not love, I don't know what is.

My therapist once told me that intimacy, when broken down, was really *"into me see."* Get it? Intimacy? Into-me-see? Now, I know that's ludicrously simplistic, but it's also ludicrously accurate.

Let's get back to my family.

My family was poor. Not food-stamps or Haiti poor. But poor.

We rented an old two-bedroom cinder-block house with a dirt yard in Olympia, and my dad got a job working with kids at the high school. It was a program for juvenile delinquents and troubled teens just out of jail. He taught art and English and Spanish and made $5,600 a year. I truly have no idea how we lived off of that. Kristin was a housewife, as most women were in those days, and had never learned to drive for some reason, so she was truly a stay-at-home mom. I remember my dad's shaggy juvies often dropping by the house in their bell-bottoms and leather-fringed vests. Kristin would stare as if the Manson Family had just stopped by for a chat.

Here's how I remember our poverty: We drove an old, used Edsel from the fifties and then a 1972 powder-blue Ford Pinto, replete with exploding gas tank. I drank powdered milk instead of regular and got all my clothes from the Salvation Army. I had about seven toys and eleven books and stared in awe and wonder at the Gnip Gnops and Rock 'Em Sock 'Em Robots and Lite-Brites and lawn darts and Twisters and vibrating electronic football sets that the other kids in the neighborhood played with. We never took vacations, and eating out was a complete luxury. When we did it was usually Bob's Big Boy, Shakey's Pizza, or this crappy restaurant that overlooked the local bowling alley, where I once found a rubber band in my cheeseburger. We never owned a washer and dryer and our weekend was always marked by a major trip to the Laundromat, where Kristin washed our clothes for the week and I wandered around trying to fish quarters out of the machines.

Never fear, dear reader. Life growing up in Olympia and then, eventually, suburban Seattle, was not all poor, sad nights and alienated TV dinners.

There was also the faith community that surrounded us. Growing up a Baha'i was a strange and strangely wonderful thing.

I remember the singing. There were lots of songs. Spirituals, call-and-response, folk ditties, chants, hymns, and upbeat kiddie tunes. As a Baha'i, I was raised to believe that all the races were one human race and that the color of our skin made us beautiful and distinct like the flowers of one human garden. We were taught as children that men and women were equal and that fighting for justice in the world was the "best beloved" of all things in God's eyes. Young Baha'is are taught that the best of human virtues are the qualities of God Himself and that as we radiate kindness, humility, compassion, and honesty we are shining with the light of the Creator that is inside every single one of us. We learned, as fledgling Baha'is, the idea that "work in the spirit of service is the highest form of worship."

This is great stuff for a kid. None of that guilt crap to bog one down. We weren't born sinful in this worldview, you see. We're noble beings who are dual natured, both divine and animalistic in our essence. God loves us, no matter what we do. There's no hell either, just in case you were wondering. (Can you imagine the despicable absurdity of a loving God creating us only to torture us FOREVER—which is a super-duper long time, by the way—in a fiery pit because we didn't recognize the divinity of Jesus or Muhammad? What a cruel, horrible God that would be! I mean, how vindictive can you get?) In the Baha'i view, after we're done in this physical world and have shed our meat suits, our souls (whatever *they* are) move on to another plane of existence and our good deeds and qualities are all that we take with us.

People were far more open to ideas of and conversations about spirituality and religion in the early seventies. Spirituality had seeped into the cultural groundwater. Religion no longer necessarily meant "Catholic, Protestant, Jew," but was a legitimate, alternative pathway that aided in ordering and experiencing the world in a more feeling, intuitive, connective way. Every Tom, Dick, and Dirty Harry was on a mystical journey of some sort or other. People of all stripes became "spiritual seekers" and were having some kind of transcendent, mystical experience everywhere you turned. Everyone was all like "Be here now" and "I'm okay, you're okay." Yoga, communes, meditation, and health food were culturally accepted spiritual paths. The Beatles went to India to meditate with the maharishi. Cat Stevens became a Muslim. Shirley MacLaine explored past lives. Steve Jobs did Buddhist retreats way before he did any corporate ones. Both "new age" spirituality and environmentalism came into being in that incense-soaked "age of Aquarius."

Our personal heroes were Seals and Crofts, the folky, long-haired, mandolin-rockin' duo that sang "Summer Breeze" and "Hummingbird" and were quite vocal about their Baha'i Faith.

Later on, as I would found the website and media company Soul-Pancake, which was inspired by many Baha'i ideas, I realized looking back that our home frequently had long, intense discussions of "Life's Big Questions," which SoulPancake was built around. Investigating other folks' belief systems, faith, and philosophy was a big part of being alive in the seventies. Our bookshelves at home were filled with books on Sikhism, Sufism, Buddhism, Egyptian mythology, and Native American spirituality. We had art books filled with paintings and sculptures from every corner of the world. An informal talk about the Faith was called a "fireside," and there were always long-haired artists and intellectuals and curious housewives in macrame vests and clogs sitting around our living room, digging into these topics with great abandon.

My dad once told me that people were so open to having these kinds of discussions in those days that you could just go up to somebody on the street and say, "Hey, we're going to have a spiritual gathering with some music at our house tonight, wanna come by?" And the random person would say nine times out of ten, "Sure, man, sounds totally groovy," or "I'm in, brother," or "Whoa! Heavy!" or something like that, and before you knew it there'd be a full house of people that resembled background actors from *That '70s Show*. Can you imagine doing that today? Going up to a group of twentysomethings in a Starbucks and saying, "Hey, you guys want to come to a spiritual gathering at my house tonight?" You'd clear out the Starbucks faster than you can say "anthrax chai latte."

I would sometimes put down my Thor and Superman comic books and sit in on these hangouts as a kid. Diverse, patchouli-scented characters would be talking about Jesus and the Buddha and God and free will and the soul and life after death and "If there is a God, why does he let innocent children suffer?" and "Is the Bible the literal truth or the metaphorical truth?" and "Isn't it just okay to be a good person and not be a part of any religious faith?" and "Did the CIA, in league with the Mafia, actually kill JFK?" You know, the questions that have haunted humankind from time immemorial.

When Watchtowers (Jehovah's Witnesses) or Mormons would come to our house, my parents wouldn't pretend they weren't home or slam the door, they would welcome them in, serve them tea, and exchange ideas about the Bible. We would politely hear their thoughts and they would politely, confusedly listen to ours.

I remember once a nice born-again lady came inside and showed us a pamphlet that had a picture of Jesus on a cloud looking positively radiant and a lion and a lamb taking a nap together on a lovely green field. She said, "You see, when Jesus returns, the lion will lie down with the lamb. Just like in the picture!" I said to her (precociously nerdy at age twelve), "Don't you think that the saying from the Bible might be metaphorical, meaning traditional enemies will lay down their weapons and make peace in the world? Not that actual lions will stop eating actual lambs? I mean, what will lions eat when Jesus returns, hummus?" (I made up that last part. Hummus hadn't been invented yet.) She paused quizzically and then pointed to the pamphlet again and said, "No, see? The lion is lying down with the lamb!"

I don't mean to poke fun at biblical literalists (actually I do, a little bit) but to point out the constant flow of ideas about religious and philosophical concepts that came and went through our sad and interesting little house.

There were so many things that were different in that befuddled, well-meaning decade. Parenting for instance.

Guide to Parenting in the Seventies

After-School Choices

A) Offer a powdered drink (e.g., Kool-Aid, Ovaltine, Nestlé Quik, or Tang) and rush children out the door, telling them to be back for dinner (i.e., when it gets dark).
B) TV.
C) Homework (optional).

Dinner Choices

American: burgers, fried chicken, meatloaf, steaks, hot dogs

Or other ethnic and cultural options:
Italian: pizza, spaghetti, lasagna
Mexican: tacos (hard taco shell, ground beef, lettuce, tomato, red sauce, grated cheddar, sour cream)
Chinese: La Choy frozen stir-fry

Dessert Choices

Ice cream: chocolate, vanilla, strawberry. Or Neapolitan (all three)

Television-Viewing Parameters and Boundaries

N/A

Hygiene

Brush the hell out of your teeth.
Bathe when stinky.

Medical Care

Visit doctor or dentist when something is broken, bursting, bleeding, or causing so much pain you can't move.

Morning Routine

Wake up children twelve minutes before school starts.

Breakfast Menu

Bowl of cereal: Frosted Flakes, Count Chocula, Boo Berry, or Lucky Charms
Healthy option: Cheerios

Lunch

PBJ

Weekends

Feed children pancakes. Rush them outside. Saturday-night sleepover at friend's house. Make sure they're alive on Sunday night.

It's a little different today. Today's parents are, as you know, referred to as "helicopter parents." There is a constant, anxious hovering over suburban children. A hypervigilant concern as to their well-being and schooling and friends and free time and accomplishments and hobbies and future and college and marriage and earning capacity and AAAAHHHHHHHH!!!!!!!

(And, at the same time, contrarily, iProducts are shoved into kids' hands by harried parents from the time they can sit upright to act as instant iBabysitters. Human interaction is greatly reduced and most modern kids spend more time looking at screens than at human faces.)

Now, don't get me wrong, I didn't have a *miserable* childhood by any means. I wasn't beaten. There were snacks around. We had various dogs and cats and furniture. You know, the things that families have around when undertaking the routine of a normal life. We had an RCA color TV that played various sitcoms of the seventies most evenings as we escaped our ennui by watching the flickering lights and laugh tracks of classic television. In fact, this appliance played a hugely important role in our lives as an easy respite and social nexus after a long, taxing day of subtle alienation.

I imagine there are hundreds of thousands of families to whom the families on the telly seemed more real, more tangible, more "familial" than their own. That's what all great television is, I believe: unlikely families. People coming together and finding a home.

The TV was my escape. Especially the comedies. I certainly loved my cartoons, my *Pink Panther*, my *Super Friends*, and my Looney Tunes, but it was the sitcoms that caught my imagination as early as age six.

I adored *F Troop* and *The Addams Family*. I absorbed Mary Tyler Moore and Dick Van Dyke in reruns. I have seen every episode of *The Bob Newhart Show* at least three times. Two hundred fifty-one episodes of *M*A*S*H*? No problem. In fact, I would sometimes watch two or three episodes a day, having memorized where and when all the syndicated reruns were playing. *All in the Family* was more real to me than my own family. We never missed a *Laverne & Shirley* or a *Happy Days*. (Even after they had "jumped the shark." Literally.) *Three's Company* was a bit "risqué" for my parents, but I was able to catch episodes at friends' houses. Mork was my spirit animal. Barney Miller was the father I never had. And I longed to someday be a Sweathog. I feasted on *WKRP in Cincinnati*. And when, thirty-five years later, I got to work with Howard Hesseman on *The Rocker*, I picked his brain for hours on that sublime comic creation.

Moving forward toward the eighties, my family and I discovered

Taxi. I had no idea a sitcom could have such heart. Besides the usual comedic shenanigans, episodes were filled with longing and unlikely romance, with hopes unfulfilled and dreams dashed. New York City became the place I wanted to study acting purely based on the haunting Bob James Fender Rhodes theme song and the cinematic opening credits of the show. It was a wistful, magical place, where you could dare to be yourself and be accepted, where artists mixed with blue-collar workers and even someone who looked like Judd Hirsch could find love.

Unlike the others at my school, I didn't revere Pete Rose, Terry Bradshaw, and Dr. J; my heroes were Reverend Jim Ignatowski, Louie De Palma, and Latka.

Because, for me, it was all about the sidekicks, the disjointed men of mayhem who provided the comic relief. The "A" story plots involving some emotional quandary of the main characters never interested me in the slightest. I wanted the zany neighbor clowns to come over without knocking and to have gotten fired from their jobs, or to need to borrow a lawn mower or have a zebra trapped in their kitchen. All those delicious "B" plot devices featuring the sidekicks made the show worth watching for me.

The idea that I would someday get to play that kind of character on an actual TV show was beyond the furthest reaches of my wildest suburban imagination.

COMPENDIUM OF
COMIC SIDEKICKS

—

My list of the ten greatest comic TV sidekicks
of the seventies

(With evaluations by renowned comic sidekick Dwight K. Schrute,
who was paid $125 per paragraph.)

SQUIGGY, *LAVERNE & SHIRLEY*

The funnier half of Lenny and Squiggy, Squiggy, was played by David
Lander. He brought an exquisite insanity to a guy who thought of himself as cool but in reality was one step away from being a mental patient. This nasal-voiced "greaser" with a spit-curl hairdo always had
a get-rich-quick scam. The beautiful thing about his characterization
was it was impossible to put your finger on what "type" of character
he was. He wasn't "the dumb guy" or "the nerd" or "the weirdo"; he
was his own very specific, off-the-wall creation. Also, his timing was
never the on-the-nose, asking-for-a-laugh sitcom rhythm. Every time
he burst into the door, you just knew something incredible was about
to happen.

Dwight: He "wasn't 'the dumb guy'"? What a moronic statement.
Squiggy was a near-subhuman cretin. However, it must be noted that
in 1979, he and his life partner, Lenny, recorded an LP under the name

"Lenny and the Squigtones." It is a masterpiece that my family and I listen to, in its entirety, each Christmas morn. If the children make any noise while it plays, their gifts are rescinded.

HOWARD BORDEN, *THE BOB NEWHART SHOW*

The clueless neighbor of Bob and Suzanne Pleshette (TV's hottest sitcom wife, FYI) was played by one of the sweetest and funniest human beings on the planet, Bill Daily, who also played the neurotic astronaut buddy on *I Dream of Jeannie*. He was able to play "dumb" in the most unobvious, effortless way. When he would pop into Bob's apartment for some inane reason, America would sit up on their sofas. Like all great comedic actors, Bill Daily never underlined a joke or a punch line, but allowed the comedy to come from his dim-witted, lovable character's perspective.

Dwight: I failed to see the humor in a television program centered around treatment of the mentally ill and thus never watched *The Bob Newhart Show*. The cast of that show should have been housed in the facility from *One Flew Over the Cuckoo's Nest* and been given care by someone effective like Nurse Ratched.

RADAR O'REILLY, *M*A*S*H*

Another sweet, dumb guy who captures your heart. His innocence was aching, as was his need for approval. I was mesmerized by this character as a child. I always wanted to know what Radar *wanted*. Did he want love? Respect? Meaning? How did he have that strange, almost psychic ability to read his commander's thoughts and know what he wanted before he did? I was captivated by his love of grape Nehi soda and his odd, specific history in Ottumwa, Iowa. He felt like a real American boy caught up in the horrors of war. Radar was someone I wanted to be friends with. So did America.

Dwight: I liked the episode where Radar killed the enemy soldier by ripping his throat out with his bare hands. Oh, wait, there was no such episode—because Radar was perhaps the biggest wuss ever to serve in the armed forces.

MICHAEL STIVIC (AKA MEATHEAD), *ALL IN THE FAMILY*

The hippie boyfriend of Gloria Bunker was effortlessly and delightfully played by Rob Reiner (director of *The Princess Bride* and *This Is Spinal Tap*, among many other great films). This well-meaning but thick counterculture loudmouth was a perfectly balanced and nuanced foil to Archie, the bigoted patriarch of the family. You wanted to both wring his neck and hug him at the same time. To this day I admire his willingness to be so unlikable and yet lovable.

Dwight: As a child, I was terrified of Meathead because I quite logically assumed his head was perhaps a large pork shank adorned with a long wig and false mustache, or a pile of sculpted venison. I have yet to find evidence that this was not the case.

REVEREND JIM IGNATOWSKI, *TAXI*

This drug-addled taxi driver was perfectly, specifically etched by Christopher Lloyd (the professor from *Back to the Future*). I loved that his character was, by turns, HUGE and terrifically real and heartfelt. This balance is incredibly hard to do in comedy. In a giant, brilliant ensemble, he really popped. In the hands of a lesser actor, he would have been a caricature, but Mr. Lloyd brought such heart and pathos to him that I longed to see him in my living room every week. The writers created a brilliant backstory for him where he was a rich, successful Harvard student who, upon sampling a pot brownie, instantly went down the rabbit hole of drug addiction and loony insanity.

Dwight: I never found Mr. Ignatowski funny because I genuinely believe his teachings and philosophies as a reverend are quite profound. Frankly, I never understood why the studio audience was laughing at this insightful thinker. Does anyone know if his parish is still in operation?

LES NESSMAN, *WKRP IN CINCINNATI*

The beleaguered news director of the radio station, Les Nessman, he of the bow tie, horn-rims, and plastic pocket protector, may have been the first "geek" on television. He's a Dwight prototype, often butting heads in his search for respect from the others in the office. His running gag of having tape on the floor, demarcating where his office walls *should* be and insisting that everyone knock on his imaginary door and mime opening and closing it, brought my nerdy heart tremendous joy on a weekly basis.

Dwight: I'm proud to be compared with the venerable Mr. Nessman. Arthur Carlson, the "manager" of the station, was a complete bumbling oaf and Mr. Nessman should have been given a chance in that position. I find the extent to which he was disrespected absolutely disgraceful. Furthermore, I wish I had thought of that whole "tape off the walls of your office" idea when I was a mere salesman at Dunder Mifflin. Would have saved me a lot of nonsense and high jinks.

DETECTIVE ARTHUR DIETRICH,
BARNEY MILLER

I loved the unflappable, intellectual know-it-all played effortlessly by Steve Landesberg. This existential philosopher was always on a quest for knowledge, and his deadpan wit was unlike anything else on the TV. He was the drily cool philosopher I aspired to be one day.

Dwight: As a fellow unflappable intellectual with deadpan wit who works in law enforcement, I endorse Detective Dietrich. However, I did not watch *Barney Miller* often, because the fact that nearly every cast member had massive bags under their eyes disturbed me.

ARNOLD HORSHACK, *WELCOME BACK, KOTTER*

Sheer, broad, idiotic buffoonery sometimes trumps all other subtler choices. A loud laugh and ridiculous hair help tremendously. This "character," played by Ron Palillo, was staggeringly huge and shocked all of America, preparing the way for Kramer and Urkel.

Dwight: I have no comment on Arnold Horshack, but I did enjoy the opening scene of *Jason Lives: Friday the 13th Part VI*, wherein actor Ron Palillo had his heart ripped out as he vomited blood.

TED BAXTER, *THE MARY TYLER MOORE SHOW*

This pompous clown, utterly lacking in self-knowledge, was perfectly rendered by Ted Knight. The anchorman's epic vanity was matched only by his stupidity. Like so many newsmen, he's completely style without a whiff of substance. Like Ron Burgundy and Geraldo Rivera.

And I'm sorry, sometimes people are just wired funny, and Ted is that. He just simply makes you laugh.

Dwight: "Simply makes you laugh" unless journalistic standards actually mean something to you. A poor reporter who, I believe, was responsible for the Symbionese Liberation Army's kidnapping of Patricia Hearst. I don't have the space here, but I'd like to expound further in a book of my own.

THE FONZ, *HAPPY DAYS*

Ayyyyyyyyyy! The Fonz was an icon. During the opening credits we see the Fonz go to the mirror to comb his hair; he stops, decides it's perfect, and does his signature "Ayyyyy" move in his leather jacket. Apparently this was the choice that Henry Winkler made when auditioning that made all the producers laugh and got him the part. All the other actors actually combed their hair in various Fonz-like ways, but it was the daringness of Mr. Winkler that set him apart and above. And the essence of that acting choice was what defined the Fonz and set his character in an entirely different paradigm from the typical fifties cool guy. He was a magical unicorn of a man who had infinite confidence and could snap his fingers to have beautiful women drape themselves on his shoulders, and yet we felt for Arthur Fonzarelli. He was lonely inside, and for all his "cool" there was a lost child in there that we wanted to get to know.

Dwight: A man with godlike powers to make machinery spring to life at the touch of his hand. A supernatural ability to induce sexual hypnosis in any woman—which he would then compulsively act upon. *Happy Days* is the terrifying tale of a town enslaved by the whims of this inhuman monster, "the Fonz."

Chapter 4

THE NERD OF GOD

IN THE MIDSEVENTIES WE MOVED TO A NORTHERN SUBURB OF Seattle called Lake Forest Park. We lived in a different but exactly-the-same tiny concrete-block, two-bedroom rental house between a Pizza Hut and a 7-Eleven just off of Ballinger Way on a leafy, green, solidly middle-class cul-de-sac. My dad was now working at Erickson Brothers Sewer Repair of Seattle (later to be known as Jim Dandy Sewer and Plumbing) as the office manager. It was a tiny plumbing and sewer construction shop that had been launched in 1908 by some craggy Swedish relatives of Kristin's. In his spare time from sending out invoices and dispatching sewer trucks to the plugged drains and clogged sewer lines of rainy Seattle, Robert Wilson would be furiously typing chapters of his science-fiction and fantasy books on a green Smith Corona. The rough-hewn, poo-encrusted men of Erickson Brothers looked at my dad as if he had just arrived from the planet Voltron.

Robert Wilson was still an artist at heart: a suburban dad, providing for his oddball family at a sewer construction company, whose bohemian dream still bubbled around inside. He literally typed out six or seven novels in that musty, mossy basement office. His second novel, *Tentacles of Dawn*, was the only one published.

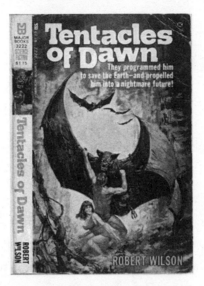

You see, there's this man who wakes up in an egg in a cave in a dark world. He fights giant bats and mutant tribes and "the Wild Wagon Women" on his quest to find "the Watcher at the End of the World," where he realizes that he is actually an android sent to bring light to Earth. It's really that simple.

Here's a compendium of some of the other books he wrote, now long lost to the world (note: I'm not making *any* of this up):

The Ghosts of Ea: A spaceship of human explorers, captained by one John Draco, returns to Earth one hundred thousand years after the planet has been abandoned, only to be held captive. They discover Earth is now a prison colony for violent aliens whom they must partner with to overthrow their evil overlords who are based on the moon.

The Curse of Gitan Mu: The diminutive monk Hikphat wanders the continent Panea, which is breaking apart, in search of a tattoo that will make him immortal. The holy order he belongs to worships a set of ankle bones and he must discover whom they originally belonged to as he travels a world peopled with slavers, monsters, and pirates.

The Chromium Kid: A semiautobiographical account of an awkward young teen growing up in a Chicago suburb while escaping into a fantasy adventure novel that serves as a guide to surviving in the "real world."

The Subways of Ur: A Roman soldier is misplaced in time and takes a subway back and forth from the frozen future of Earth to the ancient city of Ur, which was settled by ruthless extraterrestrials who are worshipped as gods.

Clarissa of Toom: A beautiful woman was created by a magician, Algoram, out of ashes, a log, a spiderweb, and some moss. She's sent out into the world to investigate if anyone else is alive after a devastating war between wizards. Clarissa travels the countryside, guided by a dial on her ring that points toward magic. She visits the Seven Cities of Stone and learns that she must ultimately return and slay Algoram, who was the one who started the war in the first place.

Arizona Hospital: In the future, after a terrible plague apocalypse, all humans live in cities built inside enormous hospitals and eat a special food called "nutrient" that protects them from mutant gene production. Special police forces, under the command of our hero, Romeo Sierra, hunt and kill mutants that are being led by a maniacal general and scientist named Doctor Corruptus. The mutants are rampant, evil carnivores . . . or *ARE* they?!

The Lords of AfterEarth: Manuel escapes his narrow-minded village and rides a giant spider left over from a long-gone civilization, stumbles upon a cult in a desert that grows people in underground vats, discovers a sunken city that rises to the surface of the ocean for one day each year, and eventually ends up at an abandoned spaceport, his final escape to the stars.

I waited with bated breath for my dad to finish whatever novel he had been fabricating so I could read it immediately. I was always his first audience, and I was instantly transported by his strange, imaginative tales, bundled in a giant pile of double-spaced typewritten pages. I was in awe of this man who could pound away on a typewriter or slosh paint on a stretched piece of canvas and actually *create* something that hadn't been there before. I wanted that. I wanted to be able to do that, and it was my father who lit the fire of my passion to be an artist of some kind.

After slugging out pulpy books and cleaning sewers during the day, he became Jackson Pollock at night. Our converted garage was my father's art studio. Upon arriving home from work, promptly at five thirty, he would put on some paint-soaked Levi's and a work shirt and head into his studio with a V8 juice (to which he added a splash of Worcestershire sauce) and a paintbrush. After cranking the Wagner, he would start to paint his enormous abstract oil paintings. I remember there was one particular phase of his work where he was painting large Picasso-esque women with their enormous breastesses fully revealed. This was terribly embarrassing to me as a young lad. Big abstract women-ladies with their boobages flying in the abstract breeze. I remember leaving him a note on his desk asking him to "please stop painting nakid women's brests" or something to that effect.

His "studio" was also stacked to the ceiling with other science-fiction and fantasy books. Their outlandish, pulpy covers sparked my imagination and drew me in. By the time I was twelve years old, and had been tiptoeing into the genre via Mr. Ray Bradbury, I was hooked.

I devoured the robots of Asimov and Andre Norton and the aliens of Arthur C. Clarke and Poul Anderson. I carried swords and cast spells alongside Conan; the Gray Mouser; Corwin, Prince of Amber; and Elric of Melniboné. I submerged myself in the dystopian futures of Le Guin and Huxley and Wells and the grandmaster of them all, amphetamine prophet Philip K. Dick. And, my personal favorite, an author largely forgotten, Jack Vance, whose hyperverbose, comic science-fantasy adventures I read and reread and reread.

I left my comic books behind for actual novels without cartoons in them. Words upon words upon words. Bloated, alternative-reality webs of pure speculative imagination. One great rule my parents had was that however many books I wanted they would buy for me, as long as I read them all. No questions asked. We didn't have a lot of money, but every month they'd purchase me an enormous stack of science fiction from our family's favorite hangout, the University Book Store on "the Ave" in Seattle.

This was the beginning of the long, inevitable descent into total and irredeemable nerddom.

I was bone-numbingly nerdy before there was even a modicum of cool attached to that now overappropriated, worn-out word. In the early eighties being a nerd meant you were reviled and got the crap literally beaten out of your gangly body on a regular basis. You were shunned, derided, and laughed at pretty much daily. There were no nerd CEOs or TV hosts or rock stars or actors or billionaires. There was no *Nerdist* podcast or *Big Bang Theory* or emo girls with "I Love Geeks" T-shirts. There were only the unwashed, cerebral misfits who slipped quietly into the side doors of the school and skirted along the lockers, trying to avoid any sudden move or eye contact that would result in a beatdown from a jock, stoner, or popular kid. It was like literally living inside a John Hughes movie.

I was repeatedly mocked, derided, shoved, punched, and laughed at by a good majority of the people I was in school with in Seattle. Certainly having the name Rainn didn't help much. I would sometimes dream longingly of being named Gary or Doug or Carl, strong, simple names that didn't draw much attention. I heard "Rain, rain, go away" chants most of the way through elementary school. Hysterical rain puns "rained" down on me incessantly.

I remember a band trip where tiny bully Terry Kostas and a bunch of his minions somehow decided they were going to kick the crap out of me and my dork posse at some future point in time. I was terrified beyond measure and escaped with nothing worse than being socked in the stomach with a monkey wrench by his version of Crabbe or Goyle in metal shop one day.

Another thing about the seventies and early eighties was that bullying was just accepted. Think of the great bullies in classic old movies: Johnny Lawrence from *The Karate Kid*, Ace (Kiefer Sutherland) from *Stand by Me*, the Socs from *The Outsiders*, Scut Farkus from *A Christmas Story*, Biff from *Back to the Future*, the entire senior class from *Dazed and Confused*, and, of course, the Heathers. The idea that there would someday be an anti-bullying campaign of some kind would have been thought of as ludicrous back then. Being bullied was good for you, according to cultural beliefs. It toughened you up and thickened your skin. It was the natural order of things. Darwinian. So geek- and nerddom* had a very high cost to it with zero perks. Only bruises on your self-esteem. And your body.

---

*A note on nerd culture: These days, the pandering and commodification of all things nerd is ridiculous and insulting. Although it must be glorious to be able to be bookish nowadays and not have to deal with getting crotch-punched and derided on a daily basis, the commercial acceptability of geek lifestyle is simply a

My obsession with all things fantasy and sci-fi dovetailed into real life with the advent of the second-greatest game ever invented (next to chess, of course), Dungeons & Dragons. For the twelve of you who don't know, D&D is a role-playing game where you pretend to be a wizard or thief or warrior and you endlessly battle fictional monsters in treasure-laden dungeons while eating Cheetos.

My friends and I would leave school on a Friday afternoon to dive into a weekend-long Dungeons & Dragons marathon extravaganza. Myself, John Valadez, Steve Wilmart, Mike Wentzel, Chris Cole, George Evans, and Shawn and Tim Higgins (our malevolent dungeon master, who spookily resembled Art Garfunkel) would live in a different world from Friday night at four p.m. until around Sunday at six p.m.

This world was filled with orcs and morning stars, dexterity points, labyrinths, twenty-sided dice, healing potions, action miniature figurines, and intricate maps, painstakingly etched onto graph paper. It was fueled by Fritos and Dr Pepper and the desire to "level-up" our characters until they were invincible. This was the world of the imagination. Scrawny, self-hating wimps transformed into fierce barbarians and dazzling wizards all across the basements of America.

I would most often play Ragnar the Radical, my eleventh-level fighter who was adept with both bow and sword and, because his moral alignment was "chaotic neutral," could do whatever he damn

---

grotesque capitalistic manipulation. Nerds buy things: movie tickets, video games, apps, and electronics. They tell others to buy things as they are tastemakers and bloggers and fiercely loyal and snobby little capitalists. Corporations figured that out around 2005 or so and started to try to cash in. Especially Hollyweird.

Another aspect of nerddom that drives me bonkers? The incessant and obsessive attention given to entertainment by this subculture. Video game releases, movie openings, comics, superheroes, collectibles, role-playing games, cosplay, TV shows, movie star castings, *Star Wars* and *Trek*, and celebrity train wrecks. One of the signs of the decline of an empire is the culture's insatiable need for

well pleased. Which was tremendous fun. I would spend my days in class not paying attention to the teacher but sketching Ragnar over and over again. Ragnar fighting an ogre. Ragnar shooting arrows into the shield of a Frost Giant. Ragnar looking majestic in his cape on top of a snowy mountain at sunrise, gazing off at the horizon, knowing that there was more evil to fight with his "Reaping Strike."™

---

entertainment. Think about those Romans, bored out of their skulls, eating bread and watching circus 24/7 as the barbarians surrounded their gates and their culture disintegrated. If one–one hundredth of the energy that our country spent on "entertainment" were focused on service to the planet and/or humanity, we could make an incredible difference in the world and be remembered as the greatest, most altruistic culture that Earth has ever produced.

Note: Do not, however, abandon entertainment to such an extent that it would put me out of a job or jeopardize my employment in any way, shape, or form. I got mouths to feed, babe.

ARTIST: Rainn Wilson, circa 1980

I also played Queekag the monk, who was a martial arts expert but, because he couldn't wear any armor, was a sitting duck if we got attacked by a bunch of goblins with crossbows, let me tell you. I admire Queekag to this day. His resolve, his discipline, his mystery, his bo staff. More of a man than I'll ever be. I suppose in some ways, Queekag was the male role model I never had. The man I still to this day strive to be. Itinerant, wise, self-sufficient, spiritual but an ass kicker at the same time. Influenced, obviously, by Kwai Chang Caine, the Shaolin monk from the seventies TV show *Kung Fu*, so deftly played by David Carradine. And by the Buddha.

Schedule of D&D Marathon Extravaganza

Friday

4:00–9:00 p.m.: Play Dungeons & Dragons, usually at Shawn Higgins's house.

9:00–9:30 p.m.: Order pizzas and run around outside with broomstick swords and garbage-can-lid shields until the pizza guy got there.

9:30 p.m.: Chug Dr Pepper from the two-liter bottle and make fun of Shawn's Adam's apple (which was like a second head, it was so huge. It was like the little alien baby in *Alien* had gotten stuck in his pale, freckly esophagus and lay there, threatening to burst out of his rubbery neck. Hi, Shawn!).

9:45 p.m.–1:45 a.m.: Fight monsters and get treasure.

2:00 a.m.: Go spend the night at John Valadez's house, watch wrestling, and eat rocky road ice cream.

Saturday

9:30–10:00 a.m.: Count Chocula.

10:00 a.m.–2:00 p.m.: Play D&D.

2:00–3:00 p.m.: Run around in the woods with Chris Cole's bow and arrow and shoot it at a bunch of old tires.

3:00–9:30 p.m.: Strive to finish clearing out the dungeons of Aktar, making sure to find Hosgurd's key (which we would need to get the treasure from Klur the Copper Dragon, of course).

9:30–10:00 p.m.: Snack on fruit from the giant boxes of free produce the Higginses had stacked in their garage from their divorced, absent father who ran a food distribution company and supposedly sent bananas and apples over by the pallet in lieu of making child support payments.

10:00 p.m.–2:00 a.m.: Attempt to finish level nine of the dungeon and slay Klur the Copper Dragon in order to obtain entrance into the Castle of Garadrel.

Sunday

10:00–11:00 a.m.: Eat runny scrambled eggs with parents (eye-roll a lot, classical music plunking away in the background).

11:00 a.m.–7:00 p.m.: Finish the Castle of Garadrel. Celebrate with Twizzlers and Slurpees and some furtive, adrenalized glimpses at a stack of *Cheri* porno mags that Tim had found at the bottom of some old boxes in the corner of their basement. (This was the late seventies. Porn wasn't as ubiquitous and "one click away" as it is now. We had to *work* for our porn back then!)

7:00–9:00 p.m.: Do all of the next week's homework while watching *Columbo*.

About once every month or two we would forgo a day of gaming in order to head out to one of the rare gamer/comic stores in the Seattle area. The best one was in Kent, Washington, which was a two-hour bus ride away. The trip would be a daylong event but totally worth it. A bus full of dork meat, meandering its way to the hobby shop, where we would stock up on the little metal miniature figurines of orcs and trolls and warriors and the model paint to adorn them with, the multisided dice that drove the game, and, most important, the dungeon maps and books of monsters and spells that were our bible. I will never forget the musty smell of those stores and the mystery of their aisles, filled with magical possibility and the strange, almost-always-bearded man grumpily gargoyled at the cash register, reading *The Sword of Shannara* by Terry Brooks for the seventh time.

Before Hollywood discovered the world of comic book nerds and sci-fi geeks, before the cultural tastemaking explosion of Comic-Con, there was a special yearly event at the saddest Hyatt in the world: Norwescon.

This was (and still is!) a yearly fantasy and sci-fi convention that would draw out all the nerd vermin from the mossy burbs of Western Washington. There was a *huge* bookstore and D-level actors who had once guested on *Star Trek* signing glossies. Favorite sci-fi authors like Philip José Farmer and Frederik Pohl were treated like rock stars there, signing copies of their books and walking the halls like members of House Lannister. And the capper was a big party called the "Masquerade" on Saturday night, where you were encouraged to dress like a Klingon or barbarian or alien.

My dad would go every year to sign a handful of copies of his book and speak on various panels, and I would proudly watch him among the other author-gods. Yes, there were actual panel discussions on science fiction, fantasy, comics, and gaming. I remember once ducking into the back of a conference room where a team of dandruffy professor types were intensely pondering whether it would be in character for Conan the Barbarian to boil water during his travels.

There was a "screening room" (i.e., dilapidated conference room) that had movies showing in it twenty-four hours a day. That is where I first saw *Silent Running* with Bruce Dern, *Zardoz* with Sean Connery, and *The Fearless Vampire Killers* by Roman Polanski. The unwashed sci-fi hippie contingent who didn't have the money to get a hotel room would simply sleep in the screening room in their sleeping bags with loud, poorly projected sci-fi movies blaring and flickering around them all night long.

I even played an elven thief in a Dungeons & Dragons competition, taking second place at age fifteen. A group of ten lost souls sat in a boardroom at the Hyatt, playing various imaginary characters for an *entire day*, while outside in the real world, hearts were broken, sacrifices undertaken, connections made, babies born, tears shed, and lives lived. Not in the Evergreen Room at the SeaTac Hyatt, though. There, chaotic-neutral dwarves and half-orc magic users pranced about in imaginary caves for hour after hour seeking treasure, glory, and magic scimitars.

Eventually, because of my dweeby exploits, I would be given the key to a magical, mythical city. A city that others can only dream of. The renowned municipality of Nerdopolis. I would also be made its lord, mayor, and spokesperson (as you're about to read).

Chapter 5

THE BASSOONIST

———

I ASK YOU TO SAVOR THE FOLLOWING SENTENCE: FOR SEVERAL years, off and on, I was a member of the following clubs at school: marching band, pep band, orchestra, debate club, computer club, chess club, Model United Nations, and pottery club.

Note: The above list does not include my aforementioned role-playing gaming, Baha'i youth activities, medieval weapons sketching, kung fu movie obsession, or vast Columbia Record and Tape Club* cassette collection featuring Journey, Styx, Asia, and REO Speedwagon.

---

* The Columbia Record and Tape Club was the most brilliant scam perpetrated on young Americans since the Vietnam War. For one dollar you'd get like twelve cassettes sent to you just for joining. Then you'd have to buy a handful of tapes at the "regular" amount (which was like $16.99 or some similarly astronomical price) over the course of the year. You'd get mailed a brochure of new releases, and if you didn't mail the postcard back saying, "No, thanks, I don't want anything this month," they'd automatically send you their selection of the month and *BILL YOU FOR IT*. It was a duplicitous scheme, preying on knuckleheaded teens who didn't have the wherewithal to return a postcard every month and who would end up with a Peter Frampton cassette they never wanted *and* a bill for $16.99. It did, however, launch many a young person's Van Halen cassette tape collection!

And then, if that wasn't enough, I decided to play the bassoon.

Boom. Universe explodes, then implodes. Then explodes again, quickly folding in on itself, only to create infinite other bassoon-shaped universes.

Let's dig a little deeper, shall we?

Having studied piano as a kid and then clarinet at Kellogg Middle School, I went to my band teacher and told him I wanted to quit clarinet and play tenor sax. Saxophone was way cooler, you see. Guys in the sax section would crack jokes and wear sunglasses in class sometimes. Clarinet wasn't pathetically loser-ish (I mean, it wasn't French horn!), but it certainly wasn't the most masculine of instruments. Sure, there was a clarinet-like instrument in the cantina scene in *Star Wars*, but let's face it, clarinets are for girls in braces and Woody Allen. (Who *loves* girls in braces. Ba-dum-dum!)

My band teacher, John Law (real name), really pulled a fast one on me. He said something to the effect of "Well, you *could* play the sax, but we've just got *so* many saxophones right now. Wait a minute . . . ," he paused for dramatic effect and lowered his voice conspiratorially, "you know what's *really* cool and unique?" I was all like, "What? What's really cool and unique?!" He was like, "The bassoon." And I was like, "Wow. What's that?"

And with that ridiculous manipulation, a bassoonist was born.

The bassoon is absurd. They should be banned for being horrible, unnecessary, and adenoidally grating.

It takes like an hour to assemble one. They're enormous and are made out of Lincoln Logs, aluminum twigs, and paper towel tubes. There are these tiny double wooden reeds that you have to soak and trim and tend to all the time. There's a strap that you actually have to sit on when you play so the whole thing doesn't fall onto the floor like a bundle of garbage. And, after all that folderol, it ends up sounding like an anemic donkey with laryngitis.

Later, after I was digging into my bassooning, Mr. Law was thoughtful enough to let the entire class know that originally the bassoon was called the *fagotto* in Italian because it resembled a faggot (bundle of sticks) when unassembled. That went over really well. People just *loved* commenting on me and my enormous *fagotto*.

I ended up playing the bassoon for the next five years until I graduated high school. For better or worse, I spent my adolescence tethered to that bastard woodwind, my siren, my spirit animal, my nerd crucifix.

I would also occasionally play in the pep band and marching band as a . . . wait for it . . . xylophonist. My eventual high school, Shorecrest, was known as the Highlanders and thusly the marching band wore kilts and knee-high socks. If you went to a Shorecrest game or pep rally in 1982 or '83 and saw a tall, pimply, gangly teen in a tartan kilt with a xylophone strapped to his skinny chest, that was probably me. Also, it should be noted that the "cool" guys in marching band would go "commando" under their kilts as they played "Tequila" and "On, Wisconsin!" and floppily marched around like pubescent idiots.

As if the bassoon, xylophone, and science-fiction obsession weren't enough, I then took up an interest in chess. It's as if the sirens of dweebdom lured me inexorably into their pimply lair, from which I never really returned.

So I joined the chess club at Shorecrest High School. The team was centered around two guys whose names sounded like *shoe*: Terry Hsu (Chinese dude) and Jeff Schuh (white dude). They were really good at chess and taught the rest of us giblets a ton. Terry was first board and Jeff second. Other team members were Blake Kremer (third board), me on the fourth board, and George Evans coming in at number five.

You see, a chess team is comprised of the five best chess players, and you put them in order from first board to fifth. When you play another team, they bring *their* five best and you both have at it in a silent room with a handful of awkward, acne-draped spectators. We did pretty well with the "shoe" brothers and went to the state championship one of the two years I was on the team. We even beat the fancy-pants private school, Lakeside (alma mater of Bill Gates). We crowed about that victory quite a bit, I can tell you.

Once the cheerleaders mockingly made a bunch of chess team banners for the school entranceway that said things like CONGRATS CHESS TEAM STATE CHAMPS 82! and stuff like that. Everyone at the school snidely guffawed and thought that was a total hoot, and we slunk past the banners in shame. Jeff Schuh, however, had purchased a chess letterman's jacket with a giant knight's profile on the back and wore it around proudly. He was a nerd rebel and didn't care what the majority of Highlanders thought of him. Like Spock and Potsie Weber from *Happy Days*, he immediately became our dweeb hero.

Sometimes we would attend weekend-long chess tournaments. I played in several of these and got my ass handed to me by the chess-farts of the greater Seattle area. At one of these competitions, I saw the most peculiar detail of nerddom that has ever been witnessed before or since by man or immortal.

I dare anyone to top this: a guy with mold growing in his ear.

IN. HIS. EAR.

I can't remember what this chess spectator looked like, but I won't ever forget the yellow-orange fuzzy mold growing in his ear hole. It's seared into my adolescent memory banks more starkly than my Farrah Fawcett poster.

Let's ponder the reality of this ear for a moment.

Something was probably in his ear hole to begin with. A clump of debris or a speck of food or something. And then, realistically, for mold to *begin* growing it would take at minimum a week, right? And then for it to fully bloom into a dull yellow flower the size of a sugar cube, another two or three?

I'm no hygiene expert, but that means that this person had, at the *minimum*, not showered for three to four weeks. *Probably* he had not let water or a washcloth touch the interior of his ear hole for over a *MONTH*!

Now, let's take a moment to ponder what might have been growing on other areas of this person. His murky bits. The clammy, ripe nether regions. Picture the furry tendrils of fungal growth that must have been entwining his taint and scrotuscus. Close your eyes and imagine you smell the moist, spidery growths that might have been carpeting his armpits.

I think of you often, ear-mold guy at the chess competition. Where are you now? Engulfed in mold somewhere, like a carcass on the floor of the jungles of Borneo? Being trod on by ants? Swarmed by roaches? Perhaps you are the mold king now, perched on a fungal throne, crowned in yellow fuzz, chessboard in hand.

Sometimes, after a long day of role playing (not the sexy kind), or chess battles, we nerd hooligans would sneak out at night, toilet-paper some houses, set off some illegal fireworks, and run around the neighborhood like skinny commandos. This gradually became a more and more regular part of our weekend adventures. There's something exhilarating and powerful about sneaking through yards and scuttling down dark suburban streets at three a.m., the normally bustling neighborhood silent except for the occasional dog or delivery truck. We would "T-P" friends' houses and strangers' houses and enemies' houses, leaving spiderweb-like strands of toilet paper all over their trees and cars and mailboxes. Eventually, toilet paper got a bit boring and we dreamed up more and more exotic defacing strategies.

We would buy jumbo boxes of plastic forks from the local Safeway earlier in the week and "fork" someone's house. John Valadez had the idea of "Cheerio-ing" someone's house and eventually, in a brilliant turn of dadaist surreality, we would "taco" people's houses, using hundreds of taco shells to decorate their lawns. We called ourselves the Taco Terrorists and would leave the initials "TT" in whipped cream on the victim's driveway. This was all great fun and seemed to be building to greater and greater Banksy-like stunts until one night we got arrested by the vicious scum at the Lake Forest Park Police Department. The guy at the local 7-Eleven had dropped a dime on us after we bought a huge bunch of toilet paper and Cheerios at four a.m. After there was a *whoop!* of sirens in the 7-Eleven parking lot and a searchlight hit us, four or five of us (minus John Valadez, who scuttled over a nearby fence) were stuffed into the backseat of a cop car like sardines, and we had the brilliant idea to stash all our contraband under the car seats.

I remember feeling gloriously innocent as we told the officers that we were simply out for a late-night walk, and then it all came crashing down as the other cop walked in from the car with an armful of toilet paper, Cheerios, shaving cream, taco shells, and fireworks. "Oldest trick in the book," the officer said, Baretta-style. They called our parents to come get us, which was incredibly humiliating. I was terrified about what my dad might say or do, but he was silent the entire way home and then, as we pulled into our driveway, turned to me and said wisely, oddly, "If you're going to do that kind of thing again, the important thing is not to get caught." That ended the fierce but brief campaign of the Taco Terrorists cell of Lake Forest Park, Washington.

Let's descend ever deeper into the nerd museum (nerdseum?) of my past, shall we?

Model United Nations is pretty much the greatest thing ever.

Similar to Dungeons & Dragons, MUN brings escapism, imagination, and role playing to its participants. Instead of warriors and monks, however, you pretend to be diplomats representing a country's best interests on an international level. You see, there's an imaginary UN conference and you, or you and a pal or two, show up to represent a country of your choice, like China or France or Bolivia or Costa Rica. The goal is to team up with allies of yours and attempt to pass resolutions that work in your country's best interest as well as blocking the diplomatic efforts of your enemies. You know, like how the world works.

It's total mayhem. Resolutions are drawn up. Notes are passed. Votes are taken. Debates rage. Countries are courted and insulted, variously. And, if you do your research on your country and its history as well as the faults and incongruities of other countries over the preceding decades, the interactions can get both passionate and intellectually stimulating. And the coolest thing? Getting to sit behind a little placard with your country's name on it. Also, getting to pretend that you just flew in on a jet, secret documents in tow.

The most fun was to represent crazy, rogue states that were a little off their rocker. Nicaragua and China were a lot of fun. Arab League states were a total blast and Iran sublimely, nuttily awesome. Plus, you could wear towels arranged like turbans on your head. The resolutions you could introduce could be completely unreasonable and you could rally the entire Muslim, anti-American world to get behind you and cause total imaginary global chaos in a high school gymnasium or conference room.

One time, at a weekend conference at Seattle University, my MUN pals and I decided to represent the US of A. Boy, was that a mistake. We were the punching bag of the entire conference. Having to stand up there and defend all the various boycotts, invasions, embargoes, bombings, military fundings, and hypocrisies our country was engaged in was a near-impossible task.

The greatest fun of all was attempting to effectively emulate the perceived cultural identities of the countries we were representing. It was a great precursor to my acting days. Only instead of roles, I would portray countries! Along with my main partner in eggheaded crime, John Valadez, I represented at various points in my career as an imaginary diplomat: Saudi Arabia (crazy), Syria (batshit crazy), North Korea (triple batshit crazy), the USSR (evil empire), China (rogue nation!), Cuba (double weird rogue!), Chad (love the name), France (boring), and Canada (so boring it makes your head throb until you pass out and find yourself watching curling reruns at three a.m.).

At MUN conferences there would be a ratio of about 85 percent dork dudes and 15 percent smart girls. And you can bet your UN Security Council resolution 286-B that the entirety of the attention of the 85 percent who were dork dudes was entirely focused on the remaining 15 percent. Needless to say, it's entirely preposterous to be looking to meet girls at Model United Nations conferences. But that's how my posse rolled, yo. I remember I was completely crushed on a girl from Shorewood High School, our school's archrival, who was representing the United Kingdom. Even though I was Saudi Arabia, I went along with everything she proposed because she looked like a cute, pimply Tina Fey. John Valadez was the only one with the cojones to go up and actually talk to her. *And* he actually got a date!

John Valadez was my best friend growing up. He was half-Mexican and we idiots called him "spic" and "wetback" because we didn't really understand how racism worked back then. For some reason, he hung with the nerds even though he was good with girls and good at sports. He was a little dude and I was a tottering Sasquatch, and together we made a preposterous pair. Our love for D&D was matched only by our love of band and MUN and kung fu movies and especially, above all else, comedy.

It was John and I who shared a sense of humor. We would stay up every Saturday night in those first years of *SNL* to watch Steve Martin and Elvis Costello and Buck Henry and Devo and the ne'er-do-wells and scalawags of comedy. We played our Steve Martin, Cheech and Chong, and Bill Cosby albums until they wouldn't play anymore. When we had sleepovers, we would watch Johnny Carson's monologue in case there was a stray joke that we could actually understand at the age of twelve or thirteen. It was he and I who memorized Monty Python sketches from top to bottom. In fact, I would take my toaster-size Panasonic cassette recorder and put it up in front of our boxy color television to record entire episodes of *Monty Python's Flying Circus* as they played on PBS at midnight. I had all of *Monty Python and the Holy Grail* recorded on a series of cassettes that John and I would play over and over, singing every classic Eric Idle ditty and reciting every John Cleese catchphrase.

John and I later became roommates in college at the University of Washington and eventually both went to NYU together, where John would go to film school. He went on to make many very successful, award-winning documentaries for PBS and is still quite short apparently.

Everyone who is at all successful in comedy has had a secret comedy dork life in their adolescence. Whether it's sitcoms or stand-ups, wallowing in the muck of comedy and repeating classic routines and jokes through your teenage years is what gives every aspiring comic or comedic actor the seed of their absurdist imagination that later takes flower.

Looking back on this phase of my life, I'm incredibly grateful for these little tide pools of weirdo culture I swirled around in. In them I found my voice, my intellectual and artistic curiosity, and my passion. Stuck in basements and classrooms and practice rooms with the oddballs, the misfits, the bizarre ones, I felt at home. I still do to this day.

The amount of laughter and strange humor that was fermented in those bizarre petri dishes was staggering. To quote Barry Manilow: "Misfits aren't misfits among other misfits." (Note: I have no idea what Mr. Manilow was talking about, as he is obviously not a misfit but the insanely handsome voice of a generation. Adored by billions, he glows with the power of a thousand suns and sings like the angel Gabriel himself with the piercing might of a galactic supernova mounted on the forehead of Zeus.)

These days, the teenage years are considered a time for socializing with a focus on dating and popularity. When relieved of the pressures of dating too young, I believe a young person is better able to focus on who they really are and find themselves in that crucial time when your personality is beginning to germinate. It's all that time reading, dreaming, and goofing off with fellow oddballs where our best selves get to evolve as teenagers.

I have always seen myself as an outsider. Not the outsider as portrayed in the movies by chain-smoking, brooding dudes with motorcycles and leather jackets, but the person who views himself as truly different and takes a keen, cold, critical eye to what society deems normal.

Later, when I would attend the Graduate Acting Program at NYU, my great acting teacher Ron Van Lieu would say to me that I needed to play misfits and outsiders. He predicted that it was playing characters who lived on the fringes that would bring me to life as an actor. That stuck with me always and has been a source of great strength as I've painted characters who are always on the other side of the fence looking in, who can never quite fit in or belong, who live in their awkwardness.

Becoming a "celebrity," especially to someone who has always believed himself to be an outcast, is one of the strangest transitions a human being can ever go through. I always longed to be loved more than anything. And to belong and be accepted. And then, when that "love" became the type where I was recognized most everywhere I went, where I was lauded and complimented in restaurants or airports, asked to be in countless strangers' cell phone pics, simply for appearing regularly on the television screen, the experience was brain-meltingly bizarre.

I'll never forget the time I first knew I was famous, when total strangers started calling out my name and waving at me from cars as they drove by. I would look up, startled, quizzically wondering what friend or relative of mine it might be when said Dwight fans would shout out, "Hey, Dwight. WE LOOOOVE YOU!!!!" And that very first time I went into a Starbucks to find the word *Dwight* had been scrawled on the side of my coffee cup, the baristas snickering knowingly. Very strange, I would often think, mind reeling. Here I am, the former pimply bassoonist, chess enthusiast, and player of an elf thief at Norwescon, and now, a few short decades later, hailed as a weird TV icon by complete strangers. Exhilarating and incredibly challenging at the same time.

Chapter 6

HOW ELVIS COSTELLO
MADE ME AN ACTOR

<T>TWO THINGS HAPPENED TO ME WHEN I TURNED SIXTEEN. I discovered punk rock and I moved to Chicago.

In suburban Seattle there were two radio stations: KISW and KZOK. If you didn't listen to those you were pummeled into oblivion by the rockers that be. They played one kind of music only: **CLASSIC ROCK** ROCK rock rock rock rock!!!!!

Then, out of the blue, a friend gave me some cassette tapes she had recorded from her hi-fi player: the Clash's *London Calling*, the Police's *Reggatta de Blanc* and *Outlandos d'Amour*, Squeeze's *East Side Story*, and Elvis Costello's *My Aim Is True*. My world was turned upside down and inside out in an instant, and my ears pinwheeled in delight.

After years of Billy Squier, Van Hagar, Air Supply, and Styx, I had never dreamed music like this existed anywhere. Sure, classic rock was awesome in its way, but the bloated, obvious, macho crooning and endless midtempo guitar solos were becoming an ear-sickening cliché. Nineteen eighty-two brought us some great radio fare, such as Queen and the Cars and Cheap Trick and Blondie and ELO, who all crafted some delightful tunes, but the angry young men of punk and new wave, with their whip-smart lyrics and rebellious melodies, made musical and lyrical explosions that completely captured my soul.

I listened to those cassettes until they snapped and I had to repair them by unwinding the brown ribbon, securing the snapped break point with dabs of Scotch tape, and rewinding with a pencil in the spokes.

Soon thereafter I would discover XTC, the Psychedelic Furs, Oingo Boingo, Gang of Four, the B-52s, Joy Division, X, Black Flag, Talking Heads, the English Beat, the Specials, and many more bands from that incredible era of music.

The music did a lot more than just entertain me. For a lot of us in that post-punk time, the music opened up a new way of thinking about the world. It was sarcastic and edgy and emotional and raw and perfectly defined our subculture's view that we were the smart outsiders looking in at all the bloated, indulgent, hypocritical crap of our materialistic culture.

In 1982, when my fairly miserable family found out my dad had gotten offered a pretty good job as an administrator at the Baha'i National Center in Evanston, Illinois, we jumped at the chance.

The only drawback was that I would have to leave my very first girlfriend, Jill. She was pretty in a Northwest-girl way (solid, fresh faced, and at home in the moss) and universally renowned as being the smartest person at Shorecrest. She found my loser idiocy charming for some odd reason. We had started dating a mere month or so before I knew I was moving. This "dating" consisted of going to movies and then spending a few hours making out and holding hands and feeling somewhat guilty about it. I was devastated as my family packed up our meager belongings and drove east, like a trio of Baha'i Joads. I listened to sad songs on cassette tape over and over again, the prairies and mountains streaming by outside, as I piloted the family 1981 Mustang hatchback filled with boxes of sci-fi books and my parents followed glumly behind in a U-Haul. (What did they talk about over those two thousand miles, I wonder.) Once I got into my new high school, Jill was quickly forgotten about, alas. Such is youth.

New Trier High School was (and still is) a very well-known institution. It was in the tony suburbs north of Chicago and was nationally renowned for its academics and arts programs. Because most schools are funded by local property taxes, the school was *flush* with cash. It had a *huge* drama department, a dance wing, a TV/film program, and a radio station with a huge blinking radio tower on top of the building. Many famous people had gone there, American icons such as Ann-Margret, Bruce Dern, Charlton Heston, and laugh-a-minute former secretary of defense Donald Rumsfeld.

We moved into literally the only apartment building that was within the school's expensive radius. It was a 1970s three-story bland edifice across the street from the "El" station in Wilmette. We lived in a two-bedroom, eight-hundred-square-foot, shag-carpeted box, while the kids I went to school with lived in impressive North Shore mansions of some kind or other. I'm not claiming poverty, just a certain kind of street cred that comes from being a character straight out of a John Hughes movie: poor, geeky, new wave kid moves into rich Chicago high school and finds self. (And, speaking of John Hughes movies, I was most certainly metaphorically in one, because New Trier was the high school most of his films were modeled on. The exterior was even featured in a different classic of the era, *Risky Business*.)

I saw an opportunity in coming to this new school and I took it. I did two things immediately: I started attempting to dress a version of "new wave punky bohemian" (instead of "suburban Seattle widelegger," with feathered hair and grotesque wide-legged jeans), and I signed up for acting classes.

One great thing about moving as a teenager is that you can reinvent yourself. When the privileged prepsters of New Trier met the new kid named Rainn with ripped-up Levi's, rectangular sunglasses, and a skinny piano tie, they had an entirely different perception of who I was from the folks I'd left behind in Seattle. I was like geeky Anthony Michael Hall with just a dash of dashing Andrew McCarthy.

Then, it happened. My past and my future collided, imploded, and exploded over the course of one three-minute period of time in Mr. Routenberg's* acting class during the first week of school. It was the perfect storm of my reinvention, where new wave music and my future life as an actor all came cascading together like a supernova. It was like a volcano flew directly into a cosmic superstorm and they both ignited like a bazooka at an AC/DC concert. Fasten your seat belts, America. It's that big.

So the very first assignment Mr. Routenberg gave us was called "Private in Public" or "Private Moment." The task was to come into the classroom with some props from home and "live" in front of the audience as if you were alone and in private. It was like the audience was peeking voyeuristically into someone's real, unadorned life. The point of the exercise was to allow us as actors to experience simply "being" in front of an audience instead of performing, illustrating, or "indicating." ("Indicating" is one of the worst crimes an actor can commit. Instead of experiencing a moment or an emotion, the actor performs

---

* Mr. Routenberg passed away in 2006. When I heard, I was very sad indeed. He directed me in *Story Theatre* and *Pygmalion* and brought out the best in everyone he worked with. He was so kind and loving to the students he directed, and I wouldn't be an actor if he hadn't been in my life. I miss you, Mr. Routenberg, and promise to pick up my cues.

and amplifies that moment in such a way that the audience will "get it." For instance, instead of just feeling angry, the actor will make his face red and shake his fist, thus "showing the audience" what he is feeling. Guilty!)

Not exactly getting the point of the exercise, I brought in a boom box and Elvis Costello's *My Aim Is True* on cassette. I fiddled around in my imaginary bedroom for a while and then put the song on in front of the class. I danced and sang and lip-synced and pranced around like a maniac to the kinetic rhythm of the song. Was it a private moment shared in front of a public audience? Well, kind of. After all, I would sometimes act out similar rock-and-roll fantasies in the privacy of my bedroom, but mostly it was a straight-up performance of what I do best, goofing around and looking like a total doofarooni.

The class went ballistic. Here was this new, odd alterna-dude in his black blazer and English Beat T-shirt doing some cool, funny shtick. And then, when the bell rang, all these incredibly pretty drama girls came over to me and asked my name and complimented me and patted me on the back and smiled and told me I should audition for the upcoming play and welcomed me to the school and the class and asked me to sit with them at their lunch table.

I was struck dumb. My face was flushed. My heart and brain were on fire. Oprah talks about "aha" moments. Well, this was like an "*AAAAAHAAAAA!!!!*" moment. I felt a sense of purpose and belonging, and in that exact instant, an actor was born.

That was one of the defining moments of my life. We can all boil down our lives to a handful of specific moments, I believe. A crossroads, a thin beam of light through a pinhole in the side of a shoe box where time stands still. Most of those moments happen to us between the ages of sixteen and twenty-four. That's when life is richest and ripest, and the vibrant memory banks are pulsating with maximum power, energy, and emotion.

I wish I could say that I became an actor because of my love of the craft and my soul's mission and my heart's longing to express itself. Nope. It was the girls. Girls, the thing in God's glorious universe that I knew the least about and terrified me more than anything. But isn't that what drives us all, anyway, at the beginning? Attention from the opposite sex? Status? Power? Self-esteem derived from external validation?

I suppose what we strive for is to ultimately let go of those more selfish, animalistic forces and seek a more mature, reasonable, balanced, and enlightened sense of purpose. Altruism, perhaps. Moral imperative. Service. God. The universe. Compassion. Nowadays I like to think I pursue my craft for the art, the challenge, the transcendence of the thing. Or to provide a service by getting a good laugh from an audience. But sometimes it all just begins with the girls.

I can still see me there, folded into the little desk in the corner of the acting classroom at New Trier High School in 1983, being chatted up by Bess Meyer, Terri Kapsalis, and Tria Smith, glowing with possibility. I have great compassion for that gangly, pale sixteen-year-old, his life moving in an entirely new direction thanks to a desire to reinvent himself, a gift for goofing off, some attention from girls, and his new spirit guide, Elvis Costello.

And so, after that fateful day, I DID audition for the fall production of *Time Out for Ginger*, a ridiculous play from the fifties, in which I played the dad of one Ginger, a girl who wanted to join the football team and caused an uproar in small-town America. (I wasn't very good, FYI.)

Those were good and fruitful years at New Trier. I acted in a ton of plays and made a lot of good friends. Chess, MUN, and D&D faded away and roles in *Ah, Wilderness!, Cyrano de Bergerac, Pygmalion, Story Theatre,* and *Oklahoma!* became the center of my universe. (Although I still played the GD bassoon for some unknown reason. I just couldn't stop wrapping my lips around that crazy *fagotto*, I guess.)

I had crossed over. Not from the movie cliché of unpopular to popular. I had crossed over within subgenres, you see. I had moved from regular old geek/nerd to the very top of the geek/nerd hierarchy, *DRAMA* geek/nerd. And the reason that drama geeks are at the pinnacle of that food pyramid of geekdom? It's not the tragedy/comedy logo or *Cats* pins on the raincoats. It's not the black eyeliner on both the boys and the girls. Neither is it the ability to burst into song or a tap dance in the school hallway at the drop of a theater reference. No. The thing that separates theater dorks from the rest is one word . . . you guessed it . . . once again . . . *girls*. There were and are and always will be pretty girls who sing and dance and act and improvise and joke around and are willing to make fools of themselves. *And*—and this is the most important point of all—*and* they're willing to hang out with geeky guys and even go to wrap parties and occasionally make out with them. This sets up drama geeks as the *lions* of the dork Serengeti.

Once, while playing Alfred Doolittle in Shaw's *Pygmalion* (the original play version upon which *My Fair Lady* was based), I had a magical moment onstage, the kind when the acting gods blow their golden muse breath down on you. I was in Professor Higgins's apartment (who, by the way, was played by the incredible actor Jim True-Frost, who later joined Steppenwolf and then created Detective "Prez" Pryzbylewski on *The Wire* as well as many other memorable roles), railing on about "middle-class morality" when I spied a pile of prop candies lying in a bowl on a downstage table. Without missing a beat, completely unrehearsed on opening night, in front of an audience of several hundred people, I made some grand gesture toward the folks upstage and with a deft sleight of hand, picked up the bowl, effortlessly sliding all the candies into my pants pocket. The audience erupted in a wave of laughter. Oh, lordy, that felt mighty good. And that's what we actors go for, those intangible, miraculous moments when something clicks and you are living a spontaneous, creative life in the shoes of the character, connected to the audience and flowing with the mysterious, gooey stuff of life. (Translation for atheists and materialists: Your synapses fire, causing a spontaneous behavior, which triggers a pleasant surprise auditory response from the viewers and consequently pleasure endorphins are released into your cerebellum, causing you to want to repeat the action for another release of chemicals in your opiate receptors.)

Deep inside of my selfity self, over the course of my gradual immersion into the world of high school theater, I sensed there was something *to* this acting thing, and that occasionally I had the ability to make people laugh, and that when I did that, I felt a pleasure greater than the great sexy-gasm itself. I had an inner mission that began to percolate. Perhaps, I thought, I might actually be able to do this acting thing as a career. This was the deepest, tiniest little flower of hope that I had ever before nurtured. Could it be? Could there be a universe in which I, northern gangly loser, could even consider the possibility of a world in which someday, somehow, people would cast me in plays and *pay* me to act in them? It seemed absurd, too far-reaching, too hubris-y. After all, I had never, ever *met* an actual person who made their living being an artist. But there was only one thing left to do: ask my drama teacher.

Suzanne Adams was the perfect companion teacher to Mr. Routenberg. While he was serious and soft-spoken, she was a wild child: emphatic, passionate, energetic, sensitive, demonstrative, and a little bit "cuckoo bird." But she was better than any acting teacher I had in college (until I went to NYU). Ms. Adams would make us improvise our parts as if we were animals, improvise on cue, and dig for the truth with great abandon. She had a glorious mystical side that I really responded to and was always talking about how we were all made of luminous stardust (this was WAY before Deepak Chopra, mind you), and she would literally pray to the gods of the theater before shows.

So I went into her office after class one day and fitfully, timidly, cautiously asked her . . . "Do you, uh, think, uh, that maybe, um, one day I might, perhaps, I could one day, maybe become a professional actor someday?"

Again, one of those pinhole moments that is tattooed into my memory. There was a pause, then she cocked her head, looked at me, and positively beamed. Dramatically—think Dame Maggie Smith— she said, *"Oh, yes!* I absolutely think you could do it. But you must study hard and work even harder! Apprentice yourself to the craft and you must go to college and travel the world. And study many different subjects like English and history, and you must read constantly! But I think you'd make a terrific actor, you're very talented indeed!"

Again, I was glowing with the glow of a thousand glowing moons as I left her office, crackling with possibility.

Here was a thing that I seemed to do pretty well and that made people laugh and girls like me AND I might get to do it as a career???!!!

Without her kind words and encouragement, I probably would not be an actor today. Had she said something to the effect of "Well, I can't say, it's a terribly difficult path and maybe you'll make it and maybe you won't. . . . It's awfully tough to make it as an actor and there's a pretty good chance you'll fail," I might have become an English professor or a radio DJ or a bassoon instructor. Not that there's ANYTHING wrong with those professions, mind you. Some of my favorite people are professors and DJs. Bassoon instructors, not so much.

Teachers can make such a profound impact on our lives and should be honored as heroes, I believe. They're working for so little money, under such difficult circumstances, usually for the love of the service to the children. Many of us owe who we are to certain teachers who appeared at just the right time, in the right place, and had just the right words to say to propel us on our journey.

(ACTIVITY ALERT: Take this opportunity, partway through this ridiculous book, to reach out to a teacher who made an impact on you and THANK THEM. You'll be so glad you did. And so will they!)

There was another teacher who had a profound effect on me during those fertile years—Ms. Raissa Landor, my English and Great Books teacher.

I had always gotten As at Shorecrest, while doing most of my homework the night before in about half an hour. New Trier, not so much.

I wrote my first paper in junior-year English class, on *The Scarlet Letter*, the night before, just as I always had in Seattle, and Ms. Landor, she of the screechy sandpaper voice and fright-wig hair, handed it back to me with a big fat scarlet D on it.

I'd never gotten a D before. Not even a C. I was stunned and held the paper in front of me with horror, like I had just been served with a subpoena or the results of a paternity test.

She said something to the effect of "I know you're new, but this just isn't gonna cut it here."

After class, Ms. Landor generously and patiently gave me some introductory instructions on the basics of how to write an essay, and I realized with a grotesque sinking feeling that I had no idea what it was to write something vaguely academic, that my Seattle education to that point had been pretty much a sham, and that I would need to start all over again with the whole "learning" thing. I think I swallowed hard (like an actual clichéd gulp) and came to a cold, hard understanding that I would need to really step it up here in John Hughes Land in order to get by.

I did ultimately step it up, so much so that Ms. Landor recommended I move into the top-level English class for the rest of the year. I adored quirky, brilliant Ms. Landor so much that I signed up for her senior-year cult.

Great Books was a yearlong English elective that should be in place in every school in America. All you did was read from the great works of literature and philosophy and debate the ideas behind them with your classmates. You were graded on the cohesion of your thoughts, your participation, and your grasp of the material. THERE WERE NO ESSAYS!

We read from Plato and the Bible and Rousseau and Kant and Nietzsche and Freud and Victor Hugo and *The History of the Decline and Fall of the Roman Empire* by Gibbon and many other writers I can't remember.

She exactingly instructed us on how to seek out the questions the authors were exploring in their works and how to fill the margins of our great books with notes and comments and thoughts in order to extract some possible answers. Great authors are constantly posing questions through their work, enormous philosophical, moral, ethical, and spiritual dilemmas with life-affecting reverberations.

Ms. Landor spoke with great zeal about Life's Big Questions (sound familiar, SoulPancake fans?) and the ancient human discussion that began in the caves and continued through ancient Greece and Rome all the way through to the cafés of Europe and the coffee shops of Greenwich Village.

You know, all the biggies: Is there a God? Do we have free will? Do we have a purpose? Is there such a thing as true love or a soul mate? What makes a civilization flourish? Is there an absolute morality or do we create our own? Are we noble beings or animals in our essence?

You get the idea.

She told us once that if we could prove or disprove the existence of God she would give us an A. So future academicians Jay Greene and Randy Kamian tried to do just that. They got As but were unable to really settle the whole God question.

So much of the seeds of my later project SoulPancake would be sown in that dynamic, fascinating, yearlong mind cult that was like a front-row seat at the feet of Socrates on the steps of the Acropolis. Thanks, Ms. Landor and your outlandish hair!

New Trier gave me an incredible hyperjump into my artistic and intellectual life, and there were so many experiences I had there that I'll be forever grateful for. Like RADIO! I got my own radio show as a DJ on the school station, WNTH, and that was one of the most incredible events of my young life. To get to play the songs I obsessed over for a listening audience of *sometimes literally DOZENS* of people! My show was called *Uncle Rainn's Story Hour*, and I would often read Dr. Seuss books on the air and have friends bring puppets to be puppet guest DJs.

And ROCK AND ROLL! I was in my first and last rock band. We had one gig in a church basement. We auditioned for the Battle of the Bands and didn't get in. Which was hard to do, let me tell you. The band was called Collected Moss (get it? A rolling stone collects no . . .) and we were atrocious. We were like rock and roll threw up in a mall and a bad guitarist slipped in it and did a solo on his back for nobody while Muzak was still playing. I was the lead singer, and I sounded like Lou Reed with a hint of Tom Brokaw. The band did not share my affinity for the music I liked. They liked classic rock and especially (gags) the Grateful Dead. So this was our preposterous set list that reflected our various tastes (guess which songs I picked):

"Suffragette City," David Bowie
"Fire on the Mountain," the Grateful Dead

"Mystery Dance," Elvis Costello

"Magic Carpet Ride," Steppenwolf

"Blister in the Sun," Violent Femmes

"Behind Blue Eyes," the Who

"Should I Stay or Should I Go," the Clash

"Sympathy for the Devil," the Rolling Stones

"Dancing with Myself," Generation X

And, finally, an ode to Cream, featuring a long, plodding instrumental bluesy jam with *tons* of guitar, drum, and bass solos.

We broke up after a month.

And, finally, the focal point of my youthful existence, the swirling white nexus of heat and light at the center of my adolescent galaxy: girls. I had several meaningful relationships with some truly lovely and brilliant young women at New Trier. I experienced the miraculous ups and downs of romantic love. Mostly the downs. The dumping and being dumped. The pain and passion of youthful infatuation. You know, like in *Jersey Shore*; *Beverly Hills, 90210*; and Shakespeare. When I was in the hormone-fueled despair of heartbreak, I often used to sleep in my closet in a pile of dirty clothes. Out of isolation and self-pity, my shag-carpeted closet with the mirrored sliders was my adolescent loser womb. This was perhaps my strongest memory at age seventeen. Me, racked with despondency at having been dumped, lying in a pile of stinky T-shirts, gazing at the dappled popcorn-foam ceiling, thinking of whatever girl had left me bereft and forlorn.

But my New Trier experience provided me with the spark to continue on toward college as an artist and actor, more confident in my abilities than ever and with an artistic and intellectual curiosity that has served me ever since. And, most important, it gave me the courage to finally and irrevocably give up the bassoon.

THE GREATEST ALBUMS
OF THE EARLY EIGHTIES
(IN NO PARTICULAR ORDER)

—

THE CLASH, *LONDON CALLING*

One of the greatest albums that will ever be made ever. So achingly smart and angry at the same time. Terrific melodies that disguise political angst and turmoil. It was like England was on fire and these guys took musical pictures.

Not a punk album per se, the Clash at the time were expanding their musical horizons with ska, R&B, dub, reggae, and rockabilly.

I remember playing "Lost in the Supermarket" on a date with a girl who had previously only listened to Joni Mitchell and her confused look as she struggled to understand what was sonically going on.

TALKING HEADS, *THE NAME OF THIS BAND IS TALKING HEADS*

An adrenalized sneak peek into one of America's greatest bands in live performance. This album was filled with sweaty, mysterious rhythms and disjointed lyrics. There's a strange dynamic in Talking Heads: the stiff, intellectual bark of David Byrne mixed with the kinetic groove of one of the swingingest new wave funk bands ever assembled. There were strange new lands explored on this album: futuristic cities, psycho killers, as well as odes to air and drugs and feelings.

David Byrne, with his gigantic suit, was someone I could relate to, an alien trapped in a twitchy human body.

XTC, *ENGLISH SETTLEMENT*

This band has been largely forgotten, but their gorgeous instrumentation tempered by edgy lyrics and a pastoral snarl made them my personal Beatles. The lead singer, Andy Partridge, had a nervous breakdown and swore he would never tour again, so the band holed up in some tiny bucolic English town, and their music became less punky and angry and more orchestral album after album. His adenoidal voice and twelve-string guitar soared through "Senses Working Overtime," and I was hooked for life.

The song was on constant play through my first Sony Walkman's foamy earphones.

SQUEEZE, *EAST SIDE STORY*

Difford and Tilbrook were the new Lennon and McCartney to us pre-hipsters in the early eighties. Their melodies were just so damn catchy and beautiful. And they weren't afraid to be really smart and super edgy at the same time. They were never sentimental but always clever. They made strangely uplifting and hopeful music in a dark musical era. I still don't know what half their songs mean.

Plus girls just love Squeeze, even today. Lads, trust me. When on a date, set your Spotify to Squeeze and wait for the sexy magic!

ELVIS COSTELLO, *IMPERIAL BEDROOM*

This early-mid-period Elvis album has avalanches of lyrics cut with a palpable longing. There's a lush beauty and sadness here that the spokesman for my generation of angry nerds was never able to capture again. I still have the entirety of "Beyond Belief" memorized from repeated listens. Go ahead, quiz me. His earlier, punkier stuff rammed up against his orchestral production in a glorious way on this album, which perfectly bridged post-punk to modern alternative rock.

R.E.M., *RECKONING*

Who were these freaks in their caps and scarves whirling around onstage singing indecipherable lyrics about weird Southern mythological stories?! There was so much anguished feeling underneath all of that kudzu noise! And what the hell was Michael Stipe saying?!

When I saw them play live at a gymnasium at MIT in 1985, the brainy audience was baffled by a lead singer in a raincoat and a Cubs hat who faced away from the audience toward the back wall, twirled around, and drone-howled poetry for the entire two-hour set. Meanwhile, Peter Buck and Mike Mills were rocking out like midseventies Stones.

I got to see them a few years back on their final tour, and I cried like a baby angel when Michael Stipe sang the glorious "I'm SOOOOOORRRRRY" chorus of "So. Central Rain."

LAURIE ANDERSON, *BIG SCIENCE*

Performance art made new wave rock and roll. This oddly affecting spoken-word tapestry mesmerizingly dissected the disaffected modern world. Stories of downtown New York for those of us who had never visited downtown New York. The furthest thing from Van Halen that you could possibly listen to. The best album to drop a reference to if you wanted to impress artsy college girls in glasses who doodled on their jeans in ink and eventually make out with them.

HÜSKER DÜ, *ZEN ARCADE*

A punk concept album?! Thirty years before Green Day did one, this Minneapolis trio erupted an epically loud soundscape song cycle about some dude who runs away from home and goes through all kinds of weird, horrible experiences, only to discover it was all a dream. Hardcore punk opera.

I've seen both founders, Bob Mould and Grant Hart, live, but I wish I had seen the Dü, as they were supposed to have been one of the best live bands ever.

THE REPLACEMENTS, *LET IT BE*

Drunk-punk poets of the northern plains, steeped in anger, heartbreak, and a sneering sense of humor. Catchy, jangly tunes that were equal parts Stones and Ramones.

"Unsatisfied" is a song every teenager should sing at the top of their lungs, forlorn and misunderstood, as I did so many times later in life, driving my 1973 Volvo through rain-slicked Seattle streets circa 1985.

X, *WILD GIFT*

A boyfriend/girlfriend outfit from Venice, California, X was the most literate punk band around. And they made at least five great albums through the early eighties. Just listen to their names and quiver in delight: John Doe, Exene Cervenka, Billy Zoom, and DJ Bonebrake. Listen to "White Girl" and you will know exactly what makes the electric ghosts of Los Angeles dance.

VIOLENT FEMMES, *VIOLENT FEMMES*

Having heard some of their advance singles at WNTH, the New Trier High School radio station, a bunch of us headed out to see the Femmes at one of their earliest concerts. It was at a small Chicago club in 1983, and there were about eighty people in the audience. The music was electric and stripped down at the same time. The drummer stood and played a snare drum and cymbal in the front center of the stage. Our little acned faces were melted. About a month later their stuff was all you heard on the radio.

THE SMITHS, *THE SMITHS*

Punk rock meets Frank Sinatra meets Oscar Wilde. Morrissey's poster with his perfect, perfect hair hung on my wall with thumbtacks through most of my early college years. I had never heard someone summarize my feelings so exactly. Moz was sick of love and sex and romance and was heartrendingly alone. But we knew it was mostly an act. How could he be so alone with hair like that?

Chapter 7

A *CHORUS LINE* MATINEE

———

I LEFT THE NORTH SHORE OF CHICAGO FOR TUFTS UNIVERSITY in Boston and was thrilled and excited to plunge headfirst into the whole college-experience thing. I was also a bit relieved to be leaving my parents and the quietly unhappy condo they inhabited.

I had been rejected by Brown, Stanford, and Oberlin and accepted by the universities of both Michigan and Illinois. But it was Tufts that I fell in love with after a visit there, and I was thrilled to be a part of its well-regarded experimental theater program.

Tufts was beautiful. It's the quintessential New England college campus, with lots of leafy trees, girls in preppy sweaters, and cool old Pepperidge Farm–type buildings. Plus it was in Boston, which is where half of America goes to school on any given day.

My roommate was a guy named Rob from Prescott, Arizona, who had LONG hair and big muscles; played endless, terrible electric guitar solos; and drove a truck. He was not your typical college New England–y roommate. I wanted a more typical roommate. You know, like someone from a Wes Anderson movie or Vampire Weekend.

Someone who was always reading Sylvia Plath, Rousseau, and *Spin* magazine. Not a future member of the WWE or *Duck Dynasty*.

I would always try to be friendly to Rob as he noodled along to Jethro Tull albums that he blasted on his HUGE stereo system, and he always totally ignored me. It wasn't until months later that we started hanging out and he revealed that he had found out before school that I had gone to New Trier and had heard from a friend that the school had a lot of rich preppies at it, so he made up his mind beforehand that I was probably a total butt like James Spader in *Pretty in Pink* and decided to essentially ice me. Isn't it funny how we make up our minds about people? Rob turned out to be a really smart, funny, great guy, not a muscle-headed moose like I had judged *him* to be.

I continued my passion for acting by diving into the thriving theater department at Tufts. Theater. The study of acting can become a heroin-like obsession and can take over your life. Theater departments at colleges are like fascinating little cults that suck away your time, energy, and very soul (evil laugh). Unlike a cult, however, they give back with a glorious production of . . . *PIPPIN*!

Just kidding. We never did any goofy musicals. We were *ARTISTES*, DAMN IT! We did inexplicable Beckett plays and experimental Shakespeare productions that drew confused audiences that numbered in the tens. College campuses all over this great nation are filled with pale, eccentric misfits, spending literally every extra second of their college time building sets, hanging lights, rehearsing scenes, and goofing off backstage. I was one of those dramatic misfits and I LOVED it. I had truly found my home.

(A couple years or so ago, I got to go speak on the campus and I swung by the [newly redone and recently relocated] Tufts Arena Theatre. I skulked around backstage and watched the students having a technical rehearsal for some kind of crazy play. The energy was *exactly* the same. The camaraderie and fun. The air and the hush and the way dust motes floated in the light, which splayed sharply across the space, casting dramatic shadows. As I silently peered from behind a pillar at the actors on the stage, there was an experience of timelessness, nostalgia, eternity, and peace. It was as if it were almost thirty years previous and I had simply jumped back in time/space in an older, beefier man-suit. It was one of those perfect, transcendent, magical moments we live for. I sure hope there is a theater department in the next world. Sign me up for the general auditions if there is.)

I got to do some stellar plays at Tufts, including *Uncle Vanya* with the very, very young (and strikingly handsome) Hank Azaria. I played an old man character and Hank played a forlorn, studly Russian doctor whom the ladies were always swooning over. He was amazing in the role and we all knew that he was going to be a big star one day. I played this ancient pompous professor (at age nineteen!) and tottered around indicating "senile Russian man" in heavy "old age" makeup like a reject from *Bad Grandpa*. I also met David Costabile there. He's the amazing actor from *Breaking Bad* and *Billions* that you've seen in about a thousand TV shows and commercials and is one of my very best friends to this day.

I was about two months into school when I got the call. My parents were getting a divorce. As much as I knew it had to happen (and really should have happened loooong beforehand), I was pretty shook up by the news. On top of everything that was new at Tufts and the incredibly difficult workload of freshman year, it was greatly unsettling to know that our bizarre little spiritually and emotionally constipated family unit had come to an end. There were obviously no cell phones or Internet back then, so the communication about this major life change happened with a calling card over the pay phone in the common area of the third floor of Tilton Hall. Plus, as I've stated previously, a Roomba could communicate better than my parents, especially about anything having to do with human feelings. My dad was pretty devastated by the whole thing and it was excruciating to know how much confused pain he was in and not be able to be there for him. I got pretty depressed after that; the excitement and buzz of the new school faded away and things started to become very gray—the leaves, the sweaters, the Pepperidge Farm buildings. Even the theater became more of a chore and an escape rather than a place of crazy, creative love.

A saving grace for me was that my birth mom, Shay (formerly Patricia), had gotten back in touch with me a few years previous and wanted to have an actual relationship. She lived not far away in Salem, Massachusetts, and I would see her and her husband (number four, Chuck: great guy, thick Boston accent, clam digger, children's shoe salesman, new age polarity massage therapist) a good deal that freshman year.

This process of reacquaintance started at about age fifteen or so when we were still in Seattle. Shay wrote me and said she wanted to be more involved in my life and get to know me better. I was a bit skeptical as she had written in this same way several times previously and then I'd not hear from her for years. Still true to her sixties roots, she would occasionally pop by our Seattle home, inspired and obsessed with some new new-agey health trend that she was championing, like dried seaweed, vitamin E oil, or super blue-green algae. Then she was gone in a flash like a hippie Lone Ranger, not to be heard from for a couple more years.

But this time Shay meant business. She started calling every week. She started asking what was going on in my life and taking a great interest. She sent me birthday cards and shipped me out on a Greyhound to see her in her tiny house in scenic Wapato, Washington (which was not in the slightest bit scenic and directly abutted one of the poorest Indian reservations you've ever seen).

As odd as my birth mother was, she was a much better, wiser communicator than my other parents. We would have long talks about these weird, confusing things that were always bouncing around inside of me called "feelings." She was very intuitive and insightful, and these talks and our new relationship helped me a great deal in my jumbled adolescence. Sometimes the people you need come into your life at just the right time. Shay was that. When I most needed a mom, she was suddenly there for me, and for this I will always be grateful.

In fact, Shay took such an interest in me and my activities that once she decided to invite a bunch of her friends over and have me dungeon master (DM for short) a game of D&D at her Wapato house. That was a night I wish I had on film: a fifteen-year-old version of me taking a bunch of adult faux hippie Baha'is through a monster-filled dungeon in a tiny cinder-block house next to an Indian reservation.

I learned a great deal about Shay in those years, where she had been, what she had done, and why she would disappear so much.

As the details about those "lost" years began to emerge, they were more amazing than anything you could possibly make up. As shockingly absurd as this timeline is, there is a very sad underbelly of the hippie generation revealed in it as well.

1. Lived on Queen Anne Hill in Seattle with a goat named Angel of the Morning. She attempted to live off of the milk from said goat.
2. Got engaged to a Jewish fella while reading Exodus, converted (briefly) to Judaism, and took a boat to Israel with him and lived on a kibbutz, where she changed her name briefly to Sarah and where a chicken once laid an egg on her pillow.
3. Got married and traveled in a camper van to Berkeley (of course), and then got a job as a house parent at an "awareness house" for drug counseling.
4. Even though she was not a druggie, she joined a cult-like treatment center for heroin addicts in Mendocino called the Family. They would do an exercise of emotional "attack therapy" called

the Game, where the participants would berate each other to break down the addict inside them. She left after a year, when it was discovered that the leaders were all secretly selling and taking drugs.

5. Became a drug counselor at a rehab in Bismarck, North Dakota, where she played a lot of Ping-Pong, hung out with Native American bead makers, and had to eventually flee when a crazy patient started stalking her.
6. Moved to Salt Lake City and got heavily into feminism and women's rights while working at a local YWCA, leading marches, seminars, and "consciousness-raising groups."
7. Married another guy and they got jobs for the Park Service at the Dungeness National Wildlife Refuge in Washington as rangers.
8. After being married a year, she left for Yakima, Washington, and became executive director for the YWCA there, heading up a program and shelter for battered women.

This is about when I got to know her again. But here are a few more scrumptious details from the years that followed. . . .

1. Decided to help form a Baha'i theater company along with a (literal) Gypsy friend and moved to Salem, Massachusetts, to launch it.
2. Got a job as a witch at the Salem Witch Museum, where, in a witch hat, she would scare tourists for ten bucks an hour.
3. Became a yoga teacher in 1990 and is still one to this day! (A very good one, I might add.)

Now, to back up a bit. I mentioned previously that there was a significant, impactful event that happened with my mom around her leaving my dad and me when I was a child.

When I was in my early twenties, having graduated from NYU

and having begun my career, I finally asked Shay about the divorce. It really was the first time I had ever asked her about it in a direct way. This would turn out to be one of the most important conversations I would ever have. (Note: We were in a graveyard for some reason. Surrounded by the dead of Salem, which probably included some famous, actual, historical witches. The graveyard location made this conversation that much more memorable. In fact, any conversation you have in a graveyard is made about 20 percent more meaningful and resonant simply by the association with the location. Try it! Call it the Rainn Wilson Graveyard Conversation Challenge!)

As the words "So *why* did you and my dad really get a divorce?" left my mouth, Shay's face transformed.

"You mean your dad never told you?" she said, stunned.

"No," I said.

(My dad, when prodded, would always just say sadly, vaguely, wistfully, "Oh, I don't know, we just went our separate ways, I guess.")

She was shocked and had assumed my dad had told me (and everyone else for that matter) the entire sad, seedy story.

So she perched on a headstone and filled me in.

Shay had become an actress in the late sixties and had performed in several plays. The fact that I had never known or heard of this and was finding this fact out in my midtwenties after I had become a professional actor was pretty mind-blowing. She had fallen in with some crazy experimental-theater types and in one somewhat infamous production had run around in the play naked with her body painted blue. (The Blue Woman Group?)

Shay told me that my dad did not look too highly on these pursuits and was a bit put off by all the crazy hippie/bohemian shenanigans of the theater artists. Apparently they were too "out there" even for my wackadoodle dad.

(As a matter of fact, when I was a teen and started taking an interest in theater, my dad always acted rather strange about it, almost like he wasn't sure I should go in that direction. I always thought that was a little bit bizarre, as he was always so supportive of my other artistic pursuits. He wasn't negative about it; there was just this odd air of trepidation and concern when it came to my interest in it.)

Shay explained that all these theater shenanigans finally brought the marriage to an end. When I was about a year and a half or two years of age, Shay came to my dad and told him that she had been having an affair with the director of the play she was in. My dad begged her to stay in the marriage, but she decided to go off with the director dude and left us.

My dad was beyond devastated, apparently. When I eventually told him of this discussion and sought his point of view on everything, he described that time as the lowest of his entire life. He couldn't sleep and cried for weeks, abandoned and alone, caring for his gargantuan toddler in the rain.

He painted a small, personal masterpiece after these events that perfectly sums up his feelings.

Yes, that's a male figure lying prone on an operating table with a naked woman and a knife standing next to him. You can clearly see the words *kill*, *money*, and *lamb* in the painting. I think you get the idea.

Shay only stayed with the hippie director for a couple months (around the time she had the goat) and then tried to reconnect with my dad soon after. But by that time it was too late. My sad dad had fled the country for the jungles of Nicaragua and quickly remarried on the rebound. The rest you know about.

I remember a wash of conflicting feelings coming over me in the graveyard that day. (It's odd sometimes, isn't it, that we can feel two or three very different things at the exact same time?) I was shocked by the events of the story, astounded that these details had never been shared with me by Shay or my dad previously. But mostly I felt relieved. Suddenly the whole family history made sense and the puzzle pieces fit together. I sighed deeply with both anguish and peace.

Many things are fascinating to me about this tale: the fact that I was only finding out about all this secret family history in my mid-twenties, the underlying idea that my discovery of and fascination with acting probably had some mysterious genetic components to it, and the realization that my dad's reticence about my devotion to acting had its roots in some devastating heartbreak. And, most of all, a serious understanding of the kind of guilt Shay had felt and why she had such a hard time being a part of my life when I was a child. She was filled with such disgrace at her behavior, about the affair, the leaving of my dad and the abandoning of her child, and the fact that she thought that the whole world knew about all of it, which my dad, out of principle, had kept secret and I am now trumpeting to the world (with her permission), that she avoided us, constantly moving and changing up her life as a form of escape from the shame.

Shay turned out to be a great mom to me, all things considered. She was a loving mentor, friend, and teacher right when I needed her in my late adolescence and early adulthood, and I'm very close to her and her husband, Chuck, to this day. After a wonderful, invigorating, but depressing year at Tufts, I went back home to be near my newly divorced parents, knowing I wouldn't go back to Boston in the fall. I felt inexorably drawn back to them, their misery, and the city of Seattle, where they had both relocated. Kristin had begun selling her silver jewelry at the Seattle Public Market (which she still does to this day). My dad was back managing the office at Jim Dandy Sewer and Plumbing, licking his wounds and trying to pull himself together. Why he was hurting so much from a divorce from a woman he didn't really love, I have no idea. Life, I guess.

After several months of driving marine supplies around the city (see the list entitled "Shitty Jobs"), I signed back up for college at the University of Washington. Another school, another drama department. I had some good teachers and did some terrific productions there, but the greatest event was meeting my future wife, Holiday Reinhorn, in an acting class.

We didn't date but became good friends, and both of us felt quite a romantic spark doing a scene from the existentialist classic *Waiting for Godot* together. At one point during the darkly comedic scene, we gave each other piggyback rides, and that was always my favorite part. (Does that sound weird?) She would ride horses in her off time and was always showing up to acting class wearing fancy jodhpurs, a kind of tight-fitting riding pant. It's an exotic and flattering pant, the jodhpur. Even more so than other types of flattering pants, such as bell-bottoms, skinny jeans, parachute (*can't touch this!*) pants, and Hillary Clinton pantsuits. In fact, I highly recommend jodhpurs as an everyday pant for both sexes!

She was a mesmerizing girl with a bizarre sense of humor and a crazy genius brain, and I was secretly smitten. Especially when I saw her play May in *Fool for Love* by Sam Shepard in a sexy tour de force. She had a boyfriend at the time, so I held back from making my feelings known. Little did I know that the payoff wouldn't be until years hence. (More on that later. You can read all about our relationship in chapter 11, "Volcano Love"!)

I moved out of my dad's new sad bachelor apartment and got a funky little pad with John Valadez in Wallingford, right next to the Dick's Drive-In, where I sometimes ate two or three delicious fried meals a day.

It was around this time that I got my first real post–high school girlfriend. Diana was an Indonesian Australian with long dark hair and a very arresting look. Like most Aussies do, she had just spent a year traveling the globe and was stopping in Seattle for a spell on her way back to her native land. She was staying nearby with some friends and I was infatuated. We spent three love-filled, postadolescent weeks together, me playing Bob Dylan songs on the guitar and trying to seem intense and tortured, her saying mysterious and exotic things in an Aussie accent while looking mysterious and exotic.

The only drawback was, however, that she most likely gave me scabies (probably from one of the thousand youth hostels that she stayed at on her around-the-globe tour). If you've never had scabies before, what a treat! They're microscopic little vermin that live in your skin. When you lie still to go to sleep, that's when they come out to play. These little buggers emerge from their tiny skin caves and eat your dead skin and scamper about on your skin lawn. The sensation is not something I would wish on my worst enemy. It's like you're being tickled by microscopic ticks with feather dusters just as you're nodding off to sleep. The only solution is to put this noxious pink poison called Kwell all over your body and to wash the hell out of your sheets, clothes, and towels, as they spread around like . . . like . . . well, like scabies. Here's a fun picture!

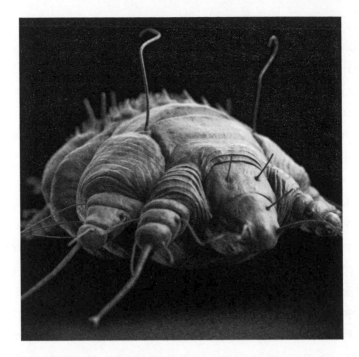

It was during Christmas of that year (1985), after I had successfully rid myself of all parasites, when I decided once and for all to become a professional actor. It was on a trip back to Boston, where I finally resolved to put all my chips on the table and pursue a career as a THESPIAN!

I flew to Massachusetts to visit Shay and Chuck and was deeply considering what to do next in my life. Major crossroads stuff. John Valadez was going to take off for India in a couple of months to do some volunteer work and teach photography at a Baha'i school there, and he really wanted me to come. I wasn't that happy being around my depressed, divorced parents or the University of Washington and was very seriously considering going with him. I was having moderate success in plays but had truly hit a rut as an actor. I was not very good. I was indicating and stiff and stuck in my head all the time. I wanted, longed, yearned to be a real actor, but I knew, after a few professional auditions in the Seattle area, that I was nowhere near good enough to make it in the real world. I knew that if I wanted to proceed in any way, shape, or form I needed some real training. There were a number of very good, legendary training programs out there and I started to look into them. But I was terrified. This would be a HUGE decision, an investment of tens of thousands of dollars and many, many years. Leaving undergrad early to enter a rigorous actor's training process was a daunting prospect.

But I also knew that to be a professional artist, there was a level of commitment that one needed to undertake that was simply staggering. I didn't want to half-ass it, be mediocre, or have acting as a "hobby." I knew that I would need to dive in completely.

My dad inspired me toward this goal. He was a painter and a writer but had a family to support and was always having to focus on his day job. I was grateful for the food and rent and solidity he provided but was well aware that this was a man greatly saddened by the fact that he never truly got to fully pursue his artistic dreams. I didn't want to follow that path. There's nothing like having a parent who didn't get to become the artist he wanted to be to focus and inspire you in your career decisions.

I was truly terrified by this crossroads and quite stumped as to what to do when I had one of the many mystical experiences that seemed as if the universe was folding itself toward me and taking a bow, inviting me onto an exhilarating pathway.

While wandering about in Boston, I decided to go see the movie version of *A Chorus Line* at a multiplex matinee.

It's a terrible movie. Don't see it. It's filled with actors and dancers and singers going on and on and on about "making it" and "getting a job" and "being discovered" and wanting to act and dance and sing. The musical itself is wonderful, but the movie is a stilted train wreck, considered by many to be THE WORST translation of a musical to a film EVER MADE. And even though I knew it was horrible, I was deeply, deeply moved. Sitting by myself, in the dark of a near-empty matinee in a theater near Government Center, Boston, I started to ugly cry. Full-on, grotesque, racking sobs during "What I Did for Love." The kind where you're sort of gulping for air. As all those actors and singers and dancers were longing and yearning to act and sing and dance, I felt a kinship in my heart, which lunged toward the screen as if it would burst.

I stepped out of the theater, tears drying on my cheeks, into one of the most beautiful sunsets I've ever seen. Red and orange light was streaming through snowflakes that had begun to quietly fall from the Boston sky. The ground, the multiplex, the high-spired churches and offices of that great city were being dusted with white. And time, once again, seemed to slow down and stop like a train pulling into a station. I gazed up into the sky and took several deep breaths, noticing that a deeply calm, passionate decision seemed to be dropping down into my body. I decided to go for it. I knew I had to become an actor. There was no turning back. It was my calling, my vocation.

The entire course of my life changed outside of a multiplex during Christmas of 1985 after a viewing of one of the worst movies of the 1980s. True story.

I told my parents and friends and dove in headfirst. The first thing to do? Apply for acting programs. I auditioned for the Professional Actor Training Program (PATP) at the University of Washington and didn't get in. Not even close. The head of the program wore an actual ascot and looked at me like I was the skinniest little weirdo who had ever auditioned for him since the dawn of time.

I then targeted the two best schools in the country that accepted people who hadn't finished undergrad, and John Valadez and I drove his parents' Chevy Impala at breakneck speed down to San Francisco for the auditions.

After a nervous, sleepless night (and a bout of vomiting at a gas station on the way), I went to my Juilliard audition, entering a large, cold loft space with a long table full of stoic panelists under fluorescent lights. I don't remember much about it other than a lot of loud sweating and gesticulating that stirred nary an eyebrow on the faces of the adjudicators. I bombed. I was rattled beyond measure. I had so much pressure on myself and my shoulders that I completely crumbled. I left, dejected. One down, one to go. The next day was my audition for the Graduate Acting Program at NYU.*

That night we stayed with our old Dungeons & Dragons friend George Evans at his communal hippie house near Stanford. He was really going off the deep end those days and would later be found up in a tree, hair down to his shoulders, wild-eyed, on the Stanford campus, shouting at passersby about the imminent end of the world. The night we stayed there, the residents of his house were having some kind of food orgy where dinner was spread out on a big plastic tarp and you'd crawl around on it naked, the only rule being that you couldn't feed yourself but only others. We opted for Jack in the Box.

That evening, once again, I was up much of the night, terrified about the audition the next day. I prayed, meditated, soul-searched, and went through what I now believe to be another transcendent, life-altering event.

After this dark night of the soul, I surprisingly awoke in total peace and confidence. I was somehow in touch with that still, inner voice inside of me that spoke to me of my own unique brilliance. I felt

---

* The program was mostly a graduate program, but they would take some undergrads like me, who would obtain their BFA instead of an MFA.

a calm strength that guided me throughout the day, all the way up to the audition. I knew what I needed to do and I wasn't going to let my own fears and inadequacies get in my way again.

The audition was for the newly appointed head of the NYU program: the grande dame genius of the American regional theater movement, founder and artistic director of the Arena Stage in Washington, DC, and internationally acclaimed producer/director Zelda Fichandler.

She was very insightful and perceptive and responded well to my Mercutio monologue. But when it came to the "sea monologue" by Edmund from *Long Day's Journey into Night*, she stopped me halfway through.

She spoke to me about the monologue and the play. About the life of the author, Eugene O'Neill, whom she had met once. She went into great detail about the circumstances surrounding the speech and the emotional need of Edmund to speak with his father, to share this intimate story of sublime transcendence with the man he longed to connect with.

She then called me forward and sat me down across the table from the other man in the room, associate dean of the Tisch School of the Arts J. Michael Miller.

"Do the monologue again, only much simpler. Just speak to him," she said. "Connect with the man sitting across this table from you."

I started up again, in a very similar vein to what I had done previously. She stopped me quietly.

"Take all 'performance' out of it. Look into his eyes and just talk to him like he's your own father. Keep it simple."

I took a deep breath and started again, this time carefully connecting with Michael and with the material. As I relaxed, the story flowed out of me. It felt real, natural, simple. Tears began to drop from my eyes for the first time doing the monologue. Tears of Edmund's intense longing to connect with his father.

I finished and there was a silence in the room. Zelda simply said, "Bravo, we'll be in touch."

And I knew I was in.

So many things occur in the course of our lives that upon reflection feel like they were meant to happen. As if God reached out a mysterious hand and opened a door to a new room. To the materialist, that mystical feeling is simply the endorphins and electrical impulses of the brain reacting to create emotional meaning in random chance. To the spiritually minded, creation, time, fate, and the Holy Spirit conspire and provide when you make the effort in showing you the path toward your destiny.

Everything in my life to that point—Shay's acting genes, the move to New Trier, the Elvis Costello exercise, scooping up the candy in *Pygmalion*, Ms. Adams telling me I had a chance to make it, the sublime decision I reached in the snow at the multiplex, the embarrassing failure at the Juilliard audition—all these things led to my going to the best possible place for me in the entire world, the Graduate Acting Program at NYU in the heart of Greenwich Village.

Chapter 8

THE ONLY LIVING
BOY IN NEW YORK

———

THERE WAS PERHAPS NO MORE MIND-POPPING EXPERIENCE in my life than moving to New York City in 1986 to attend acting school. Complete and total culture shock. I had lived in Seattle, Boston, and suburban Chicago at that point, but nothing prepared me for the explosion of Manhattan.

I rode to town in a crappy old van that had a couple of boxes and duffel bags (my entire life's possessions), along with John Valadez and Steve Wilmart. Together we had made our way from Chicago, Steve on his way to the Berklee College of Music, John on his way to India to travel for a year, and me to move to my new city and what would be my home for the next thirteen years.

We were slack-jawed and wide-eyed as we sputtered across the Manhattan Bridge and chugged on up to Union Square, where my dorm was located. It was insanity. Traffic barely moved; horns blared; loud throngs of people of every possible ethnicity roved everywhere, completely disregarding crosswalks and street signs. Seas of taxicabs surged at every red light and the *ding! ding!* of the bicycle bells of Chinese food delivery guys peppered the soundscape. It was like every

NYC movie I'd ever seen smashed into a single city block. If I'd seen a giant ape climbing a skyscraper, I wouldn't have been surprised in the least.

My first week in the city, all I did was walk. Walk and look. I remember walking from the Village up to the Guggenheim AND BACK one day, taking in the chaos of the beautiful city.

And one of the main things I remember? Socks. Every other person seemed to be selling socks. There were socks everywhere. Dress socks, tube socks, tiny, frilly baby socks, you name it. Walk pretty much anywhere in NYC in the late eighties and you'd be offered socks out of shopping bags, off of sidewalk folding tables, out of the trunks of cars. Three for $5 seemed to be the going rate. Nowadays, your only options in Manhattan are Bloomingdale's, Benetton, and Banana Republic.

You see, New York in 1986 was a very, very different place than it is now. It was a madhouse. Ed Koch was the mayor. He went everywhere making peace signs and shouting out, "How'm I doin'? How'm I doin'?!" to adoring and contemptuous crowds alike.

There was still all that chaotic graffiti all over the subway trains, like in *The Taking of Pelham One Two Three*, *The French Connection*, and *Welcome Back, Kotter*. (And this was before there was any air-conditioning on those trains, mind you. They were like hot, metal, underground torture boxes. And they used these weird little $1 coin-like objects called—get this—"*TOKENS*.")

The crack epidemic was just starting to heat up. Drugs were ubiquitous. No matter where you walked, but especially in Washington Square Park (the heart of Greenwich Village), vaguely Rasta-looking guys (white, black, and Hispanic) would come up and say, "Sense, sense?" Like a hayseed, I was innocently confused and couldn't understand what they were selling. Scents? Incense? Sex? Common sense? (Obviously I was interested in buying all of these things.) Then someone told me they meant sinsemilla and I finally got it. Ohhhh!

I remember trying to order a bagel in my polite suburban Seattle manner in a typical brash, harried NYC deli.

Counter Guy: Next?

Me: Um, may I please have a, uh—

Counter Guy: WHAT YOU WANT???!!!

Me: Um, a bagel please, sir . . .

Counter Guy: WHAT KIND?

Me: Um, just regular I guess.

Counter Guy: [rolling eyes] HOW YOU WANT IT?!?!

Me: Well, I suppose I uh . . .

Counter Guy: [increasingly exasperated] *TOASTED?! PLAIN?! SCOOPED?! CREAM CHEESE?! BUTTER?!*

Me: Sorry. Um, sure!

[COUNTER GUY LOOKS AT CAMERA, MIMES SHOOTING HIMSELF IN THE MOUTH. THEN TURNS AND ACTUALLY DOES SHOOT SOMEONE IN THE MOUTH BECAUSE THIS IS 1986 NEW YORK.]

To me, the homeless seemed an integrated part of the city. They were everywhere. They seemed perkier back then. More well balanced. Like happy-go-lucky urban hobos from a musical. In fact, Tompkins Square Park, the heart of the East Village, was essentially a nonstop homeless hoedown jamboree. Vagrants, (pre-hipster) punks, and street musicians rocked out until dawn with half-broken guitars, joints, bongos, and endless liter bottles of Olde English 800. It was always a fascinating adventure to chat up a fellow who was living in a refrigerator box and hear his history and philosophy. And we did it with regularity. In fact, it was the best way to pass a day, hearing monologues from grizzled street vets on Avenue B.

The Village was a giant, weird party. Everyone (except suburbanites) was welcome. Misfits, transvestites, hucksters, bohemians, junkies, students, cops, and the criminally insane of all races frolicked and jostled together like background actors from a Village People video.

Heading farther east, the East Village (where the NYU theaters were) was an even more lively, dangerous adventure. CBGB was there. King Tut's Wah Wah Hut. Performance spaces like La MaMa and the "Gas Station." Countless booksellers lined graffiti-and-garbage-bedazzled streets. There were amazing Ukrainian diners where we feasted on $1.50 bowls of borscht and steaming plates of kasha varnishkes. And, of course, the ubiquitous pizza places with their perfect, greasy triangles of cheese and sauce for $1.25.

There are four major north-south avenues in the East Village, Avenues A through D. This was Alphabet City. Sounds pleasant, right? Kind of like *Sesame Street*? However, the common neighborhood saying was "A stands for adventurous, B is for brave, C is for crazy, and D is for dead." D, farthest east, was where the projects were. And the hard drugs. The smack, crack, and coke.

A few dozen blocks uptown, Times Square was a seedy wasteland of abandoned movie theaters and run-down derelicts. It was a neighborhood that looked like it had watched the movie *Taxi Driver* a few too many times. On Forty-Second Street between Eighth and Ninth Avenues you could literally buy anything you wanted. I used to buy stolen calling-card numbers for twenty bucks, call Diana in Australia, and talk for hours on some poor schmuck's Sprint number.

Around me, people were selling passports, driver's licenses, stolen cars, and sex. There were peep show theaters, panhandlers, filthy bars, and rows of abandoned buildings filling the "Crossroads of the World" and the "Great White Way." Handfuls of brave tourists huddled together, terrified, as they made their way in clumps through some of the seediest areas known to man, praying to find some kind of friendly tourist attraction or a Sbarro.

Today Manhattan is a "New York"–themed mall for the megarich. The diversity, both economic and racial, the rich elbow to elbow with the poor, is swiftly evaporating. You can't move to the Village without a couple hundred grand in the bank. (It used to be you needed a couple hundred. When I moved there the going rate for a room for rent was $400 a month.)

Back in the day, there was always an uproar whenever a national chain company would open a store or restaurant in the area. I remember the outraged petitions and demonstrations against the Gap and Blockbuster and Target in the East Village in the late nineties. As the city prospered and flourished in the Giuliani and Bloomberg years, the rents started climbing up, and now you have a situation where only the very rich and the very corporate can afford to lease real estate. That's why every corner in Manhattan is a Duane Reade drugstore or a Chase Bank, and the young folks wandering the streets with their $5 lattes are mostly trust-fund kids and aspiring stockbrokers, not down-and-out, struggling artists as in decades past. The gritty Times Square of my youth is now fully sponsored by Disney, Red Lobster, and, for some inexplicable reason, M&M's.

(If I sound like a grumpy curmudgeon extolling the virtues of a bygone era, I am. Sorry. I'm almost fifty. It's what we do. Someday you'll understand, you insufferably upbeat millennials.)

I'm incredibly grateful that I got to experience the city during those years. During my most formative time, my twenties and early thirties, I got to live in the Manhattan that took place in the cinematic era of *Big, Basquiat, Desperately Seeking Susan, Stranger Than Paradise,* and *Hannah and Her Sisters* rather than the one portrayed in *Maid in Manhattan, Girls,* and *Sex and the City 2.*

And someday I hope to be in New York for its inevitable apocalyptic demise! As portrayed in *I Am Legend, Soylent Green, War of the Worlds, The Avengers,* and *Sex and the City 2.*

The late eighties were some harsh, crime-ridden times in the Big Apple. When I was in my second year of training at NYU, I got some firsthand experience with a bit of the ol' ultraviolence.

Diana and I had moved up to East Harlem. (She had moved to New York City that same fall to go to fashion school.) We lived near 105th and Second Avenue, which is still a pretty bad neighborhood but in 1987 was the epicenter of the crack epidemic. It was super-cheap rent and a beautiful apartment. It was also hell. And a terrible decision.

During the summer I had some German subletters staying in the apartment while Diana was back in Australia, and some robbers broke in through the fire escape window and took their cash and cameras. WHILE WE WERE ALL ASLEEP!

Right after that, I bought an old beater car to get around in and parked it out on the street one night. In the morning the battery was gone, stolen, the hood up. I was super bummed, as $40 for a new battery was a lot of money for me at the time. I went off to work and returned home with a new battery in the evening, only to find that the entire car had been stripped. Everything. Up on blocks. Tires gone. Parts yanked. Wires sticking out. Broken glass. I sighed. Hundreds of dollars evaporated. Just like that. I ended up using the battery as a makeshift, modern ottoman, which impressed no one.

And then, sure enough, I was mugged big-time. *Attacked* is more like it. Twice.

The first time, I was waiting for Diana and John Valadez to get off the subway at the 103rd Street station at around eleven at night. I was going to walk her back to the apartment, as I often did.

While entering the station, I saw this roving gang of East Harlem kids running around "wilding" like something out of *The Warriors* or *A Clockwork Orange*. This posse of around twenty kids, who ranged in age from twelve to sixteen, was throwing bottles, tipping over trash cans, and shoving people aside. I had never seen anything like it before. My pulse was racing as I went down into the station hoping to get away from them and not be seen, this big white misfit loping through East Harlem at night. I thought wrong. They came down into the station. Not seeing me, they jumped the turnstiles and started literally beating an old black homeless guy with sticks, throwing bottles at him, and then THROWING HIM ONTO THE SUBWAY TRACKS! I hid behind a pillar and gestured to the woman in the token booth, who, noticing the violence, nonchalantly ignored it and went back to her magazine and doughnut.

I hid in the corner until the next train pulled into the station and John and Diana got out. The gang had taken off, and the homeless guy, bleeding and staggering, had crawled back onto the platform. I decided not to tell them about the insane gaggle of hellions, as I didn't want to scare them, and we went up the subway stairs—right into my worst nightmare. We literally walked directly into and through the mob of kids.

"Walk faster," I said in a fierce whisper out of the side of my mouth as we set off down 103rd Street. They looked at me quizzically. To them, we had simply walked through an average group of young East Harlemite teens hangin' on the corner, like we often did.

We started moving at a rapid clip when I heard footsteps running up behind me. "Oh shit," I said to myself, and then THWACK. I was hit across the back of the head by a kid with a stick. Hard. I realized later that if that had been a pipe or a bat, I'd probably be dead right now (which would make writing this book more difficult than it already is).

I turned to look back; John had been grabbed and swung around, and was being punched by a trio of what looked like fifteen-year-olds.

"RUN!" I shouted, and Diana and I started taking off for the corner, John close behind. A few bottles shattered around us as we bolted down the dark street.

And there, thank the Almighty God in heaven, was a cop car. New York's finest. I pounded on the windows and we all jumped in. The cruiser screeched out, caromed down 103rd Street, and, of course, just like that, the gang was nowhere to be found. They had scattered like mice.

The cops drove us home and we were all traumatized and sweaty. Right then and there, obviously, we decided to move out of the hood. But the thing that bugged me most of all?

The dozen or so people sitting out on their stoops on 103rd Street at eleven p.m. with their little kids running around who had seen all this go down? Our neighbors for the previous six months? The witnesses to this mob of feral hoodlums? Did they call the police? Did they shout out, "Hey, cut it out"? Did they come to our defense? Not one bit. They laughed. They pointed and laughed and applauded as we were being attacked and even shouted out, "Go back to Greenwich Village" at us. That still makes me very sad and a little bit angry.

A few months later I was "gay bashed" in our new neighborhood of Chelsea. I couldn't sleep and was walking down Seventh Avenue near Sixteenth Street when a couple of drunk gentlemen, hanging out on the sidewalk in front of an Irish bar, suddenly wheeled around and turned on me. One beefy fellow called out, "Hey, faggot," as he swung at me and caught me on the side of my head with his heavy drunk fist.

Another swung me around and tried to punch me in the face, but

I ducked like Jackie Chan. (It's amazing how the old "yellow belt in Shorin-Ryu Karate" reflexes kick in under duress.) The third one came up behind me to grab me by the arms, and I took off like a cheetah. (Actually, probably more like an emu.) The angry gay-bashers called out, "Get that faggot," as they jumped in their car to give chase.

I've never run so fast in my life, and after taking a quick left down Thirteenth Street (which was a one-way street, going the wrong way for gay-bashers in cars), I hid under a stairway for about half an hour, terrified, sucking in wind like Usain Bolt.

Wanting to hurt, degrade, insult, or discriminate against a person or a group of people because of their sexual orientation is an abomination. I got a firsthand lesson in how deep and grotesque the hate and injustice toward my LGBT comrades run in our culture. A lesson that I'll never forget. (Or perhaps this whole incident was a vast misunderstanding—they hated bassoonists, were calling me *fagotto*, and were simply drunkenly slurring their words a bit. I don't know.)

Strange things happen when you put six million people on an island the size of Dodger Stadium.

Flash forward a bit: In 1991, when I lived with my future wife, Holiday Reinhorn, on Third and C in Alphabet City, there was a tremendous turf war happening between the squatters and the drug dealers. We lived across the street from a drug front, a store called Today's Candy. (Hint: It didn't sell any candy.)

The dealers would often take those giant phone receivers that the phone company uses to check the lines, pry open the telephone box on the back of our building (RIGHT outside of our bedroom window), and hot-wire it, talking in loud voices to I have no idea who.

The squatters were do-gooding hippie/punk anarchists who didn't like to obey anyone else's rules, the cops', the mayor's, or the dealers'.

One night we woke up to huge jets of flames emerging from the abandoned building right behind ours. The dealers had set fire to the squatters' building. We watched smoky, filthy anarchists emerging one by one down a fireman's ladder. Some carrying babies. The drug dealers had won. And they did. They won everything. They won the whole city, the whole decade.

I was never attacked in New York again, but those events traumatized me, and still to this day I jump back and scream at the top of my lungs whenever I see a drug dealer, homophobe, candy store, or teenager.

Chapter 9

AN ACTOR REPAIRS

———

I STOOD UNDER THE LIGHTS ON THE STAGE ON MY FIRST DAY AT NYU's Graduate Acting Program and took a deep breath. In the audience was every single student in the program and every single faculty member, arms crossed, faces saying, "Impress me." This was called "showings," a rite of passage for all students at the school. Terrifying. I had literally been losing sleep for weeks waiting for this dreaded moment, and although I didn't end up babbling or naked like I had in many of my worst acting nightmares, the only response I got from the crowd was yawns. The monologues that I had performed with such success in my audition in front of Zelda Fichandler fell flatter than pancakes on that day. I survived the experience, however, and, along with my seventeen other classmates, was ready to enter the maelstrom of becoming an actor. I had a lot of work in front of me.

The training program at NYU was like an actor's boot camp, only instead of three weeks, it was three long years. We had to be at the Greenwich Village location every morning at nine thirty and classes didn't end until six or seven. If we were rehearsing a play (which was most of the time) we would rehearse from seven to eleven p.m.

There was no time off. Any break we got was filled with other work. We had monologues to memorize, songs to work on, vocal warm-ups to attend to, scenes to rehearse, comedy bits to hone, and COUNTLESS plays to read.

If you were making a movie and needed a faculty for a Greenwich Village acting program and wanted to fill it with the most fascinating, frustrating, and eclectic human beings known to man, look no further. This group of people gave me all the tools I needed, and I'll be forever grateful to their collective genius. The faculty was truly indescribable. That being said, I'll attempt to describe them.

ZELDA FICHANDLER

The legend of Zelda, grande dame of the American theater. Zelda always had perfectly coiffed bangs that slanted across her forehead at a forty-five-degree angle and covered one eye in a dramatic fashion. She wore silk a great deal and had ENORMOUS pieces of jewelry that clattered when she would move or gesture. While doing imitations of her we would put random objects on our fingers to comedically signify her rings—Coke cans, tape dispensers, folding chairs, etc. . . .

She had founded the American regional theater movement and had some of the deepest, most memorable quotes known to man. Such as: "We're each given one life, the life of a fly when measured against eternity."

And: "There is a hunger to see the human presence acted out. As long as that need remains, people will find a way to do theater."

And, most famously, as she would repeatedly say (sphinxlike, perplexingly) to our class, *"Go out and come in again."* And we would nod sagaciously, as if we understood exactly what she meant. Sometimes we would literally go out of the classroom and come in again, hoping that was what she was asking for.

To her, you see, theater was a divine mission, a sacred excursion deep into the human condition. Artists were warriors, shamans, con men, and saints. Thank you, Zelda.

NORA DUNFEE

Life is like a box of chocolates. That old woman on the bench in *Forrest Gump* in the pink coat? That was our text teacher, the late, brilliant Nora Dunfee. She was like a mini grande dame of the American theater and had been speech and vocal coach to dozens of acting legends and even toured with the Lunts as a young girl.

Nora would dramatically drill us on Shakespearean sonnets, obscure poetry, and heightened verse, seeking to ever expand our range, tonality, and expressivity. If you said "axed" instead of "asked" or "egg-zit" instead of "eck-sit" (for the word *exit*), she would really let you have it.

She was most loved, however, for the adorable way she would fall asleep in plays, wrapped in her winter coat, big fuzzy hat perched on top of her head like a bird's nest. Once, in the middle of our endless, terrible "theater-in-the-round" production of *As You Like It*, she not only fell asleep, but she let slip her program, which floated slowly and delicately like an oak leaf straight off of her lap onto the center of the stage. The whole play froze and stared transfixed, unsure of what to do. Frank Deal, who played Touchstone the jester, picked up the program and ran offstage with it, hooting like he had found a priceless artifact, and the audience roared.

HOVEY BURGESS

Hovey Burgess ran away from home at age fourteen to join the circus. By the age of twenty he had traveled most of the United States as a clown and performer with Ringling Bros. By twenty-two he was the world-record holder for juggling five balls cascading on the floor in reverse.

He taught us circus skills. Why professional actors needed a circus class is beyond me, but boy, was it fun. We would pass juggling clubs, walk a tightrope, and even swing on a trapeze.

Hovey was famous for his punk-rock style. He hung out at the clubs and bars of the Lower East Side with his long white beard and black leather motorcycle jacket with *Siouxsie and the Banshees* airbrushed on the back. Only in New York.

LIVIU CIULEI

The late Liviu Ciulei was infamous in the theater. He was the first of a whole gaggle of great Romanian directors who came over to the United States in the 1970s. These dudes were mad geniuses. For some reason theater and Romania go together kind of like England and rock and roll or Greece and dire economic circumstances. These obsessive Romanian lunatics reinvented from top to bottom every classic play they got their hands on.

He was a sweet, gruff, grizzled, leathery Slav who looked like a cross between a dwarf, an orc, and Paul Giamatti. You could barely understand him because he sounded like Borat's great-grandfather. Every moment of his direction was expertly choreographed, and bad acting caused him to wince as if he were in physical pain.

But the most memorable thing about Liviu was his constant losing battle with nicotine. In an attempt to quit smoking, he would chew nicotine gum in gigantic wads. But as soon as we would get into the technical rehearsals of a play, he would get really stressed out and start smoking as well. Both at the same time. Golf-ball-size blobs of nicotine gum and a cloud of smoke around him wherever he went as he sucked down nicotine like a demon from hell.

JIM CALDER

Jim Calder was our clowning, commedia dell'arte, and movement teacher. Jim had traveled the world doing weird clown performances and was obsessed with the rhythms of comedy. With him everything had to do with rhythm, juxtaposition, intensity, and absurdity. His classroom was an intense laboratory in total physical imagination.

In his class, we would fall madly in love with a trash can, become the personification of trees or fire, bark like dogs, explode like volcanoes, sing nonsense songs, and wear "neutral masks," discovering the world as if we were newly born and experiencing it for the first time.

Jim was renowned for his unwittingly harsh criticism, which would be given in his sweet, Stan Laurel–esque fashion. You would finish an exercise that you had sweated and strained over, and Jim would turn to the rest of the class and say (goofily while scratching his scalp): "Not interesting, no? Kind of boring, right? Didn't really work. Fell flat, no? Oh well. Next!"

I don't think there would have been a Dwight Schrute, however, without his wicked mentorship.

PAUL WALKER

Our late theater games teacher was one of the most miraculous and inspiring human beings I will ever have the honor to meet. He looked like a vaudeville version of the Monopoly guy, with a large mustache and absurdly mismatched clothes. He was mercurial, joyous, and mysterious, with eyes that shone with insanity and wisdom.

Kids play games. So do actors. Play creates total unself-conscious freedom and an open door toward the full expression of impulse and instinct. This was the incredible playground of wonder and imagination that we explored with Paul.

The class would start with simple children's games like Duck, Duck, Goose; Tag; or Red Light, Green Light and build to ever more psychedelic, ridiculous types of play.

Some of my favorite, most memorable games:

Poet Laureate: Improvised poetry slams and readings.

Instant Greek Tragedy: Just like it sounds.

Harry Belafonte Day: Just like it sounds. Which is to say, awesome.

Sexy Nostril: You draw a random character trait and a random body part out of a hat, create that character, and improvise accordingly.

Steve and Eydie's Telethon: A completely improvised hour-long 1950s-style charity telethon with singing, cocktails, cigarettes, and stand-up comedy.

Paul's main acting dictum has always stuck with me and been a guiding principle through my long, strange acting career: "Assume your own brilliance."

Whenever you're onstage, assume that whatever you are doing is absolutely vital, amazing, and the most perfect thing you could ever be doing in that particular moment. As simple as it sounds, assuming you're brilliant helps one break through the doubt, self-consciousness, and tentativeness that plague one when acting.

Paul died of AIDS in 1993 at the age of forty-one. Anyone who had ever worked with this brilliant, fierce angel had their life touched.

RON VAN LIEU

Ron was the Obi-Wan Kenobi of NYU. Our acting and scene study teacher, he was like a pencil-thin half-owl with a shock of white hair. He was very intense. Very wise. His blue eyes could and would pierce your insecure soul. I always found myself a fearful, stuttering mess in his presence. It was from him that I really learned how to act.

The first year of training was a blur.

The whole year's focus was about stripping away all the bad habits we had developed as actors to that point. The idea was then to fill our empty actor cups with the delicious stuff of great actor training. It was a lot of work. And boy, was it bizarre.

We spent hours literally learning how to breathe. We learned about our tongues. How they moved. We stretched them like tongue yogis. We learned how our voices worked, what resonated when we made sound and how to maximize those vibrations. We learned phonetics and how to talk purdy. We spoke obscure verse and poetry with abandon. We forced our bodies to be ever more expressive and flexible. We did period dancing and movement, learning how to bow and curtsy like the cast of *Downton Abbey*.

Deb Lapidus, our singing teacher, taught us how to "act" songs and gain confidence even when we were horrible singers and croaked like toads.

I was in heaven. This is what I had wanted my entire life. I couldn't wait to go to school each morning and I delved into the process with total abandon. I was living my dream. It was like the movie *Fame*. You know the one. Where they would sing and dance to Irene Cara in the subways and on the lunch tables with a gritty New York abandon.

I would walk to NYU from the subway with Tom Waits blaring from the cheap spongy headphones of my Walkman (kids, a Walkman was like an iPod with a cassette tape in it that kept jamming and shutting off a lot for no apparent reason) and feed off the energy of the city, going to class literally pinching myself.

(I would feel this same way on *The Office* many years later, inspired and singing as I drove to my dream job, where I knew I'd get to improvise, play, and goof off with some of the most talented, funny, and cool people on the planet.)

Then I started hitting an acting bottom in my second year. I was simply not good. My acting was forced, stiff, and "in my head" instead of allowing me to inhabit the characters I was playing. I didn't know what to do about this situation and got more and more anxious. The more anxious I got, the worse I got as an actor. I started seriously doubting my abilities and believing that in truth I sucked.

Finally, the wheels fell off during scene study class one day and I finally learned how to act.

I was doing a scene from Strindberg's *Miss Julie* with Maria Vail and I was just awful in all of the usual ways: self-conscious, robotic, forced, tense. It was another sweaty, inhuman performance. We finished the scene. The observers in the class were bored and fidgety. There was a long pause. I felt sick to my stomach.

Ron Van Lieu looked at me and said, "Rainn, I believe that you're very talented. Why do you keep getting in your own way?" He was plaintive, caring, and genuinely concerned for me. I could feel his frustration and love coming toward me as he asked me the question.

I dropped my head and, as much as I resisted, started to cry. To sob, really. In front of the whole class, dressed as a turn-of-the-century manservant, sitting on a wooden cube that was substituting for an ottoman, I released all of my pain, fear, tension, and anxiety in loud, pain-filled blubbers. I wept for literally fifteen minutes and Ron didn't stop me. He just let it happen and let the class be witness to it.

We began to discuss what was really going on with me and I realized that underneath all my tension and bad acting was FEAR. Fear of rejection, of abandonment, of not being liked. I truly thought that if the audience was able to see the real me, they'd get bored and hate what they saw. In my acting I then amped everything up to try to "be more interesting." This of course only made me look like a broken acting robot, filled with gestures and tension that had nothing to do with the character I was playing or the scene I was in.

We decided to let all that go. I made a commitment to "dare to be boring." To just listen while acting. To simply breathe. To *BE* the character and see the world through the character's eyes, without amplifying my performance in any way, shape, or form.

The idea of working in this manner was absolutely terrifying to me.

The next scene I performed was from *Long Day's Journey into Night* by Eugene O'Neill. I truly dared to be boring. I just sat there and listened to my scene partner, without self-consciousness, worry, or any forced indication of listening.

To me, I felt naked, bereft, unadorned, afraid. But I could tell I was onto something. Surprise, surprise, I was far more interesting to watch when I didn't try to be interesting! Simply being and listening can be riveting if the internal life is fully fleshed out.

My classmates were extremely kind and supportive, as was the entire faculty.

To me the key to acting is listening. You can't believe how many actors "fake listen" when onstage or on camera. We all certainly know what it's like when someone is not truly listening to us in everyday conversation, how strained and hollow the conversation can feel. A great deal of the time, when we're watching actors and not responding to their performances, it's because of this specific issue.

Most of my favorite acting moments of all time are not showy moments of bravado but simple ones, when the actor's body, mind, and heart are filled with truth and a deep reservoir of emotion.

Not long after, Ron, in his office, told me those prescient words of wisdom about my acting that proved ridiculously true. He said, "You know, Rainn, you have an affinity for playing alienated outsiders. You will have great success playing comedy, and it's through that milieu that doors will open for you. Only after you're established as a comic actor, playing eccentric misfits, will people let you take on more serious, dramatic roles."

He was like an oracle.

All this would come into play again during my third year at NYU. I had been cast as Hamlet in *Hamlet*. That's right, folks, THE DANE! The Prince of Denmark. The Hambone. Hamalama-Ding-Dong. Moons over My Hamlet. Wham, Bam, Thank You, Hamlet . . . Okay, I'll stop now.

Nothing is more bowel-churning and intimidating to a twenty-three-year-old actor than to be charged with playing perhaps the most legendary and complex role of all time.

Our director for the production was a fascinating playwright who was a former Jesuit priest who had fallen in love with the theater and had entire Shakespeare plays memorized in his brilliant mind.

The only problem? He didn't know much about working with student actors and every day after rehearsal he would give us all grades. Literally. I got a report card after every rehearsal with a giant B+ or C− on it and detailed notes on what aspects of the role I needed to improve on.

The rehearsal period for an actor is a very delicate process. One is exploring, making mistakes, trying things out, spitting a lot, bumping into furniture, and falling flat on one's face. Fortunately in the theater you have about a month of rehearsals to reach the point where you're ready for an audience. Grading an actor in the first week of rehearsals, especially a young student tackling one of the world's toughest roles, can have a deleterious effect.

I felt completely stifled from all the grading and stylized theater shenanigans going on around me. I swiftly went back into my old patterns of pushing and indicating, disconnected from any internal truth of the character. (Especially with the 29,551 words of dialogue to memorize.) I started to suck. Big-time. I just knew I was going to be a complete and total lost failure in my performance in the role of a lifetime.

Once again, I had some dark nights of the soul where, instead of sleeping, I prayed on my knees on my futon in the middle of a quiet New York night, weeping for some kind of divine intervention. I was terrified, lost. Like most moments of intense personal tragedy, it was both heartbreaking and a little bit ridiculous. (Note: Curiously enough it was right before this experience that I had left everything having to do with God and religion behind. But you know what they say: "There are no atheists in rehearsals for *Hamlet*.")

Thankfully, after one of these sleepless, terrified nights, some faculty members came to an early run-through of the first half of the play, saw all the weird, bad acting and bizarre stage direction going on, and pulled the plug on the entire production.

I had a reprieve!

Ron Van Lieu decided to take the reins and direct the play, and I got an impossibly rare chance to play *Hamlet* a second time.

Needless to say, the next version was far better than the first. Ron made the production extremely stripped down, bare, and focused on the acting. It was every actor's dream and the pinnacle of my time at NYU to sit on a chair in front of an audience and do the "To be, or not to be" monologue (as well as so many others) with as much simple truth as I could muster. I wasn't great, but I was good enough and learned a ton about my craft through that experience. I can always say that I played the Dane twice before the age of twenty-four. And sucked only once.

It was getting near the end of my time at NYU and I was about ready to enter the outside world, become a professional actor, and have reality pick me up, turn me upside down, and shake me like a snow globe.

SHITTY JOBS

———

I HAVE ALWAYS WORKED. I HAVEN'T ALWAYS WORKED HARD. But I've had a LOT of jobs. Some of them okay, most of them simply awful. It's not like I had any great work ethic, it's just that 1) when I was younger, I was mostly bored and needed something to do other than sit around my sad house and read science fiction, 2) we didn't have any money, so if I ever wanted to buy something, like a membership to the Columbia Record and Tape Club, or a KISW T-shirt, or D&D figurines, I needed to get my own cash, and 3) as an adult, I had to pay the R-E-N-T!

(Note: When I saw the musical *Rent* and all those quirky bohemians were singing about how they were going to "pay the reeeeennnnnt!!!!" I just kept thinking about my life and wanting them to shut up and get actual jobs. I wanted to do a sequel called *Jobs!* Where all those perky, tortured artists were all waiters and janitors and pizza delivery guys and receptionists. You know, like everyone else in New York trying to have a career as an artist. If they would have put half the energy they exerted in their singing and dancing into getting real jobs, they really would not have had to worry so much about how they were gonna pay the rent!)

I'm grateful to all these shitty jobs, because when I graduated from acting school my sole goal was to work as an actor and not have to work any more of the horrible, degrading, monotonous, crappy, soul-sucking jobs that had gotten me to that point.

Let's dig in, shall we?

BERRY PICKER

In Washington State, child slave labor was alive and well in the late seventies and early eighties. You see, farms could get around labor laws by having very loose boundaries concerning what an employee was or wasn't. Every summer, busloads of witting and (mostly) unwitting teenagers would be picked up at local street corners and shopping malls and trucked out to a berry farm. You would work for six hours or so in the hot sun, in endless rows of berry bushes, and you'd get paid not by the hour but by the basket of berries you picked. At Bahnmiller Berry Farm of Monroe, Washington, you got $1.25 per FLAT of berries you picked and you'd be lucky if you picked one flat per hour. DO THE MATH, FOLKS! Also, you didn't get paid until the very end of the season.

I worked there for three summers. I started in strawberries but that sucked big-time. They grow on the ground, you see, and you have to squat, crawl, bend, and waddle your way down the aisles of strawberry plants. It was truly backbreaking work, and whenever I pass laborers in the strawberry fields of the San Joaquin Valley, my heart (and knees) goes out to them.

Raspberries were way easier because you could stand and reach into the thick bushes and grasp around for those pulpy little sons of bitches and drop them into the little box you wore around your waist like a fanny pack. The bushes were even high enough to provide shade a good deal of the time.

Some people were innately genius berry pickers and could fly down the aisles, leaving the bushes bare and their flats piled high with berries, racking up $1.25 after $1.25. Others were dawdlers and ate as many as they picked, chatting the whole time.

The girls at the berry fields didn't know that I was a total loser at Shorecrest, so they would occasionally talk to me and joke around. That always makes a job easier.

The whole thing was a racket, like I said, but on the bright side, it was a little like a berry-themed summer camp, and in August you'd get a big fat check (well, if you call $379 a big fat check).

NEWSPAPER BOY

I delivered papers for a few months in Seattle as a young teen. I had to fold the papers as well and pedal them around the neighborhood on my Schwinn ten-speed. That was the suckiest part. I would also have to collect subscriptions, and one time a guy with a biker 'stache answered the door buck naked. You just can't unsee that.

ASSISTANT *TO THE* APARTMENT MANAGER

As a teen in Wilmette, I worked as a kind of super at an apartment building and would empty the garbage and mop stairways and change lightbulbs and tar roofs. And the endless poo-brown garage doors at the apartment building, on Linden and Fifth? Yeah, I painted those in 1983 while listening almost exclusively to Eurythmics and U2.

SECURITY GUARD

Picture a 158-pound version of me in a blue polyester security outfit. Intimidating, right?

I worked as a security guard at two locations in the eighties.

In the summer of 1984, I was "securing" the grounds of the Baha'i House of Worship in Wilmette, Illinois.

(If you haven't seen this majestic domed temple, it is simply incredible. Built by the American Baha'i community, and completed in 1953, the Taj Mahal–esque architecture is stunning and the whole edifice vibrates with a solemn beauty. It was created for people of all faiths to come to and meditate and/or worship and is one of the seven wonders of Illinois, along with Wrigley Field, the Sears Tower, the Great River Road National Scenic Byway, the Cinnabon Express at O'Hare airport, wheat, and Mike Ditka's mustache.)

Being a security guard at the Baha'i House of Worship was very mellow. The only time I had to police any actual law breaking was when I had to grab a little suburban skate punk by the elbow and ask him to leave. I mostly just drank a lot of Mountain Dew and walked around the beautiful gardens thinking about girls.

Being a security guard at the NYU student center in 1986 was not as fun. This was a work-study job, and I mostly checked IDs at the front door. When drunk students would roll up wanting to use the bathroom and not have their IDs, I would point to the big sign that said NO ADMITTANCE WITHOUT STUDENT IDS and they would curse me out and call me names and I would just sigh and continue to read whatever Shakespeare play I was focusing on at the time.

SHIPPING AND RECEIVING/DELIVERY TRUCK DRIVER

I worked for nine months as a shipping and delivery guy at Ballard Marine Supply in Seattle. For $3.75 an hour, I would put pallets of merchandise on shelves with the forklift, mail out boxes of gear to fishermen in Alaska, and drive around Seattle in a HUGE box truck, picking up enormous orders of anchors and propellers and gaskets and marine paint. It was lonely work. A man and his truck.

The guys I worked with were hard-drinking, beefy, sailor-y types who couldn't understand my odd sensitivity and social awkwardness one single bit. Here was this pencil-necked artíste hauling around boxes of paint, propellers, metal screws, and wet rope.

We were all let go one day when it was discovered that the owner of the company was hundreds of thousands in debt and had drained all the accounts and fled the country in his sailboat, *Aperitif.*

COOKIE CHEF

Okay, I just lied. I was never a cookie chef. Like in the movie *Sliding Doors*, I often wonder what would have happened HAD I gotten the job at the Mrs. Fields cookie store on "the Ave" in Seattle in 1985.

I applied one day, desperate for a job, and was met by a real-life Dwight Schrute. He took his job as cookie store manager VERY seriously. He told me that the pay was minimum wage and that I would have to get there at five a.m. to start the baking process. It was a hard, hot, lonely job, he said, and was obviously trying to gauge my commitment. Cookie Dwight told me delightful stories of the real Mrs. Fields, Debbi, who was a former Utah housewife, model, and cheerleader who would often visit the various stores and make sure they were running up to her exacting standards. And when he spoke of her, his eyes filled with the same empty joy that cult members get when thinking of their beloved cult leader.

I laughed heartily at his stories of the cookie trade and solemnly told him of my commitment to getting there ON TIME to get Mrs. Fields cookies into the hands of hungry college students. I told him I thought it would be "fun" to work in such an "amazing" work environment and what a "huge" fan I was of the cookies, because that's what it's really all about, isn't it, the cookies? We shook hands and laughed and he told me he would get back to me soon. I waved goodbye with a cheery flick of the hand and was off.

As soon as I left, I groaned audibly. The job sounded horrific, but I had to do it. I was broke. I have never not wanted a job so much. I was already feeling sick from the odor of cloyingly sweet butterscotch that had filled his cookie office. I was forlorn, despondent, resigned as I walked away.

And the call? I never got it. I didn't pass the interview. I was shot down. And somehow, in some strange way, that was worse. Rejected from a job that a chimp with an apron and a spatula could do.

I was a Mrs. Fields reject.

TRAFFIC-COUNTER GUY

Perhaps the oddest job of my entire life (other than pretending to be a dorky paper salesman to a weekly audience of millions) was counting traffic in a carpool lane from a freeway overpass as part of a Department of Urban Studies study at the University of Washington for $6 an hour.

For a couple of weeks from three to six p.m. myself and another UW student would sit over the lanes of the 520 freeway with little metal counter/clicker thingies and click each time a car went down a certain lane. We also had clipboards and pencils, as well as coats and umbrellas, since it was cold and raining most of the time up on that forlorn bridge.

The other student was a very pretty girl and I was weirdly infatuated. It was a very strange situation to have to count all those damn cars, all the while having a crush on the girl counting cars next to you, umbrellas raised and clipboards on laps, traffic roaring around everywhere. I would try to tell some lame jokes or make halting, fitful conversation, to no avail. It felt like a deleted scene from a Woody Allen movie, and I kept hoping that it would turn cute and romantic, but no dice. At six p.m. she would grab her soggy clipboard and hightail it out of there, the dim Northwest sun sinking below the foggy horizon, cars zooming along below.

DISHWASHER

There is simply no suckier job in the universe than being a dishwasher. You spend hours on your feet in a loud, wet, steamy corner of a stinky, hot kitchen. No matter how many dishes you do, more keep rolling in. *ENDLESS* plates covered in gravy and oil and piles of uneaten foody chunks. If God were going to design a modern version of hell, dishwashing would be way more degrading and torturous than mining in phosphorous pits and being stabbed by dudes with tridents. You are also treated like crap by the rest of the kitchen staff, being the low man on the totem pole. I believe that people think there must be something wrong with you in order for you to be a dishwasher in the first place. In fact, when I was washing dishes at a seafood place named Arnies in Edmonds, Washington, the other dishwasher, Erik, was actually developmentally disabled and was, actually, better at the job than I was. I was faster, sure, but his dishes were spotlessly bereft of all gravy and stacked like the gold bars in Fort Knox.

One time I asked a server for a Coke, as I wasn't supposed to go into the bar area, and the charming young waiter thought it would be really funny to bring me back a Coke with some green beans in it. I got him back by getting depressed and eventually quitting. Be nice to the lowly dishwasher, America!

BUSBOY

I spent a summer at the Lyceum restaurant in Salem, Massachusetts (where my mom, Shay, was living), bussing tables. The Lyceum was a famous old lecture hall where Ralph Waldo Emerson and Henry David Thoreau spoke. In the best American fashion, it was then converted into a bar and grill with a dinner theater upstairs, and on Friday nights after midnight it was a hangout for local transvestites and cross-dressers (who tip GREAT, FYI!).

It's a big step up from dishwasher to busboy, let me tell you. You're in the air-conditioning, for one thing, and people speak to you like you're a human being (barely) and not a tongue-chewing automaton. I was an amazing busboy and the second a fork was set down, the offending Alfredo-splashed plate would be whisked away to the dishwasher (who I was always very nice to).

I was eventually allowed to wait tables in the dinner theater, where I would lay down prime rib in front of preppy yacht-owning drunks from Marblehead as they watched THE WORSTEST production of THE WORSTEST play, *Last of the Red Hot Lovers* by Neil Simon, on the dismal little stage.

I remember gazing up at the lead actor's offensive mugging on the stage as he hammily pulled a pair of panties up from the couch cushion he was sitting on and made a big ol' ham face to the audience, to a roar of drunken applause, and thinking to myself, Are you sure this is what you want to do professionally?

WAITER

I'm going to brag a little bit. I have waited thousands and thousands of tables. I was good. Very good. As an actor I am only okay, but as a waiter, I was masterful. To this day, I often feel like jumping up in restaurants and taking over the waiter's job when the staff doesn't know what it's doing. It drives me crazy when drink orders aren't taken in the first four minutes of sitting down. Or when waiters' arms careen juttingly across your face as they're setting something down on the middle of the table.

I can carry three plates of food laid out on one arm. I know what a "monkey dish" is. (Look it up, idiots.) I can still calculate the 8.25 percent tax on an NYC bill in my head. I can say "ORDER UP" with such authority that it will send cooks running within a three-block radius. I've served eggs at the Waverly diner and coq au vin at some extinct French place in Chelsea. I've poured gallons of mimosas for various brunches and laid down hundreds of pounds of deep-fried potato skins for deep-fried tourists.

It really is the perfect job for an actor, mostly because working at night and on weekends frees up your days for auditions. Also, free potato skins.

Of the many places I waited in NYC, by far the most memorable was Phebe's Wine and Dine (whine and dine) on the Bowery. It stayed open until four a.m. and served four very distinct clienteles: actors from local downtown theater companies (including Michael Chiklis, who was the NICEST guy, even to the waitstaff); NYU students, who would buy a $5 pitcher and tip fifty cents; beefy, loud cops from the local precinct; and, by far the best tippers, the Chinese Mafia.

The Chinese Mafia dudes were serious. They had beepers and Ray-Bans and ordered snifter after snifter of Hennessy. I would routinely get tipped hundred-dollar bills and once was even tipped a baggie of cocaine.

INSURANCE SALESMAN

People outside of LA ask me all the time: "How do you work in Hollywood? Isn't Hollywood totally corrupt and backstabby and materialistic?" Now, of course it is, but my diplomatic response is always the same: "By far, most of the people in Hollywood are truly nice folks who value their families and friends and are just trying to make high-quality entertainment. Most of what you see and hear about the grotesque, out-of-control behavior is from a handful of messed-up ego diva freaks who always make the front pages of the gossip mags. And, besides, no career is as venal, corrupt, and grotesque as the insurance industry."

After I graduated from college I got a job in an insurance brokerage office in a dismal hovel in midtown. It went by the fake moniker of Richard Noon and Associates and was lifted straight from the pages of a lesser David Mamet play.

I was hired by a guy named Kenny from Long Island who had slicked-back hair, a gold chain, and a tight pink polo shirt. He was a real ladies' man who immediately regaled me with stories from last night's conquests and invited me out to the bars with him that very evening. I declined and would continue to on a daily basis. He was always buying me sandwiches and putting his arm around my shoulders.

The job? These five or six slimeballs would hire an unwitting college student (in this case, me) to make cold calls for them to try to get them appointments to sell insurance to various companies. Sounds pretty good so far, right?

Well, they handed me a stack of cards with the contact info and names of various businesses and the name of whoever would purchase their insurance on it. I was instructed to call the company, ask for this important employee, and then *LIE* and tell the secretary that this contact person had asked me to personally call him back six months earlier about insurance for their company.

I felt HORRIBLE about lying. Even a little lie like that would tear me up inside every day I showed up. And at every place of business I called, there would be this curious brick wall and I'd be given the worst runaround known to man and even be directly scoffed at. Then I realized something important when I pulled up a certain card one particular day.

The card read: "Kissinger Associates, Consulting," contact name: *Henry Kissinger*. So I was supposed to call Kissinger Associates and tell them that Henry Kissinger had personally asked me to call back to talk to him about health insurance for his secretaries and copy boys?!

Even I, a twenty-three-year-old unemployed actor, knew that CEOs didn't buy insurance for their employees. I dug a little deeper into the cards and, using the yellow pages (remember, kids, there was no Google in 1989), realized that these were in fact HUGE companies and corporations and that these CEOs were ridiculously unreachable. I even found a card for the FORD MOTOR COMPANY, and the contact name was whatever Ford great-grandson happened to be running the company at that time.

Sample conversation:

Me: Hello, is this Kissinger Associates?

Receptionist: Yes.

Me: May I speak to Mr. Kissinger, please? This is Ron Wilson returning his call.

Kissinger's Secretary: Hello, Mr. Kissinger's office.

Me: Yes, this is Ron Wilson from Richard Noon and Associates returning his call.

[pause]

KS: What is this in reference to?

Me: Yeah, uh, he asked me to call him back.

KS: About what?

Me: Is Mr. Kissinger there?

KS: You're going to have to tell me what this is regarding.

Me: Fine. About six months ago, I spoke to Mr. Kissinger regarding an insurance policy for his employees and he asked me to call him back at this time.

KS: [scoffing] That's impossible. Mr. Kissinger doesn't deal with insurance policies. He's Henry f$c*#&@ Kissinger!

Me: [unconvincingly] Well, he told me to call him. That he really wanted to find incredible savings on insurance by meeting with one of our agents and—

KS: You're making this whole thing up! You're lying!

Me: *Yeah, well he was lying to the American public about secretly bombing Cambodia!*

[dial tone]

When I approached Kenny about this ridiculous, futile conundrum, he offered me a sandwich and a creepy pat on the back and told me to keep up the good work.

I finally was so fed up with guilt from so many lies to so many receptionists that I quit after two weeks, and when I asked Kenny when I would get my check, he laughed at me and said because I had filled out no starting paperwork, there was no record of my ever having worked there and I was welcome to go ahead and try to sue them. The laughter of Kenny and the rest of the oily Mamet cast echoed down the hallway as I dejectedly walked away.

MAN WITH A VAN

With the money my wife and I got for getting married in 1995, we bought a 1982 Chevy cargo van.

This van was our meal ticket (and instant camping spot) for the next three years. I could place a *Village Voice* ad for $27 or tack up a few flyers on telephone poles (with those tearable phone numbers on the bottom) and get more work than I knew what to do with. I would charge $65 an hour for me and the van, and then an additional $25 an hour for an extra mover. (This was also really fun for me, because I could hire my friends to work with me and joke around as we "hauled cube.")

Cash. Off the books. That's right, folks, I'm a tax cheat.

You see, mid-Americans, New Yorkers move all the time, and because their apartments are so minuscule, they really don't have that much stuff. The man with a van was a cheap, quick, and easy way to move your futon, books, lamp, and suitcases from one apartment to another.

True to my ever-questing spiritual identity, I called this endeavor the Transcendent Moving Company and my tagline was "A man, a van, a sense of Higher Purpose." The flyer had a cute little van with wings on it.

Even though I was woefully skinny and out of shape, I became an expert mover and van packer. People would look askance when this gawky, gangly, pale dude with a big head would show up to move all their crap, but quickly their minds would be blown. What they didn't see was that I was wiry/strong back in those days and was like a box-wielding, stair-maneuvering mongoose. I would haul sofas and bed frames and bookshelves and trunks up and down four-story stair-cases in every borough. I would fill and empty the van in impossible combinations like it was Tetris on wheels. I would strap mattresses on the roof with bungee cords and whiz up and down avenues and over bridges, cutting off taxis and blasting Wilco on the tape deck.

Most memorable move?

I once moved a young African American woman and her kids out of a crack den/drug front in Harlem. I mean, full-on: armed dealers on the front stoop, kids working as lookouts, line out the door of tooth-less, ravaged ghosts looking for crackety crack. It made *The Wire* look like *The Naked Gun*. As I moved them out of the building, away from the numb glare of the henchmen, I was literally shaking with fear and drenched in sweat that soaked into the seat of the van. It felt like one of the greatest accomplishments of my life to move this nice family into a nicer, safer building a few miles away.

DOG WALKER

My wife, Holiday, and I had a VERY short-lived business with the best name ever recorded: "Tails of New York." We had moved to the Upper West Side (abbreviated UWS; families, Jewy) from the Lower East

Side (abbreviated LES; artists, junkies), and we saw dog walkers constantly headed back and forth, to and from Central Park. We befriended one dude with eight panting dogs on eight tangled leashes and asked him about his business model. When we found out that you could get $15 per dog for taking them on a one-hour walk, our eyes lit up like little ATMs. We owned a beautiful white pit bull named Edison and much of our New York social life consisted of hanging out shooting (and picking up) the shit at dog parks and walking Edison all over the place. So why not make some real money at it?

We did the math. If we could do two shifts of ten dogs each, we could make $300 in a day! And there would be time here or there for fitting in the occasional audition.

Delicious. We put up flyers and started with three neighborhood dogs, who immediately started fighting with each other. They were lunatics, pulling in every direction. One, a crazy Lab puppy, loved to find other dogs' crap and immediately start rolling in it. Another, a standard poodle, would go after squirrels like a crazed Bengal tiger, frequently slipping from his collar and dashing off into Central Park. We were done after a week. Tails of New York curled up its tail and slunk away into the shrubbery of brilliant mistakes.

SANDWICH "HO"

Holiday and I and many of our friends worked at a catering company and lunch delivery place in Chelsea called Beauty and the Feast. Every late morning we would roll into the kitchen and load up these HUGE straw baskets with gourmet sandwiches. Every sandwich seller would then get a route on a map in midtown Manhattan and we'd be off to sell our wares. We were door-to-door sandwich vendors, or, as we called ourselves, "sandwich hos." We'd get forty bucks for the day and some tips occasionally. It really wasn't a bad job, although it was challenging to slog around the heat and cold of Manhattan with a fifty-pound basket of sandwiches.

The highlight? Every day, I would take my tips to a fine off-track betting establishment and bet the six to fifteen dollars I got in tips that day on the ponies. I got a lot of funny looks from the vagrants, drunks, and semihomeless tongue-chewers who spent their days there, this twenty-six-year-old in torn jeans and a Pixies T-shirt with a giant, mostly empty wicker basket with a red-and-white checked cloth inside. I'd give out a sandwich or two to the hungriest looking of the lot, just to be all friendly-like. Sometimes I would hit a horse and make a nice tidy bundle, but mostly I would lose it all to the New York State Gaming Commission and slink out of the stinky place with my basket and pockets empty.

ACTING TEACHER

After moving to Los Angeles in 1999, I was mostly able to support myself as an actor, although we definitely went through some hard times. As a matter of fact, when I got cast in *The Office*, I had been so hard up in the months previous that I had been paying rent by putting it on the ol' credit card—with those little shame-filled "checks" that come with your bill, attached to the statement like leeches.

I needed to get a money job, so I went to my friend who ran an acting school in Hollywood. I had, at that point in time, enough experience in TV and film to teach an "on-camera" class. I boned up on some teaching techniques, got prepared, and even learned how to use a video camera. I was told that the students all had scenes already prepared from another class and that we would film them, watch playback, and learn from that experience. What I was NOT told was that the students were almost all from foreign countries. Also what I was not told was that the scenes they would be presenting were all from now-canceled eighties TV shows.

When I walked into class it was the oddest assemblage of actors I had ever met, and I'd met some pretty odd assemblages of actors in my day.

It was like walking into the Muppet Babies United Nations. There was a Russian dude in a fake leather jacket; an Armenian gal with big hair; a couple of giggly, demure Japanese actresses; a Brazilian mixed martial artist in a muscle shirt; and a couple of Swedish beauties who walked like serial killers. To call the language that the students in that classroom spoke "English" would be a stretch. Having a conversation with many of them could be challenging, let alone understanding them in a scene from a long-canceled TV show.

There is a huge international population of actors in the LA area who are not native English speakers, all following their dream of Tinseltown stardom. It's hard enough to build a career even if you don't have a thick accent, which makes this a very sad side of Hollywcird.

True story: One of the most delicious scenes that has ever been presented in the history of acting was one I saw presented by two young women, one Italian, one Swedish, from the hit 1980s TV cop show juggernaut *Cagney & Lacey*.

[Int. Police Locker Room. Day.]

Cagney enters to find Lacey getting changed at a nearby bench.

Cagney: [thick Italian accent, think Chico Marx] Ehhh, Lacey! Why-a you-a hea-uh? You letta me so down outta theh today. You have-a som-a nerv-ah!

Lacey turns to face her partner, livid.

Lacey: [think the Swedish Chef from the Muppets] Cagney, you-ah awlways-ah gettin-ah so-ah mad-ah. You were the one-ah who is a-tellin' me to give you a-your space-uh. And I thought-uh we were a-partners! Get-a out-a my face-ah!

Cagney sits.

Cagney: [intense] Don't-a you tella me what to do-ah! You mite-a gotten us a-killed!!

[Lacey pauses. Then, with great intensity]

Lacey: That's-uh lie-uh! I was-uh just-uh doin-uh my job-uh!

[And, SCENE!]

You get the idea. And somewhere in a Hollywood acting studio there sits a videotape of that scene. Someone please find it immediately.

Chapter 10

THE FACE OF GOD

———

I N AN IMMENSE THEATER AT THE JUILLIARD SCHOOL, EVERY single agent, manager, and casting director in New York City assembled to watch the acting talent of all the top schools in the area perform scenes for them. This is called the "League Showcase" or something similarly grandiose and idiotic. Wait, maybe it was the "League of Extraordinary Theater Dorks."

For most of us, this was the ultimate finale and payoff of our three years together. Getting seen in a good light on this day meant the possibility of signing with a good agent, which meant quality auditions and a tremendous leg up on carving out a name for oneself in the pursuit of that most precious and impossible of all things: an acting career.

We had been working for weeks on our presentation, and because I had literally just finished performing as Hamlet, I didn't have any time to find good writing that highlighted my moderate talents, so I ended up in some very dubious scenes.

I did one from an obscure British play (Stoppard's *The Real Thing*) filled with subtextual verbal nuance, and another one where I played the Woody Allen character from Woody Allen's *Annie Hall*. Yes, me, a twenty-three-year-old Baha'i stick insect from suburban Seattle playing one of the most iconic Jewish New York roles of ALL TIME in front of hundreds of jaded New Yorkers. Terrible idea. (Although, when it comes time to remake *Annie Hall*, I AM available, Hollywood!)

It was one of the most nerve-wracking events I've ever been a part of, but my talented class comported itself quite well during our hour of various scenes and we were happy, exhausted, and breathless as we left the stage for the dressing rooms.

Now would come the tough part. . . .

An hour or two after the performances from Juilliard, NYU, and Yale, these sheets of paper would go up on an enormous bulletin board in a remote hallway. On them, all the industry executives would request meetings, headshots, and phone numbers of those actors they were interested in.

I'll never forget the anxious, shallow breathing echoing in my enormous braincase as I tenderly jostled my way up the stairs to the bulletin board, a pen and paper ready to take notes in sweaty hands. I nervously scanned sheet after sheet, which all asked for meetings and contact information from most of my various classmates.

My name wasn't listed. Not once.

I checked again. Surely there must have been a mistake? So many actors were being called in for so many meetings with so many agents and producers and casting people! I mean, this was what it was all about. Our future. Our career. My name must have been there somewhere. Surely someone who had watched the presentations had seen at least a tiny glimmer of talent in me and wanted to meet and talk to me and eventually help cast me in something. Nope. My name was nowhere to be found on that great big actor's wall of shame.

I was a reject. Me. The guy who had just played Hamlet to such great acclaim the previous month!

(In fact, a large agency had seen me in *Hamlet* and called me into their offices. They were incredibly complimentary of my work in the play and told me they would be back in touch after the "League showings." After the showcase they weren't interested. I guess the two-and-a-half-hour performance in the greatest role in the English language was overridden in their minds by the two crappy three-minute scenes they had just witnessed. Which just goes to prove the old showbiz adage "You're only as good as your last Woody Allen impression.")

I looked down at my blank notepad and, red-faced, slunk away back down the stairs, hoping not to be noticed or spoken to by any of the excited, fresh-faced young actors jabbering in the hallway.

That night was the first night I tried cocaine.

I don't remember exactly how I got my hands on it, but I obliterated my feelings of total failure with a bunch of white powder that went up my nose and exploded my dopamine receptors. I was not only successfully numbed out, I was utterly transformed.

We had a graduation party that night and the power of the coca leaf changed me from an awkward college kid to the LIFE OF THE FRIGGIN' PARTY! I actually remember dancing that night like I had never danced before. It was like David Bowie had been cloned with Patrick Swayze (or at least his less attractive brother, Gary Swayze). People kept coming up to me and saying, "Wow, I had no idea you could dance so good!" I merely grinned, my eyes looping like Angry Birds, and kept on boogying up a Bolivian disco until dawn.

You see, my moral compass had started to spin and fall into the mud during my final years at NYU. I had gradually left behind and even all-out rejected the faith of my childhood and its beliefs, entering fully the life of the Greenwich Village bohemian. Maybe it's because I was angry about childhood experiences that weren't in line with Baha'i principles. Maybe walking away from faith is a necessary step in every young person's development. I'm not sure. But if you ask me . . . it all started with sex.

While at NYU, my girlfriend Diana moved from Australia to the city and right into my dorm room. Soon thereafter we relocated to that aforementioned East Harlem hellhole. We did the "sexy time" a lot (Borat voice). I felt extremely guilty about this, as premarital sex was contrary to the moral guidelines of the Baha'i Faith. I also really enjoyed it, couldn't get enough as a matter of fact, and knew that stopping and abstinence was not a realistic option in my life at that point. This was quite a quandary.

Many of us come to a time in our lives when the beliefs we grew up with collide with the reality of the world we find ourselves living in. It's a common theme for the twentysomething-or-other.

Besides the sex, it was around this time when I became intimately acquainted with drugs and alcohol. When I started, I didn't hold back. I was like an Amish kid on Rumspringa. Or, the Baha'i version: Baha'imspringa.

I had a "friend" from acting school, a total addict, who turned me on to pot and booze in my third year of school. We would skulk around the streets of New York smoking weed and sipping from huge cans of malt liquor out of brown bags. (You used to be able to wander the streets of NYC with whatever you wanted to ingest and be pretty much left alone by the cops as long as it was in a brown paper bag. And if you were white. Which I was. Very much so.)

Besides the sex and drugs and rock and roll, there was a building feeling of unease with the whole religion thing in my life. I didn't want anything to do with morality.* I really didn't know if I bought this

---

* Let's pause here and discuss morality a little bit.
WARNING: MAJOR DIGRESSION AHEAD. FEEL FREE TO SKIP.
Here's the deal with morality: It has a really bad name these days. Young

whole "God" concept anymore. I didn't want any pressure on me from above or anyone telling me what to do. Like many young people, I wanted to do what I wanted to do when I wanted to do it and screw the consequences. I was sick of my parents and their eccentric hypocrisies, disgusted by some of the wackadoodle Baha'is I had met in New York, and tired of any overarching responsibilities to my eternal soul or the planet or a Higher Power or to anyone other than myself.

So I went from active Baha'i dork to full-on atheist dork.

I didn't want big daddy Zeus looking over my shoulder, scowling judgmentally at my every move. Real artists and scientists didn't look up to and bow down to some mythical, supernatural father-creator guy, right? (Of course, many of the most brilliant artistic and scientific minds in history have had faith in a unifying force that some people label "God," but I was unaware of that at the time.) I didn't want some obsolete books from a bygone era determining what I should or shouldn't do or what to feel guilty about.

Religion was for the weak, the old, and the old-fashioned, after all. Faith was for grandparents and fundamentalists who believed Jesus rode around on dinosaurs. (Kind of like Chris Pratt in the last *Jurassic Park* movie, except Jesus was even more ripped.)

In this brave new world we lived in, the strong made their own

---

people LOATHE the word and don't want to hear about it or be subject to it and, frankly, OLD people aren't exactly jumping to hear about it, either. However, we ALL operate under a moral code. It may shift occasionally, but we all have a sense of right and wrong, and our behavior matches that belief for the most part. (Even Hitler was a vegetarian because he thought it distressing and cruel to kill animals and wanted bodily purity. He even called meat broth "corpse tea." That's morality, folks.)

Some of us get that moral code from a religious faith, others from our parents or family, but most of us from the consensus of the culture at large. For instance, in the 1950s, sex before marriage and pot smoking were considered extremely immoral. People who participated in those activities were the worst scum of the

decisions separate from any obsolete strictures written in some ancient, highfalutin language.

Plus, I knew the biggest rebellion I could have against my parents
and the strongest move toward a postadolescent individuation would
be a total rejection of God and faith. This synced up well with the
angry young man who was emerging from inside. And all this religious blather and folderol would get in the way of the thing I had
really come to New York City for—to be a BOHEMIAN!

That was my dream. I mean, I had read Henry Miller, Charles
Bukowski, Jack Kerouac, *The Catcher in the Rye*, and *A Moveable
Feast*. I had listened to Patti Smith and Blondie and Lou Reed and Tom
Waits. I had seen all the Woody Allen films and I had even once seen
Andy Warhol crossing lower Broadway, his face clouded with inten-
sity and light.

I knew what I wanted and I was finally living it. And, for an artsy
East Village actor, there was simply no room for God, morality, or devotion. Or, at least, none that I could conceive of at the time.

In my quest for this tantalizing bohemian street cred, during my
first year at NYU, I dyed my hair jet-black and started smoking a pipe.
The hair dye I got from a box of Clairol "Midnight Black." You know

---

earth (or, even worse, actors). Nowadays marijuana use is not only accepted, it's
considered "cool," and premarital sex is the norm, most children having lost
their virginity by seventeen.

These days, the idea that you would not do something because a wise, divinely
inspired person recommended you not do it in some holy book is considered an
absurd notion. It's thought to be old-fashioned, obsolete, and inherently didactic
and judgmental to have religious teachings guide one's actions.

So how do we determine what is right? From our faith? From what our culture
currently believes is just and right? What are the implications and reverberations
of our actions? Where do morals come from? Materialists would say that morals
are somehow (inexplicably) programmed into our biology and human/animal
social impulses. Religious folks would say that it was God, speaking through the

the kind. So toxic that there's an emergency 800 number right on the box in case you accidentally dump the concoction into your eyes.

I looked ridiculous. The first issue was that I had forgotten about the eyebrows. The hair on my head was like Bruce Lee's and my eyebrows were a light brown with ginger highlights. I looked like a serial killer who had just written his manifesto on the walls of a cabin in his own blood and feces. (Which, coincidentally, were the secret ingredients in "Midnight Black" hair dye.)

And the pipe? My aunt Wendy (my dad's sister) smoked one. Always had. She was a rebellious, artistic, pipe-smoking inspiration and I had always loved her rebellious, artistic, pipe-smoking spirit.

As with most things in my life I was simply trying WAY too hard.

We were such a pretentious lot, us Village artists. I remember having one ridiculous late-night conversation with a bunch of pot-smoking artistes where the question was posed: "Would you ever do . . . a *commercial*?"

I remember a friend of mine paused dramatically and considered this disgusting capitalistic question quite deeply, stroking his goatee and drawing on his Camel Light. "I might do a commercial . . ." And

---

religious movements of the past, who taught us as a species "right from wrong" over the centuries.

Mortality in the Baha'i Faith is a bit different from morality in other faith traditions. There's no hell or sin in the traditional sense. Evil is merely the absence of good. Hell is remoteness from God, the divine presence. Sin is "missing the mark," and one should simply try to learn and do better next time. (It should be noted that in the early Greek translation of the New Testament *hamartia* is the word that is used for sin. *Hamartia* is an archery term that literally means "missing the mark." It has nothing to do with shameful evil. That came into play later.) Moral and ethical guidelines in the Baha'i system are given to us by a loving Creator as a protection and direction for us as individuals and for the betterment of our society as a whole.

then he added headily . . . "For *soy milk*." True story. (And would actually make a pretty hilarious soy milk commercial.)

We dove into big ideas and the meaning of art. We mourned the commercialization of pretty much everything in the world. (In fact, we were the *very first* group of people in history to complain that "MTV doesn't even show music videos anymore, man!") We compared Miller and Williams to Chekhov and Shakespeare and fiercely debated the intersection of politics and art. We wanted revolution but through a visceral storytelling that would grab the audience by the throat and never let go.

Later, as I was further along on my spiritual and artistic journey, I made some important realizations about this phase of my life. I came to see that my passion and zeal for my faith when I was younger had merely transitioned to a passion and zeal for art and theater. There was still a religious fervor about what we were doing. We wanted to turn people on, ignite their consciousness. Both Baha'is and downtown theater artists wanted to change the world and touch people's hearts but in different (and related) ways.

We seriously thought that we could change the world with great art and challenging, arresting works of transcendent theater. We discussed

---

Baha'u'llah writes:

"O ye peoples of the world! Know assuredly that My commandments are the lamps of My loving providence among My servants, and the keys of My mercy for My creatures."

The key thing with any discussion of morality, especially from a religious perspective, is that any whiff of judgment, condescension, and arrogance needs to be completely taken out of the conversation. And hell. And damnation. And original sin. Ludicrous ideas.

I have made plenty of moral mistakes and had lapses in ethical judgment. (Trust me. I'm not just saying that to sound humble.) Most of us have. But the culturally taboo topic of morality I find fascinating.

But what do I know? I'm just a bassoonist.

how doing the right production of *The Cherry Orchard* at the right downtown theater in the right church basement for the right audience of twenty-seven could so explode the minds and hearts of the theater-goers that their lives would never be the same for the rest of time.

I had become a "born-again" theater artist!

So, now that God was out of the way (as well as the corresponding guilt), I could dive into my bohemian proclivities and downtown depravities with unrestrained gusto.

Here I was. I had graduated. The world was my oyster. My whole life was in front of me! What was next in my artistic and spiritual journey?

Depression. I was unemployed. I was broke.

Without a dime in my pocket, my old Seattle friend John Valadez and I moved to an abandoned beer brewery in the remotest part of Williamsburg, Brooklyn.

This was not the hip, fun, funky, developed world of Williamsburg today. This was the desolate crack-infested industrial wasteland of East Williamsburg circa 1989. (To give you an idea of how intense it was: There was not a SINGLE artisanal cheese shop in sight! I know, I'm shuddering at the thought too.)

The owner was a Dutch real estate tycoon (i.e., slumlord) who was salivating over the idea of transforming his various abandoned industrial buildings into "artist lofts," so he allowed my friend and me to live there for free so he could get a tax credit and lure other artists to the building. He was a giant bear of a man in a trench coat with a name like Van Dam or Don Vom or something like that, and he reeked of cigars, poo, and ill-gotten money (which he used to buy more cigars and poo).

My friend and I shared a small living space that was in an elevated crow's-nest former foreman's office that overlooked an ENORMOUS loft space. In this tiny office, we had two mattresses on sheets of plywood elevated by milk crates. Glass botanica candles from a bodega lined the shelves, along with our many books and plays and the jars of peanut butter and jelly that kept us going. I remember seeing the movie *Taxi Driver* at the time and thinking, Huh. This Travis guy's apartment is a lot nicer than mine.

It was about 15 percent really cool and 85 percent super awful and sucky. Free rent has its price. Let me explain.

(Please note, I am not exaggerating any of the below *IN THE SLIGHTEST.*)

- **THE COLD:** We had no heat in our loft for the first several months and it was one of the coldest winters on record. I remember being on the phone with my mom, wrapped in blankets, spitting on the cement floor and watching it crackle and freeze in seconds.

- **THE FILTH:** We were not the cleanest duo and other than some occasional sweeping with a push broom, we never cleaned the place. Piles of boxes, lumber, bricks, cardboard, and plastic sat clumped in the corners from when we first moved in and never actually made it out of the loft. Eventually, those piles were formed into "chairs."

- **THE TOILET:** The toilet was the filthiest, most craven porcelain monstrosity in all of Brooklyn. It was down a floor from our "loft" and frequently surrounded by surly rats the size of poodles. Fortunately they would scatter (along with the cockroaches) when you'd click the string on the lightbulb that hung from the ceiling. Getting to the toilet, especially in the middle of the night, proved to be so onerous and arduous that we did something that I'm a teeny tiny bit ashamed of. We kept cranberry juice bottles next to our mattresses and would fill them with pee rather than brave the cold, dirt, and rats. Mostly we remembered to empty them out in the morning. Mostly. Sometimes the rats would get grossed out and do it for us.

• **THE ENTRANCE:** Here was your choice: You could go in the door to the old warehouse and be met by the mad Dutchman's angry guard dog, a Rottweiler, who was chained to the wall in a similar fashion to Cerberus. This ferocious creature would bark and lunge at you repeatedly, but if you slunk along the far side of the wall, he didn't have enough length of chain to allow his jaws to reach your flesh. (He was surrounded by piles of poo and yes, we yelled at the crazy Dutchman and called the Humane Society repeatedly, but to no avail. I would throw him pizza and Slim Jims, but it didn't make him like me any more.)

OR

You could climb up eight feet on the outside front wall of the loft on a series of brick handholds and get directly into the loft via a steel loading-dock door. This was a slippery, cold, and tricky maneuver but was still more palatable than dealing with Ol' Brooklyncerberus.

• **THE SHOWER:** We had none. There was no shower. There was not a place to wash one's naked body. There wasn't even hot water. This is not good. Helpful hint: If you're thinking of moving someplace, you'll want to see if that place has a shower of some kind. Otherwise you will be completely miserable.

So what I would do is pack a towel, soap, and shampoo in my backpack, and one of the central focal points of any given day would be to find a place to bathe myself. I discovered a secret shower in the basement of the Tisch School of the Arts building that came in very handy (it's not there anymore . . . or maybe it is, and I'm not telling you). More often I would stop by friends' houses to "say hello" and then, as if by afterthought, would say,

"Oh, hey, do you mind if I take a shower?" It was a grotesque manipulation, I know, but my body is a temple and I needed to keep it clean. I once dated a girl simply because she lived very close to the L train, was home a lot, and had a beautiful shower with plenty of hot water. God, I miss that shower.

- **CRIME:** There was oodles of crime and drugs around our abandoned brewery. My roommate saw someone get shot in the playground across the street. We could look down from our steel loading-dock door and see folks smoking crack and shooting heroin and passing out in an abandoned lot. One night a bunch of teenagers started throwing rocks at our door and windows for some reason at the *exact same time* as I needed to get into the city for a date. I was screwed. I was forced to wend my way through the rat-infested, mazelike brewery building to the back side, where it abutted a lumberyard. I scrambled out of a fire exit, down a steep dirt embankment, and into the lumberyard, where I was lucky not to be shot by the very surprised security guard as I made my long way out and around to the subway entrance a few blocks away. Believe it or not, when I arrived for my date, I discovered that "I just clawed my way through rats and dirt and lumber to be with you" is NOT considered an effective opening line.

Around this time I started seeing a Wall Street corporate lawyer who doubled as a drug dealer. We'll call her Jesse. She was all business during the week, wearing those lawyer-y outfits and carrying a five-hundred-dollar leather briefcase. Jesse would look at briefs and spreadsheets and case files and legal precedents (or whatever lawyers do; I've only seen two episodes of *The Good Wife*) during the week, but on the weekends it was a different story.

She had what she called her "magic bag." It was a small zippered leather bag with various pouches and sections, each one containing a type of drug. She had pills of various shapes and colors, mushrooms, heroin in a tiny Ziploc, perfectly rolled joints of both hash and marijuana in leather loops meant for pens, and, most important from my standpoint, she had lots and lots of cocaine.

Apparently she had some kind of coke connection from some Bolivian hooligan. (Note: Use of the words *cocaine*, *Bolivian*, and *hooligan* in describing your girlfriend's social circles is what relationship specialists refer to as a "red flag.")

We didn't have what I would call a very mature relationship.

She gave me drugs. I gave her . . . I don't really know what I gave her. I suppose I was entertaining in my own weird way.

We spent several weeks together doing insane amounts of drugs. I remember her getting mad at me for trying to snort incredibly pure white piles of powder with a one-dollar bill once. She insisted on using hundreds or at least twenties. I thought that ridiculous. I would have used a Krazy Straw, a flower stem, or a toilet paper roll. One time, I did. I didn't care. Besides, I didn't have any twenties or hundreds. Here I was, an unemployed actor who could barely afford a falafel, inhaling thousands of dollars' worth of drugs from the well-manicured hands of a Wall Street lawyer/drug mule.

When on the drug, I was articulate, charming, snappy, and filled with boundless ideas and enthusiasm. When coming down or waking up the next day, I felt like the lowest, most grotesque form of hungover sloth-beast, miserable and self-hating. Remember how Robin Williams once said, "Cocaine is God's way of telling you that you are making too much money"? God was warning me—and I didn't even HAVE any money!

I remember going to a party at a beautiful loft in SoHo filled with models tottering about on enormous high heels. I snuck in with some of my druggie bum artist friends from the Lower East Side and I started smoking a HUGE Cheech and Chong–size joint in the corner with them, judging everyone there from the comfort of my big army jacket.

After countless drags on some very powerful herbage and several lagers, I suddenly felt a wave of nausea, paranoia, and insanity come over me. I went to the bathroom (which was built into the loft space with walls of plywood and an open ceiling so you could hear the party going on all around you). I started to pass out; the music was throbbing in the background and I fell to my knees. My head was spinning like a Vitamix®. After a few minutes like this, I started vomiting up whatever pizza or bagel I had ingested that day. Then the knocks at the door started. I propped myself up on the toilet trying desperately to not pass out. I looked in the mirror and my eyes were red as beets. I crawled over to the bathtub and started running cold water over my head and hair so as not to lose my feeble consciousness. It worked. The swirling brain slowed down. I got up after a few more minutes, the knocking and outraged calls of drunk models and their boyfriends echoing through the throbbing disco music; stumbled my way to the door; and opened it.

There I was in all my glory. Vomit on my army jacket and chin, my hair dripping with water. Water all over the floor. I pulled myself up tall and started out through a small crowd of angry SoHo-ites. "Have a very good evening, laaadies," I said as I strode along upright, out the front door, and into the icy winter evening.

I spent countless nights in drunken stumblings and almost vomiting in taxicabs. Speeded speedily through parties and bars. Wafted, red-eyed and high, through many late-night conversations. And woke up desolate, fried, embarrassed, and sad on countless mornings during those years. Good bohemian times.

Once I even tried smoking cocaine with a guy I knew from NYU who later wound up destroying his life and career with crack addiction. That event made my hair stand on end like each strand was a tiny sparkler. And I, middling addict that I was, got scared enough and somehow found the wherewithal to quit all cocaine for good soon thereafter.

I quit pot smoking not long after that as well. After I saw the *Face of God*.

It was Christmas morning in the ice-cold loft. Instead of breakfast I "waked and baked" with a large joint I found on a filthy table downstairs (probably laced with something). I lit it and went back upstairs to the crow's-nest office/bedroom to read, surrounded by several groovy lighted glass candles. John was on the phone down in the warehouse area when all of a sudden I started to seriously freak out. I mean like on-a-whole-other-level freak out. My heart started racing. Sweat started pouring off my brow. Muscles in my arms and chest started contracting and relaxing. Visions of heart attacks and imminent death were swirling through my psychedelic-Christmas drugged brain.

I started shouting to John downstairs for help. He was a bit buzzed himself and thought I was messing with him. I was shouting, desperate, as I dragged myself, heart like a jackhammer, to the door of the crow's nest at least ten yards away. I could see John on the phone with his mom, trying to focus on the call, holding up his hand to silence me and trying to hold in his laughter at my "antics." Sure I was going to die, I needed to get his attention so he could call 911. I knew I could never make it down the stairs, so I grabbed something to throw. The nearest throwable object? A lit glass candle. And I chucked it down at him like a grenade. The glass shattered. Still nothing from him but stifled giggles. I got pissed. I grabbed another one. And another. Lit glass candles rained down on John like the London Blitz as I hollered from above, "HELP ME, YOU ASSHOLE!" and he just turned away, continuing to try to restrain his laughter as he spoke to his mom. Eventually a pile of trash in the corner burst into flame from one of the candles. There was a long pause and I remember hearing him say: "*I gotta go.*"

He stomped out the fire and ran across the shattered glass and up into our dank, dark elevated bedroom to find me, having just vomited into the trash can, covered in sweat on the floor, crying like a baby.

"Call 911!" I hissed at him, clutching my heart, which was still going off like a Haitian voodoo drum. John, lucky for me, ignored my pleas and instead chose to read to me from "Raise High the Roof Beam, Carpenters" by J. D. Salinger as I slowly "came down."

It was somewhere in here that I saw the Face of God. True story. It was a large, luminous face, like the sun, rising. No actual features like a nose or mouth or anything. More of a presence than a face, really. It expanded infinitely in gorgeous colors across a horizon like a Mark Rothko painting. Mighty, awe-inspiring, beautiful, ancient, and terrifying. And I remember saying to myself, "Wow. That's the Face of God."

I tearfully swore to that incredible, unforgettable Face of God™ that I would never smoke pot again.

And I never did.

I just stuck with the booze for the next ten years. Hey, I never said anything to the Face of God about the booze.

But—and trust me on this one—the best drug of all is love.

Chapter 11

VOLCANO LOVE

—

L ET'S FAST-FORWARD A WEE BIT. WE'LL GET BACK TO MY JOUR-ney in and out of moral confusion and bohemian depravity very soon.

It's a year or so later in our story and, on a break from doing a Shakespearean theater tour for the Acting Company (see the list entitled "Adventures in Theater"), I went to Seattle to visit my dad. The first thing I did was look up Holiday Reinhorn, the mesmerizing girl from my old University of Washington acting class, who still tickled my memory banks. I had been thinking about her for years, frankly, and was excited at the idea of reconnecting.

To try to find her, I actually looked her up in the white pages. (This was back in the day of these things called "phone books." Pre-Internet. Pre-Google. Pre-Facebook. Pre-Chatroulette.) And, for some strange, miraculous reason, Holiday Reinhorn was actually listed in the Seattle phone book.

I called and we spoke briefly and set a time for a date. When I walked into Holiday's house, an eclectic abode filled with rabbits and cats and that gorgeous white pit bull, Edison, and I saw her in a beautiful vintage 1950s dress, a red cardigan, lumberjack boots, and sporting a Day of the Dead arm tattoo, I was gobsmacked.

I don't believe in love at first sight—it simply doesn't make any sense—but that's what happened to me on that night. And, to be quite honest, even through the most arduous times we've had (and we've had plenty), I've been deeply in love with her ever since.

For the record: Holiday is just awesome. Dark sense of humor and dangerously smart. With a giant heart and a lovely Modigliani face. I hope you get to meet her someday. But don't touch her inappropriately because then I'd have to punch you in the tooth.

A devout feminist in college (she pioneered a women's studies degree from the University of Washington), she used to wear earrings made out of steak knives and carry around a book about women artists with a giant Medusa face on the cover called *Angry Women*. Her worldview became a bit more compassionate and varied when I met her, but I always respected her commitment to equality.

We had a series of amazing dates during those few weeks in Seattle that kicked off an incredible, passionate, sometimes difficult, but mostly mind-blowingly awesome twenty-four-year relationship and twenty-year marriage.

Holiday, who had been doing plays around the Seattle area as well as some other odd jobs (such as working at the Pacific Northwest Ballet box office and making giant vats of hummus for a local hummus company), had been planning on moving to NYC before I ever got reacquainted with her. Sure enough, with a little coaxing from me, a year later she shipped out her books, clothes, pit bull, and collection of animal skulls and antique lamps, and we began an incredible life together.

My wife was an excellent actor, and she moved to NYC to be a performer. After a few auditions for some dumb plays, she completely shifted gears as an artist, however. Her heroes were the performance artists of the downtown scene: Spalding Gray, Anna Deavere Smith, the Five Lesbian Brothers, Eric Bogosian, Rachel Rosenthal, Karen Finley, and most of all, our idols, the Wooster Group.

Within months she was performing what she had written at many great downtown experimental theaters, such as PS 122, Nada, and Dixon Place. It was in some performance-writing workshops with María Irene Fornés and Sarah Schulman, and studying with Mabou Mines, Playwrights Horizons, and Circle Rep, that she found her calling as a writer.

Holiday's first pieces were absurdist performance monologues that she would present in theaters and bars and underground clubs. It was super fun to watch her perform outlandish theatrical works like "Liver of a Tourist," "You Are in the Mood for Love," and "Fish" in some of the most outrageous locations in downtown Manhattan.

I'll never forget her dressed as a male CIA agent, replete with mustache, having a conversation with his talking German shepherd (played by John Valadez in a tuxedo) about the fact that his upcoming divorce would be interrupting this year's New England fall foliage tour, onstage at the downtown lesbian performance space the WOW Cafe Theatre, in front of an audience entirely dressed in cigarette-fumed clothes and motorcycle boots.

These strange and funny monologues soon began to turn into stranger and funnier short stories, and before you knew it she had written a handful of amazing fiction (check out her hysterically twisted short story collection, *Big Cats*) and had gotten accepted to the most prestigious writing program in the country, the Iowa Writers' Workshop.

It's too hard to do justice to a twenty-some-year relationship in a silly book with a bassoonist on the cover, but if there is one aspect of our time together that best sums up our union and what Holiday brings to my life, it's our many travels.

Holiday and I spent a great deal of time zooming throughout the wilds of the Northeast in my dilapidated "transcendent" moving van. Every few months we would throw a foam mattress, a cooler, and our pit bulls in the back and go van camping in the Catskills, Berkshires, Adirondacks, and other sad excuses for East Coast "mountain ranges."

We've camped under the redwoods, snorkeled with dolphins, dined in exquisite Parisian restaurants, and watched baby sea turtles exit their eggs by moonlight and barrel toward the waters of the Pacific in Costa Rica. We've wandered the alleys of Marrakech and Istanbul and the moors of Scotland. We've hiked through Israel and the Okefenokee Swamp, the mountains of Central Oregon and the barren hills of Haiti.

In 1992, in what turned out to be perhaps our strangest adventure, we traveled to El Salvador to visit my friend Phil, a poet and political activist who was working with the trade unions and the Farabundo Martí National Liberation Front, or FMLN. The FMLN were leftist rebels who had just signed a peace treaty to set aside their rebellion and form a political party. Holiday and I ventured through the countryside and up to this volcano called Guazapa that was still occupied by the very, very dangerous and armed FMLN army and surrounded by land mines placed by the very, very dangerous and armed Salvadoran military. We spent a couple of days up there hiking through the various battle zones with former rebels still carrying their AK-47s. We saw craters from bombs dropped from American airplanes (the United States was not-so-secretly funding the corrupt military dictatorship of El Salvador and its death squads for decades in its bloody fight against leftists, unions, Jesuits, farmers, students, various nuns, and those in favor of democracy), bullet casings scattered across the jungle floor, and caves filled with snakes where the guerrillas would hide when bombs were dropped. Holiday and I slept on the cement floor of a hut, under a dirty sheet with parrots barking in the trees, mosquitoes mosquitoing, and former rebels cleaning their guns all around us.

We would look at each other, sipping on coffee that had been boiled in a coffee can from local beans, as if to say, *"Is this really happening? Are we really doing this?!"*

An even greater, more outlandish adventure on a volcano, however, has to be our wedding.

We decided to get hitched in 1995. There was no proposal, just long, heated discussions about the pros and cons of marriage. Holiday was against it for the most part, as she was wary of being a woman losing her identity in the traditional male-dominated roles that we were familiar with in most marriages we knew. Plus she had turned down seven previous proposals already. I really wanted to get married because I couldn't imagine being with anyone else as I loved her so damn much. Also, I wanted the tax credit. (Yes, there is a little bit of Dwight in me. Always has been, always will be.)

Holiday and I decided to get married as close to Mount Saint Helens as we could muster. We loved the metaphor of that former mountain. Plus, much of our family lived nearby in Washington and Oregon. We had access to a gorgeous piece of land next to the Kalama River just about fifty miles from the ashy remains of the volcano. And for the ceremony we created something akin to a piece of downtown NYC performance art.

As our various friends and family were ushered to the location of the wedding by a bagpiper playing "Amazing Grace," Holiday (who looked stunning in white go-go boots and a white minidress) was rowed down the river by her father in a raft filled with flowers. As the bagpipe crescendoed, I pulled the boat to shore and helped her out onto the sandy bank. Participants read from the Bible and Baha'i prayers but also from Lewis Carroll and other favorite playwrights and poets. Our pit bull, Edison, was the ring bearer (replete with a fashionable velvet ring pouch around her neck), and we were officially joined by Holiday's stepdad, Ed, a lawyer who had been made judge-for-a-day in Cowlitz County. After I kissed the bride and we were pronounced man and wife, Holiday and I built a fire. The attendees filed past and, having written hopes and dreams and prayers and well-wishes for us on small pieces of paper, placed them lovingly in the fire. Then we all had a salmon barbecue and jumped in the icy river (with our dog). It was a pretty glorious event, and looking back on it I wouldn't change a thing. It was a bizarre and profound expression of our love. And a hell of a lot of fun.

Back to NYC. After shacking up deep in the East Village and then on the Upper West Side (where the local denizens had never *SEEN* a pit bull before), we lucked out on the apartment of the century. Folks, I'm going to straight-up brag here for a second. Bear with me.

We lived in a giant two-bedroom in Fort Greene, Brooklyn. It had thirteen-foot ceilings, a bay window, tons of light, wood floors, a DECK, and, best of all, cost us seven hundred dollars a month. Yes. You just read that right. A two-bedroom in a great, diverse neighborhood in Brooklyn for SEVEN HUNDRED DOLLARS A MONTH!

(Four years later, after Holiday had received her degree from the Iowa Writers' Workshop and I had done a bunch more plays that no one really saw or cared about, we were "bought out" of said apartment by our landlords so they could sell the building for oodles of cash. We were paid sixty-five grand to move. It was more than three times what I ever earned in a year. We thought we were rich and would never have to work again. Like the Beverly Hillbillies. Of course, six months later, after paying off credit cards and some student loans, having some sushi dinners, and moving to LA, most of that money was sadly gone and we were broke-ass broke again.)

It was a glorious place to live. We got another little neighborhood pit bull named Harper Lee and proceeded to get to know the locals really well at the dog park. They were truly the most diverse group of people in the world. Young artsy students from the nearby Pratt Institute, well-off African American professionals (Fort Greene was the neighborhood *The Cosby Show* was supposedly set in), some folks from the nearby housing projects, and, of course, offbeat bohemians like us. We would have huge parties and invite the neighbors AND their dogs to the party. The mutts would run around the apartment in a huge mob, chasing a ball or wrestling over a dirty sock, thundering around like a herd of bison as the eclectic of Brooklyn sipped Rolling Rocks and talked about art and life and pets. Occasionally someone would be brought down with a thud when the pack slammed up against the back of their knees, but the party would always pick right up again after a few seconds.

We've been through so much together on our spiritual and artistic journey through marriage and travels and life. Our ups and downs and sidewayses could fill another entire tome. We grew up together. We became artists together. Ate frozen burritos while watching the sunset in Red Hook together. We even spent some difficult time in separation and therapy, dealing with issues concerning ourselves and our coupleship. I won't fill more of this book with those many stories, but I truly believe I'm the luckiest man on the planet to have such a brilliant woman with the biggest possible heart to journey alongside me. Also, she's hot. So that's cool.

I'm going to skip even further ahead in the timeline to tell you the final story, however, which is also the most harrowing. Of all the adventures Holiday and I have had, the most horrific and transcendent was the birth of our son, Walter, in 2004.

It's a grueling tale and if you're squeamish and/or pregnant, I advise you to skip ahead. It's a bit bloody and scary too, with gory details about vaginas and fluids and whatnot. Just wanted to warn you. Also, the story does have a happy ending. So eventually there will be much rejoicing.

After we tried to get pregnant for over a year, my seed finally took. We were older at the time. I was thirty-eight and Holiday was forty. My sperm were a bit decrepit and spun to the left, and her eggs were already sipping mai tais in Palm Desert. Finally (right after shooting the *Office* pilot, actually), the pee stick glowed with its magical plus sign. Her eggo was officially preggo.

The pregnancy was a breeze and health-wise everything went incredibly smoothly.

Then, just two days before her due date, a bunch of really weird blood clot thingies started periodically coming out of her vagina. We scooped one of those suckers out of the toilet in a Tupperware one day and took it in for inspection. We went into the swanky Santa Monica hospital where we were scheduled to give birth, and our (horrible) ob-gyn dismissed it as this common thing called "bloody show" and sent us right home. Boy was he wrong.

At three a.m. the night she was due, Holiday got up to pee, and instead of peeing her water broke, and instead of water it was bloody water. Tons of it came pouring out of her into and around our San Fernando Valley toilet. She called out and I ran in to find her toppling over, pale as paper, about to pass out. I had no idea what to do. Blood was everywhere. The love of my life was about to lose consciousness, perhaps worse, and what was happening to the baby inside her?! I started to panic.

I did what I had learned from that time I had almost passed out at that SoHo party with all those models: I hoisted her incredibly pregnant body over to the tub and started running cold water over her head as it lolled around (along with her eyes). She was about to completely give in to unconsciousness. Blood continued to come out of her as I called 911. No idea if keeping her awake was a good or terrible idea, but she stayed conscious and later thanked me for my Clooney-during-*ER*-like impulse.

I had never been so scared in all my life. Neither had she. But things were about to get a whole lot scarier.

Within ten minutes an ambulance was at our door and a bunch of confused firemen types tromped into the bathroom to find my completely wet, nearly naked, nine-months-pregnant wife almost passed out on the linoleum floor covered with blood and amniotic fluid. They were more than just a little bit freaked out.

And that's one thing about this story that is so weird. On the TV, when there's a medical emergency, everyone knows EXACTLY what they're doing, or at least looks like they do. In this debacle, NO ONE seemed to have any clue what to do next. All of these "health professionals" seemed completely lost, confused, and in over their heads.

Now, ambulances in the middle of the night don't just take you to the fancy hospital of your choice in Santa Monica. No. They take you to the nearest place, no matter what it's like. So there we were at a hospital that shall not be named in one of the seediest parts of the San Fernando Valley at three in the morning. The emergency room was full apparently, so Holiday was wheeled upstairs somewhere and left in a hallway. I raced over to find my ashen wife barely conscious, on a gurney, uncovered, still bleeding.

I was shaking and sweating and had no idea what to do or how to act, whether to scream at someone or go hide in the corner. Everything completely breaks down when there's blood and a baby involved. I was a basket case.

Thankfully, Holiday was incredibly brave through this living nightmare. She was tearful and terrified but never lost it or broke down. She maintained a steely, calm resolve and a trust that somehow it would all work out.

Even when the nurse brought over a portable ultrasound and couldn't find our son's heartbeat. Even when said pathetic excuse for a nurse then handed my wife the ultrasound paddle thingy and said in a loud, panicked voice (and I'm not making this up), *"I CAN'T FIND THE HEARTBEAT, I CAN'T FIND THE HEARTBEAT! HERE. YOU LOOK FOR IT. YOU KNOW WHERE YOUR BABY IS!!!"*

Holiday showed incredible fortitude when that same nurse later shouted over to us from her desk down the hall: "I'VE PAGED THE DOCTOR ON CALL OVER AND OVER AGAIN, BUT HE'S NOT CALLING BACK! *HE'S NOT CALLING BACK!!!*"

Staying as positive as she could, Holiday just kept praying and breathing slowly, even after we finally found the heartbeat, which was quite low and growing fainter by the minute. She remained serene and focused through her terror even when I went over to another gum-chewing nurse and screamed at her to please leave her damn paperwork at her desk and please come over and help clean up and tend to my wife *WHO WAS BLEEDING TO DEATH FROM HER VAGINA IN YOUR FILTHY HALLWAY!!!*

Finally, after what felt like hours, after many hushed prayers and an ever-deepening profound realization that we just have so, so little control of what happens to us as human beings, either outside or inside our fragile bodies, a doctor slammed through the hallway doors like Superman.

He took one look at the situation and started barking orders at the lame nurses like a champion. Finally, someone acting like a doctor on a TV show.

"WHY ISN'T THE OPERATING ROOM PREPPED?! WHEEL HER INTO THE O.R. WHERE'S THE ANESTHESIOLOGIST?! GET HER READY FOR A C-SECTION, STAT!"

(Note: I'm not sure if he actually said "stat," but if he didn't, he should have.)

It was like God sent us an angel in the form of a rumpled, bald, Iranian ob-gyn named Dr. Foroohar, who promptly saved Holiday's life and delivered us (in record time) a beautiful, perfect baby boy.

Someone brought Walter out to me as I was deep in prayer in the hallway and it was there, having been through two hours of living hell, that I had my most sacred and memorable moment ever.

I'm not sure if you've ever held a fresh soul in your hands before, but if you ever get the chance, take it.

Walter was about three minutes old when I held him in my arms in that Van Nuys hallway not far from where his mother had been frantically, tearfully searching for his pulse with an ultrasound paddle not half an hour earlier.

I held him in his little blanket and looked into his gigantic blue eyes, and he looked right back into mine with a strong, quizzical expression that said, "What the *HELL* is going on here?! WHO ARE *YOU*?!" Tears rolled down my face as I peered into his eyes and through them. Down. Into and inside the essence of this tiny, wide-eyed, gorgeous boy.

I had the most profound experience of seeing his newly born, infinitely precious SOUL. His "beingness." Not his personality. Not his consciousness. Something beyond both of those things. There was an entity there, wrapped in a blanket, and the two of us were connected for life.

Now, the only dead body I've really seen up close was that of Holiday's wonderful grandmother Alice, who passed away the year after we were married. When you see a lifeless form, you realize so clearly that we are *not our bodies*. As I gazed down at her corpse I knew the "Alice-ness" of her had dissipated and gone somewhere else. Evaporated. There was just a pleasant, empty shell that remained in a coffin of wood, devoid of any life or soul or spirit or being. This body I was gazing at had carried the living essence known as Alice for almost ninety years, but that essence was gone now, and the husk had been discarded. Alice was not her body. None of us are.

With Walter, it was the opposite. Here was this soul that had been cooked for a good while in utero, which had now emerged and was inhabiting this brand-new tiny body. His eyes were little portholes into his being. Which was being held in my shaking, grateful hands, the two of us, eye to eye in that Van Nuys hallway at four a.m.

Little Walter was brought to Holiday, who was sweaty, grateful, and gray as a ghost, as she came out of anesthesia in the dank, cold "recovery basement" of the hospital. We were together as a family at last, and in classic Wilson fashion, he knew exactly where to find the milk.

She recovered just fine, although she stayed in the hospital for four more days with incredibly low blood pressure, having lost four pints in just a few hours. Her mom, Mary, and sister, Amy, flew into town, and the five of us camped out in that hospital room for all four days, grateful as any humans could be that Holiday and little Walter were alive.

My wife was a wonder of strength throughout this horrific ordeal. I was a total mess, and she dealt with the pain and chaos like a fighter and a saint.

In fact, this seems to be the story of our relationship as a whole. You'll often find me panicked and acting like an idiot, while Holiday offers incredible perspective, shows strength in adversity, and, for some strange reason, puts up with my incessant assholery. But it is our willingness (with another tip of the hat to M. Scott Peck) to *extend ourselves to support each other's spiritual growth* that has made this marriage not only survive so many ups and downs but prosper as well. And for that I am volcanically grateful.

ADVENTURES IN THEATER

—

Throughout my life in acting, I have had some strange, outlandish, and wonderful experiences, both as an actor in training and as a professional. I have done countless plays and roles on TV shows over the years. I've done many movies and taken and taught many classes and workshops. Throughout this panoply of acting adventures there are some truly bizarre and memorable experiences that I want to set down in type before I keel over.

Let's visit some of these, shall we?

EXPERIMENTAL THEATER EXPERIMENTS

Experimental theater is weird. Way weird. I like weird. Weird is cool. Especially when it involves masks, rolling around on the ground, making loud groaning noises, and gesticulating and prancing about like a possessed tweaker in sweatpants. The THEATER!!!

At Tufts, when I was in my misty cloud of depression, I stayed on campus for winter break instead of going home to my divorcing folks, who had just relocated from Chicago back to Seattle, separately. How did I spend this festive time of year when families come together to celebrate their gratitude and give loving gifts to one another? Simple. Locked in a church with a Polish "Theater of Cruelty" director who didn't speak a word of English.

The Tufts theater department rented out a local church and brought over this woman, Rena Mirecka, from Jerzy Grotowski's infamous theater company in Poland. The company was infamous for isolating themselves in a commune in the woods and rehearsing plays for years. They called it the Poor Theater. There were no orchestras or moving lights and sets and costumes. It was the actors' voices, faces, and bodies that were used to tell the story to an alienated (again!) audience. Myth, ritual, ceremony, dance, music, and raw emotion were the central elements, not props and effects and artifice.

There were about twelve of us. We would gather at nine a.m. and not leave until six p.m. What did we do? Well, nothing and everything. We just waited to see what would happen. There were some drums and bells and bowls of water and oranges and flowers. Some idiot in sweatpants would start banging a drum and then a dance would erupt somewhere. Or a game of tag. Or a song. Or a jumping contest. Or a person would start quietly sobbing in the corner.

This. Went. On. For. Hours. And. Days.

It was like an acid trip without the acid (in fact, she wanted us to not consume alcohol or caffeine during the entire week). There was something oddly magical about a series of physical events launching themselves from some random impulses of a group of people in a space. Ceremony, dance, ritual, spirituality, and group psychology all woven together.

Occasionally we would gather and start walking around in a circle. For an hour. No, I'm not kidding. The ensemble would walk around at a brisk pace in a circle for a full sixty minutes. Nothing gets you crazier *en la cabeza* than a forced circular march. They should consider using it at the rehabilitation camps in North Korea. Why did we do this? I honestly have no idea. To break us down to be more free? To get us out of our heads? To learn about shapes? I really don't know. But ultimately, I just loved the experience.

At the University of Washington, our chain-smoking Marxist, feminist theater professor had us do Bertolt Brecht scenes while wearing paper bags on our heads. We cut out eyeholes and a mouth hole and performed intense scenes about political injustice and class. This would alienate the audience and teach us, theoretically, to use our bodies, gestures, and movements to reveal character and tell the story. We became real-life political sack puppets!

At NYU, one of the greatest experiences of those three years was taking an amazing clown workshop with Gates McFadden (the actress who played Dr. Crusher on *Star Trek: The Next Generation*). As part of this two-week adventure in red noses, pratfalls, and absurdity, we did an infamous exercise, appropriately called Ring of Fire.

In the Ring of Fire, you would come out onto the stage as your clown character and there were only two rules.

1. You had to try to make the audience laugh.
2. Once you made the audience laugh, and only then, could you leave the stage.

I remember my turn, the nervousness and terror of the moment as I walked out onstage under the bright lights. For some reason I decided to deeply pretend that my clown character was a prostitute at a truck stop and was flirting with various truckers as they walked and drove around. Apparently, my trying to be sexually seductive to truckers in a dress and clown nose was pretty funny; I made the audience laugh and got to sit down. Phew!

Some people were fairly effective and got laughs right away, with deftness and vulnerability. Others, not so much.

They would try some piece of shtick or physical comedy, which would immediately fall flat. Then they'd dive back in and try something similar, which also wouldn't work. Then they'd try again. And again. It would be painful. "Trying to be funny" just doesn't work, you see. They'd get stuck. Just stand there. Gigantic awkward pauses. Sometimes an excruciatingly long amount of time would go by, and in two people's cases, they ended up onstage for almost an hour. It was brutal. You could tell they were pissed off and confused and resentful under their clown nose and ridiculous outfit. Sometimes people break down and cry under the strain and pressure. And, oddly enough, as soon as they do, the audience laughs and the teacher tells them to sit down.

It was an incredible lesson in acting.

You see, when the actor/guinea pig was attempting to "be funny" and "get laughs," it was akin to watching dentistry.

As soon as the clown character was real, open, vulnerable, breathing, and feeling in the moment, they were hysterical and a joy to watch.

I attempted to apply these principles in the role of Dwight, sometimes effectively and sometimes not. You tell me.

After graduating from NYU I worked with many great experimental theater artists and directors, including, briefly, Richard Schechner and a company he had formed called East Coast Artists. I was introduced to their work when I saw their production of Goethe's *Faust* in which, at a certain point, Faust pulls down his pants and literally POOPS OUT HITLER. Out of Dr. Faust's butthole comes an actress as a wet poo-Hitler, replete with tiny mustache and loud goose-stepping speeches. It was awesome.

Richard was known for his enormous belly, which looked like he had swallowed a yoga ball, as well as for standing on his head and crossing his legs. He would often watch the proceedings in this manner, on his head, giant stomach floating weightlessly, legs folded and crossed on top. Like an upside-down Buddha.

One exercise we did with Schechner was these emotion circles. This was inspired by Antonin Artaud's quote that actors are "athletes of the heart." (Artaud also once famously said: "I call for actors burning at the stakes, laughing at the flames.") Across a gigantic floor were all these circles with different emotions written inside each one, like an enormous game of Twister with various emotional states. We would jump from one to another and seek to totally emotionally and physically embody the corresponding feeling. If you had captured the actors leaping circles from Grief to Ecstasy to Rage to Envy on a video camera, the viewer would have been positively assured that they were looking into the very worst possible insane asylum.

Later on, I did a workshop with a personal hero of mine, the experimental theater director and actor Andre Gregory. He is an amazing man and artist, and his films *My Dinner with Andre* and *Vanya on 42nd Street* were HUGE inspirations to me (watch them!). For a few weeks he once gathered a group of lost actor souls in a loft in the Garment District, and we would do these strange body exercises called plastiques.

We would take our shirts off for some reason (the guys at least) and do a crazy communal dance in which we would isolate various body parts and find movements and gestures that our knees or pelvis or elbows would make to one another. It was countless sweaty hours of contorting and undulating our various body parts, communicating like we were inhabited by demons and/or aliens.

Then we would do various Chekhov monologues and cry.

———

Richard Foreman is an infamous downtown theater director. He's a tiny, maniacal man who moves his actors around the stage like insane, jerky puppets. I did a production of Suzan-Lori Parks's play *Venus* that he directed, and besides climbing around on a movable jungle gym in period Victorian clothes, I spent a good part of the play with a mask that featured an enormous penis on it. I was the "penis-faced man" in a sideshow of freaks. I dabbed at my "nose member" occasionally with my hanky, looking forlorn. Somewhere at the Public Theater there exists a photo of me with a big fat dick face. (Note to publisher: Replace existing bassoon cover with dick-faced-man cover immediately.)

TONIGHT I FEEL THE MAGIC OF THE THEATER

My very first theater job was in *Twelfth Night* for Shakespeare in the Park in 1989, where I got paid $210 a week. This particular production was noted for being incredibly star-studded and directed by an acting coach who had never directed a play before. I found myself on the first day of rehearsal surrounded by Michelle Pfeiffer (who had never acted in a play previously), Jeff Goldblum, Stephen Collins, Gregory Hines, Fisher Stevens (whom I understudied), and John Amos. A nervous twenty-three-year-old beanpole, I was terrified, giggly, and starstruck. The production was hacky and mediocre, although Mary Elizabeth Mastrantonio (*The Abyss, The Color of Money*) was great as Viola. It was an amazing first acting job and I was elated. I loved watching the rehearsals and joking around with the crazy stars.

The most incredible moment of the entire production (besides the gorgeous Michelle Pfeiffer beginning a three-year love affair with gawky, squawky Fisher Stevens!) was when the acting coach/director gave the cast a mind-bending speech right before opening night. He said, literally, "F&*^ Shakespeare. F%$* the text. Don't worry about that s%9$. Just be yourselves! The audience is here to see *you*. Have a blast, do what you want, and forget about Shakespeare."

For the young understudies and ensemble members, most of whom had just graduated from Juilliard and NYU and Yale, this was the EXACT OPPOSITE of what we had been taught for THREE LONG YEARS. Also, I don't imagine that the casts of plays at the Royal Shakespeare Company often get "F*@# Shakespeare" speeches from their directors.

We were astonished and not surprised when the cast took him at his word and mugged up a storm, ignored the demands of the text, danced whenever possible, and even started doing "the wave" with the audience during the course of the show. Sure enough, the audience ate it up and the critics SAVAGED the production.

I once did the worst production of the worst Shakespeare play ever written, *The Two Noble Kinsmen*. (Note: It's one of those lame plays everyone's pretty sure that Shakespeare may have had a hand in but didn't really write.) The two leads were myself and the actor Peter Jacobson (Dr. Chris Taub from *House*). He is about five feet five and extremely (what's the PC way of saying it these days?) "ethnic." Side by side with me at six feet two and 165 pounds of pale geek meat, we were the most ridiculous set of warrior brothers you've ever seen on-stage.

The absurdist, impractical, and stupid set we performed on had a door in the center of the back wall, which leaned in toward the audience. This door would never work right and occasionally, at the most inopportune times, would just swing wide-open with a thunderous crash in the middle of a scene. There was usually an actor waiting for their entrance behind it who would be fully exposed to our minuscule audience and would look up and dash away in their tights.

I will never forget this one scene where the Widows of the War

Heroes™ walked out in a strange procession, all in black, carrying the ashes of their dead war husbands in urns, singing a dirge. Once one of the widows tripped on our ridiculous set during a performance and SPILLED the ashes of her dead husband all over the stage. Everyone froze. No one was quite sure what to do. The widow, after an excruciating pause, slooooowly knelt down and began solemnly sweeping the remains of her ashy husband back into the urn with her hand while continuing her atonal chant. I have never laughed so hard in my life. Peter and I still chortle about it to this day. (Note: This production was *FILMED*, people, and is on file somewhere at the Lincoln Center library.)

After I graduated from NYU, I went on tour with the Acting Company for over two years. The Acting Company is a prestigious theater troupe that was founded in 1972 by John Houseman out of the Juilliard School, specifically for young actors to cut their teeth in a traveling repertory company after graduation from actors' training programs. There were many famous alums of the company from its early days, such as Patti LuPone, Kevin Kline, and Frances Conroy, as well as in its later days, including Keith David, Hamish Linklater, and Jesse L. Martin.

As I was sick of doing all my "shitty jobs" in NYC and had no agent, I signed up to go on the road, playing Peter in *Romeo and Juliet* (yeah, thought so. You're racking your brains right now. You've never heard of him, have you? No one has. He's the assistant to the nurse. One of the smallest parts in all of Shakespeare) and Speed the clown in *The Two Gentlemen of Verona*. After doing one incredibly difficult yearlong tour, I signed up for yet *ANOTHER*, playing Demetrius in *A Midsummer Night's Dream* alongside the great Jeffrey Wright (*Boardwalk Empire, The Hunger Games*), who played Puck.

We lived on a bus that used to drive Reba McEntire's band around filled with sixteen actors, and there was a semi with all the sets and props. We went to hundreds of venues in over forty states in that first year, performing Shakespeare in places where people had not only never seen Shakespeare before but had never seen a *play* before. Gillette, Wyoming; Terre Haute, Indiana; Stillwater, Oklahoma; Burlington, Vermont; Marquette, Michigan; Valdosta, Georgia; and Bozeman, Montana. I've played them all and dozens more. Sometimes we performed a ten a.m. student matinee in a combo auditorium/cafeteria and sometimes evening shows in beautiful, restored turn-of-the-century theaters. We acted in three-hundred-seat college theaters and college amphitheaters that sat two thousand.

Out of sheer boredom, we would often invent little games to get us through the tedium of doing our hundred and fifty-seventh matinee.

Withered Hand: We had to play a scene completely straight and with tremendous focus and passion . . . but with a withered, immobile hand at our side.

Bunny Hop: We had to hop like a big ol' bunny rabbit at an exit of our choosing. (I always wonder what the audiences must have thought, watching Mercutio and Benvolio hopping offstage like kangaroos in period garb. Did they think it was a "theater thing"? A character choice? A figment of their imagination?)

Car Keys: At some point while onstage we had to search our Renaissance pants as if we were perplexedly looking for our car keys.

Pass the Battery: Someone would start the play with a battery in their hand and then, over the course of doing a scene, would pass it to someone else; that person would do the same thing, and so on until everyone in the company had held the battery in their hand.

And my personal favorite:

> **Mascot:** We had to incorporate the name of the mascot of what-ever school we were performing at into the play somehow. Every-one needed to say the word *panther* or *patriot* or *cowboy* or *fighting Scotsmen* as their character and have it perfectly scan into the iam-bic pentameter of the Shakespearean verse without drawing any attention to it.

There's an entire book that could be written about those endless, te-dious miles, the debauchery, shenanigans, and incredible amounts of laughter we shared as a company of twentysomething wannabe clas-sical actors, but this isn't it.

I'm grateful for those years. While most actors were waiting ta-bles in New York, hoping for their big break, I was getting direct per-formance experience while logging thousands of miles in a stinky bus filled with a bunch of neurotic narcissists (myself included). It's where I cut my teeth as a performer: snowball fights, poker games, late-night guitar jams, motels and crappy food, farmland and telephone poles, poetic language, and physical comedy. I felt, finally, like a professional actor.

One of the strangest theater adventures I ever had was doing the Os-car Wilde play *Salome* with Al Pacino. He had already performed it on Broadway for months, but it was a work he loved coming back to again and again. He was doing a remount a year later in Stamford, Connecti-cut, and I did a monthlong run as the Page of Herodias. It was a nice role of a boy/page who poured wine and fell in love with a soldier at the beginning. After my acting section was finished, my blocking was literally to kneel by the side of the stage with my ornate wine decanter in my short, sexy, ridiculous biblical robe and sandals and just stay put. I got to watch Al Pacino perform for an entire month from a distance of twenty feet and it was a master class. He played the role of mad King Herod, who was obsessed with Salome and brought her the head of John the Baptist on a tray. In the play, Herod speaks for page after page after page in grand gestures and tremendous, poetic Wildeian language. The fascinating thing was watching Al at work, as every night was completely and utterly different. Tickets were outrageously expensive ($125) and some nights he was an exploding volcano that put on the performance of a lifetime, finding nuance and passion and flourish in every line. On these nights, you literally had no idea what he was going to do next or how he was going to spin a line, and it was electric, dangerous, and riveting. Other nights, he was TERRIBLE. He seemed to be fumbling, internally focused, and lost in some kind of stutteringly boring inner exploration (making the ticket price a total waste of money). What I learned as a young actor is that no matter how many times you've played a role, every single performance is an excavation, a rehearsal in front of an audience, where you play, dig, explore, and unleash your spontaneity to bring a fresh vitality to the character and an unpredictable magic to every moment. Hopefully, the actor can temper this process, however, to allow the audience to get their money's worth on a nightly basis. Also, some nights I would be covered in the manic spittle from Pacino's endless monologues, which I imagined a kind of literal theatrical baptism.

One of the saddest, most tragic theater experiences I ever had was doing *Long Day's Journey into Night* at the Arena Stage. I played the youngest son, Edmund, and my father was played by the bighearted Richard Kneeland. (My brother was played by Casey Biggs and the mom was played by the late actress Tana Hicken, who is one of the greatest actresses of the American stage. Her performance in this play was truly one for the ages.) Unbeknownst to us, Richard was a recovering alcoholic who, as the show progressed, relapsed and kept relapsing, deeper and deeper. Pretty soon he was getting drunk every day and showing up drunk to many of the shows. Doing a three-hour Eugene O'Neill play is hard enough. Doing a three-hour Eugene O'Neill play with a sloshy, surly, forgetful old drunk guy was sheer torture. During one performance he was doing the famous "unscrewing the lightbulbs to save money" scene and was so buzzed he started to fall off the dining room table he was standing on. He literally toppled backward. I ran over and (somewhat effortlessly, somehow) caught him, saving him from cracking his head open. I was pissed. We confronted him, cajoled, threatened, pleaded, begged him to go to meetings and get help, but he was too far gone. He controlled his drinking during the shows, giving a beautifully nuanced performance, but began getting stinking drunk in the final act and becoming smashed after them. He was found dead a few months later in his San Diego apartment, having fallen and hit his head. Alcoholism is a devastating disease that destroys lives and families. RIP, Richard. You were one of the greats.

This isn't quite theater, but since it was a "live performance," I'll include it here. I was once a corporate shill for Nortel Networks at the Jacob Javits convention center. I remember getting paid $1,500 per day for three days' work, and that was more money than I could have ever possibly imagined in those days. I had to memorize about five interminable pages of the worst technobabble, Internet bull crap mixed with IT jokes and "perform" this monologue every fifteen minutes for audiences of anywhere from zero to eighteen people in a cavernous convention center. I had one of those Madonna mics on the side of my head, and a black turtleneck, and my script was timed to go with various images on a wall of television screens. People would walk up and ask for free T-shirts and I would politely tell them that they would have to wait patiently and receive their priceless Nortel Networks T-shirt at the end of the presentation. They would sigh disgustedly and sit in the audience, willing to undergo a twelve-minute brain-numbing monologue in exchange for a cheap T-shirt. The opening line of the presentation is one that still haunts me for its brilliant horribleness.

Nortel Networks Script

[Narrator appears onstage from behind a wall of televisions. Photo of Charles Dickens is revealed on the myriad of screens. Narrator turns to the audience.]

Narrator: It was the best of times, it was the worst of times. [points to screen] Charles Dickens. Now *THERE'S* a content provider. . . .

[Narrator smiles, waits for laughter. Silence. The laughter doesn't come. Ever. Narrator shoots himself in the face. Blood on the dance floor. Lights go to black. A scream. The Internet explodes. Everyone is given a free T-shirt.]

Chapter 12

I BOMBED ON BROADWAY

I'M NOT HAPPY. SORRY, PHARRELL.

Let's flash our story forward to 1996. I'm thirty and I have everything I've ever wanted. I've been living the so-called bohemian lifestyle that I always dreamed of. I have a beautiful bohemian woman to share my life with in our beautiful bohemian apartment. I have been working with some of the greatest bohemian directors in the theater in some really interesting and challenging bohemian productions. I eat bohemian dinners with a bohemian fork (hand-whittled and wrapped with a hemp rope). I am (mostly, except for occasional Transcendent Moving Company jobs) making a meager but steady living as an actor. This is everything I ever wanted, right? When I went adolescently trembling into Suzanne Adams's office in my senior year of high school to ask about the remotest possibility that I could ever someday be an actor, I never could have dreamed that twelve years later I would be where I was: in New York City working as a professional actor.

And yet . . . *Why wasn't I happy?!* You set a goal, your life's dream;

you pursue it; and *then* you become happy. Isn't that how it's supposed to work?*

Well, there I was, not happy in Brooklyn. And I wasn't exactly sure why. I would wake up in the middle of the night deeply, deeply sad. Alienated. Disconnected. Disconsolate. Then I would kick myself! "Why are you feeling this way?! I mean, look at the amazing woman asleep beside you. Think of all the incredible theater you're doing. You have everything you've ever wanted, including a kick-ass van! Your dream has come true and yet you are not happy, jerk-face." Remember the scene in *Fight Club* where Ed Norton beats the crap out of himself? That's what I was doing to my heart, soul, and self-esteem on a daily basis. I was filled with stresses and it was uncomfortable to be in my body.

Perhaps all humans feel this way deep down inside. Maybe it's a part of the human condition, occasionally feeling that we are isolated dots of consciousness in a meaningless universe that's whirling around outside of us like sad fireworks. This was in the pre-smartphone era, after all, and maybe I was—we all were—a bit less simply distracted from what Louis C.K. would call "man's essential aloneness," and I was able to get more deeply in touch with my core existential angst without the presence of a tiny screen to check and double-check endlessly throughout

---

* A note about happiness: In 2014 I did a talk at the University of Southern California about happiness. I'm not what you would call a joyful person, but I believe I have a few minor insights into what DOESN'T make you happy. One of those things? The myth that happiness is something to be *pursued*. "Life, Liberty and the pursuit of Happiness" is total bull balls. You can't *pursue* happiness. What does that even mean?

What it really means, the pretty overt subtext to our national motto about that "unalienable right," is that nothing should get in the way of a citizen's trying to accrue things. In other words, I have the RIGHT to go out and get crap without neighbors or the government or institutions getting in my GD way. It should really read "LIFE, LIBERTY AND THE PURSUIT OF ACCRUING CRAP." And

the day. (For instance, while writing this last paragraph I checked Twitter twenty-eight times. Got mostly LOLs and one "YOU SUCK.")

To quell the angst, I used something that ultimately gave me far *more* angst: alcohol. I drank a good amount every single day through those many New York years. I rarely passed out in pools of my own (or someone else's) vomit, but I definitely used alcohol as a constant daily coping mechanism and leaned on it as a consistent emotional/social lubricant. The dizzying high from beer and spirits was a constant in my life throughout my twenties and early thirties. But you can only rely on being buzzed for so long before it starts to wear thin and the troubling noise you've been trying to blot out and force down starts echoing up through the cracks.

I had a thought that started sneaking up on me around this time. Perhaps, I thought to myself, the reason I'm not happy is that I don't have meaning. I don't have purpose. Or maybe it's that my previous purpose—becoming a professional actor and doing life-changing plays—simply wasn't a completely real or satisfying life course. Maybe I had thrown the baby out with the bathwater when I jettisoned my faith. (Not literally. I never got THAT drunk!) Maybe, just maybe, I should give more thought to this whole question of . . . oh boy, here we go . . . GOD.

---

implicit in that "right" to buy, stockpile, and obtain is that eventually, once you have the right home on the right plot of land, the right mate, the right family, the right job, the right savings, the right everything, THEN you will be happy. It's an "if-then" proposition. And it just doesn't work that way, I believe.

The ancient Greeks had a different word for happiness. They often used the term *eudemonia*, which translates best as "human flourishing." That's such a rich, complex, evocative term. Think about it: human flourishing. That includes art, service, contentment, connection, community, challenges, and endeavor!

What if our "right" in the Declaration of Independence was "Life, Liberty and the pursuit of HUMAN FLOURISHING"? That would create a much deeper and more varied dialogue on what human flourishing actually is. How can the indi-

I related to that great Catholic monk, writer, and mystic of the highest order Thomas Merton, who described himself as "loving God and yet hating him; born to love Him, living instead in fear and hopeless self-contradictory hungers." Was I living in hopeless self-contradictory hungers? Yikes!

I started fitfully asking my friends about God. (I greatly enjoy talking about topics that almost always clear the room, the dinner table, or a party. Topics like God, death, fate, Palestine, and Charlie Sheen.)

This is always a tricky conversation. It's such a loaded word.†

To a person my bohemian friends had the same response to the whole God conversation. When I asked them if they believed in God they always said the same thing: "Ummmm . . . *kind of.*" They would say, "Well, I don't believe in a judgmental old man on a cloud with a beard, but I *kind of* believe that there's *something* out there, some loving, creative power in the universe. I have a sense of something more out there."

---

vidual and community BOTH flourish? How can we help one another to greater and greater flourishment? (I know, not a word.) How do we create a living society where growth, enlightenment, and peace are nurtured in all our political and cultural institutions?

But I digress. Happiness is not something "just around the corner" or "over the hill" or that can be enjoyed as soon as you have a certain level of material comfort. It's a moment-to-moment choice. Joy and contentment come from daily, hourly, minutely, secondly decisions to be grateful for what you have. With every breath. Savoring every moment. Focusing on the good. On service to others. On the sacred, whatever that word means to you. Happy?

---

† This was something my friends and I would tackle when we started SoulPancake, the website and media company. We wanted to redefine words that had become so icky over time. Words like *God* and *spirituality.* Even philosophy, which was once a meaningful conversation about things that were relevant to one's life and choices, has now become a useless, highfalutin, academic exercise that, to quote Baha'u'llah, "begins in words and ends in words."

"Kind of." I got this same answer from just about everyone I spoke to.

This just didn't sit right with me. How could there "kind of" be a God? I mean, you can't "kind of" be pregnant, can you? You either are or you aren't. I mean if Beyoncé responded with "kind of" when asked if she was pregnant, she'd be hounded to the ends of the earth for more specifics. But as for the presence of an all-encompassing deity, "kind of" is enough for people to say, "Cool, no more questions."

I mean, either there IS an all-knowing, all-loving, all-powerful creative force behind this universe and perhaps infinite other universes, or everything has always "just been," and through an accident of random molecules somehow we humans ended up with consciousness. Either there is a *meaning* to the time we spend alive on this physical plane or the only meaning in this universe of stuff and energy is the meaning we create for ourselves. We've either been "created" and have eternal souls that will exist after we slough off our meat suits, OR everything in the universe is just random, beautiful matter bumping into itself and somehow we accidentally evolved from sea paste to monkeys to humans and there is no "divine" presence beyond us, and, when we die, it's lights out, end of consciousness, end of story.

(Socrates [aka Plato] spoke of his lack of fear of death because it was either an eternal, blissful sleep of nothingness or a glorious transition of his eternal soul to another state of being.)

To quote the great Thomas Merton again: "A life is either all spiritual, or not spiritual at all."

Am I missing something? It's really two choices, right? There's not a "kind of" option.

There certainly is the agnostic option: to actively say that one just doesn't know, or can't ever know, if there's a Creator. This option allows one to stay open to evidence of His existence. But that's a little different from kind of believing there kind of could be a God.*

I moved from atheist to agnostic along this phase in my journey. But I was an agnostic who wasn't going to passively wait for some evidence of God to be dropped in my lap. I was going to go on a MISSION, gosh darn it. A quest for God and for the truth about this miraculous, challenging, strange, and awesomely dazzling universe we are born into.

I started by working my way through many of the central holy books of the world religions. I started with the Bible, Old and New Testaments (a bit thick, but worth it); the Koran (same, only thicker); the Bhagavad Gita (action and adventure ancient Indian style!); the Vedas and Upanishads (mystical!); and the Dhammapada (the Buddha speaks). But it was when I started reading books on Native American spirituality that something clicked.

I read about Wakan Tanka, the title for the Creator in the Lakota Sioux tradition. Suddenly things started to make sense. *Wakan Tanka* translates as "the Great Mystery." It/He/She is an all-loving, all-powerful essence that connects all things. It moves through nature. It is the wind and the light and the sun, and it binds us to the animal kingdom and plants and the leaves moving in the trees. Wakan Tanka courses through the seven directions: north, south, east, west, up,

---

* A note about agnostics: I completely accept someone not knowing if there's a Creator or not. Here's my issue: In my experience people often use being an agnostic as a convenient, unevolved fallback position. For instance, they simply say, "I'm an agnostic," and then don't do any soul searching or spiritual questing. OR they say because you simply "can't ever really know" that this excuses one from a committed examination. I know because I lived under both of those banners for many years.

For me the greatest proof of the existence of God is the existence of LOVE. Love, like God, can never be proven in a laboratory, on a chalkboard, or with a computer program, and yet we KNOW it exists. No behaviorist can ever tell me

down, and INSIDE, toward our very hearts. Toward love itself. It connects us through time as well, to our ancestors, throughout the history of Earth, like the Force from *Star Wars*. (See? That made my nerdiest fans perk up!) Both ancient and imperishable. Running through and yet beyond every thing and every not-thing. Mysterious. Ultimately unknowable but everywhere.

Sounds awesome, right? All of a sudden, I had a window into the concept of God and He started to make sense to me. The immature God-view of the unapproachable old man scowling down on me faded away as I started to ponder Wakan Tanka and feel His/Her/Its presence all around me. It was the idea that the Creator could be felt in nature and time, that He was a force for healing and connection and love that moved through the wind and the sun and art and our cells, that opened my cynical young heart to the possibility of a more evolved vision of God.

I was speaking to my poet friend Phil, an unrepentant atheist/agnostic (whom we had visited in El Salvador), about my new infatuation and fascination with Wakan Tanka while we were watching a Yankees game. They were down in the bottom of the ninth when Darryl Strawberry stepped up to the plate. He swung and missed. Phil said, "Why don't we put this Wakan Tanka theory to a test? Pray to Him and ask Him to let the Yanks win the game."

---

that the profound feelings I have for my son and wife, say, are simply a result of chemicals and electricity causing my brain to form a connection to my offspring to preserve my heredity and species. I know in my bones and heart that I love my family and that this *crazy little thing called love* (Queen!) is *more than a feeling* (Boston!) but rather a powerful force in life beyond the mere *material* ("Material Girl," Madonna!). The same holds true for art, beauty, and music, by the way. Their incredible effect cannot be reduced to an electrochemical formula in the brain. Can anyone PROVE that there is a thing called love that is anything more than some impulses in the brain? I don't need proof. I know it exists and that it is glorious, life-changing, transcendent, and spiritual.

Sounded reasonable to me. So I stopped leaning against the door-jamb and stood up, hands in the air, shaman style. I said, "Oh, Wakan Tanka," in some ridiculous, formal voice that sounded vaguely like a character from *Dances with Wolves*. "Oh, Wakan Tanka, Great Mystery. Oh, Father spirit of the seven directions, of nature and our grandfathers, thank you for the air we breathe and the sunlight that gives us life." (Or something to that effect. I can't really remember what I said.) "If it is your will, please allow our team to win! Show us that you exist by helping Darryl Strawberry to hit a home run. Um, thank you, oh Wakan Tanka. Sir. Peace out."

I have no idea why I was so stilted and vaguely racist during my heartfelt prayer, but as I came out of it I heard a *thwack*! Darryl Strawberry had just hit a two-run walk-off home run that won the game in the ninth inning.

We were stunned. Our jaws dropped like oven doors.

We looked at each other curiously. Hmmmm.

Okay, it most certainly could have been a coincidence. But it sure got my mind spinning. Even skeptical Phil was a bit agog.

Maybe I was onto something.

I dove even deeper into my spiritual quest. I mean, what else was I going to do in my long unemployed months in between acting gigs? Be productive? That would defy the principles of lazy, shiftless actors since the days of Shake-a-spear-a!

I went to several church services. I attended Buddhist meetings and meditation workshops. I continued to read and read and read. I even started to fitfully, anxiously, confusedly "pray." To surrender. The concepts of Wakan Tanka and God merged and fused in my mind's eye. I started to ask for help on my journey from a power greater than myself, something infinite and unknowable. (Baha'u'llah, the founder of the Baha'i Faith, calls God "the Unknowable Essence," "the most manifest of the manifest, and the most hidden of the hidden.")

Then an event happened that forced me to greatly deepen and broaden my path to a Higher Power. I had a nervous breakdown on Broadway.

Joe Dowling, the great Irish director whom I had worked with for both the Acting Company and at the Guthrie Theater, called me and told me he wanted me as the goofy romantic lead character in an old English Restoration (post-Shakespearean) comedy called *London Assurance*. It was going to be performed on the main stage of the Roundabout Theatre in Times Square.

I had a lead role in a Broadway show! I was ecstatic. Up to that point I had done a bunch of regional-theater plays, Off-Off-Broadway stuff, and various tours but nothing close to something of this caliber.

In the months and weeks leading up to the rehearsals, I grew increasingly nervous. The pressure was building inside. I felt an intimidating stress mounting within me about how I would need to really shine in this role. A stressful voice in my head began prodding: "This play could get me a better agent! This role could land me a Tony nomination!! This is my chance to get an amazing *New York Times* review!!!" The pressure continued to increase and build through rehearsals and eventual performances until, you guessed it, I totally sucked in the role.

I bombed on Broadway. But—and isn't it funny how life works?—it turned out to be one of the best experiences of my life.

In rehearsals I was stiff and disconnected. I had, for some weird reason, decided exactly how to play the role in my head. All my choices were pre-decided. They were also broad, fakey, and strangely puppetlike. I could feel myself throwing out all of my training and rehearsed the play by doing strained line reading after strained line reading.

I knew I was sucking and I didn't know what to do. I could tell internally and also from the quizzical, almost sad looks I was getting from the rest of the cast. Joe pulled me aside after a couple of weeks and spoke to me quite seriously about his concerns with me in the role. He urged me to relax and just explore the play and have fun in the rehearsal process, but try as I might, I just couldn't. I was in a gigantic, pressurized acting rut that I couldn't escape.

All of a sudden we were getting close to having an audience. I freaked. I began waking up in the middle of the night shaking and sweating. I was terrified. I knew that I was about to suck in my first big show. Holiday was in Iowa at the time, and I spent many tearful hours in the middle of the night (me, again, panicked) with her on the phone as she consoled and counseled me (her, again, offering incredible perspective).

That's when the prayers started. When all else fails, sometimes you just get on your knees and ask for help. And I did. Over and over again. I reached out for assistance from Wakan Tanka/God/Creator/Whatever. I was stuck. I was lost and terrified. I literally didn't know what else to do. The prayers didn't make me a brilliant actor all of a sudden, but I do believe they were a factor in a transformation I made as an artist and person at this pivotal juncture.

I started to understand that I had been doing the role for all the wrong reasons: to impress people, to gain accolades, to gain fame. I was looking outside of myself. Trying to be something that I wasn't. For others.

In fact, this was the story of my life as an actor in New York up until that point. I was always seeking to impress others with my work and control how I was perceived by people in the industry. I had wanted to be some external drama school ideal of an actor-man. This was often giving me a stiff, kind of formal demeanor in my acting and presentation and would lead to much nervousness and self-consciousness.

London Assurance broke me open like an egg. I didn't want to be that kind of fakey artist anymore, performing out of obligation, neediness, and a desperate need to be liked. I knew that ultimately I needed to be *myself,* and screw whatever other people thought of me. I felt this newfound commitment to freedom in my bones and it was a revelation. After this Broadway fiasco, I learned how to relax and breathe and play. I embraced the natural nerdy oddness that was me. I was never going to be some formal idea of a "classical actor-man," beloved by casting directors and the *New York Times* and rocking an ascot.

I gotta be me, Wakan Tanka–damn it!

As the previews went along, I did see some eventual improvement. I was able to relax a bit here and there and get a few occasional laughs in the role. Was I good? No. But at least I wasn't completely horrible. I got mostly poor to middling reviews, but at least I didn't get raked over the coals.

But, more important, after the show closed I was filled with much greater purpose and inspiration in my life and work.

I fired my lousy New York agents, who hadn't even bothered to see me in the play, and strode out onto Forty-Fifth Street, manifesting a newfound sense of myself as an actor: unemployed but inspired.

What I hoped would be the greatest triumph of my career ended up being an excruciating nightmare. But it was through that artistic trial that I came to find my voice. I felt the energy of God and prayer behind this entire adventure on Broadway, and it pushed me to continue and deepen my search.

Ultimately that yearning magnet inside of me came to know, to believe in, to have faith in, a Creator. I just couldn't wrap my mind around an empty universe, filled with scientific laws but no meaning. It just didn't make sense to my bones that once upon a time (fourteen billion years ago) there was this teeny tiny dot of something and then a big bang and all of a sudden there was space and time and unlimited matter and energy all exploding with unimaginable force as the universe as we know it was ripped into being for no real reason. Try as I might, I couldn't imagine all this "stuff" around us and the incredible majesty and mystery of the push and pull of scientific rules that spin all the galaxies like plates and adhere us to our mud-ball home with this inexplicable (and, as of yet, unidentified) force called "gravity," existing simply on its own by chance and accident. The idea that my little blip of incredible consciousness and the miraculous consciousness of seven billion of us on our celestial/terrestrial home in the Milky Way was arrived at by the random confluence of molecules evolving for no purposeful reason from oceans to beaches to condominium complexes just didn't add up. A Creator-less creation didn't make any sense, try as I might to understand it. My spidey senses felt the presence of a mighty Love-Being behind and inside the curtain of the stuff and energy and beauty of the universe. And that Love-Being . . . get this . . . was the ancient Roman snake god, Glycon. (Joking! Just wanted to flip out anyone who's still shaking their head at all this God stuff. But seriously, Google Glycon sometime. An entire Macedonian cult was devoted to this snake deity, who turned out to be . . . a hand puppet. You can't make this stuff up!)

I then dipped back into the faith of my childhood. I read most of the Baha'i books that I had skipped or neglected as a young'n. I started with *The Dawn-Breakers*, the history of the earliest Baha'is (called Bábis at the time), who had been slaughtered by the thousands in countless grotesque ways by the Persian government and the Muslim authorities in mid-nineteenth-century Iran. My heart was drawn in by the tales of the heroic sacrifices of those early believers. It gave me a context for the historic rise of the young religion. I read the principal works of Baha'u'llah, the prophet founder of the Faith: The Book of Certitude, the Gleanings, the Hidden Words, the Seven Valleys, the Epistle to the Son of the Wolf. I read his son 'Abdu'l-Baha's writings and talks contained in *Some Answered Questions* and *Paris Talks*. The four-part biography *The Revelation of Baha'u'llah* by Adib Taherzadeh was instrumental in my gaining a deeper understanding of both his teachings and struggles. The list goes on. Suffice it to say I eventually quit the booze and came to RE-believe in the faith of my family and my childhood. It made the most sense to me. It seemed like the most advanced, evolved, and applicable of the world religions. Baha'u'llah's plan, both mystical and practical, for the spiritual healing of humanity, for increasing the bonds of love and unity on our planet, resonated deeply within me and I felt newly inspired. I was finally ready. As Kahlil Gibran famously wrote, "Faith is a knowledge within the heart, beyond the reach of proof." My heart had the knowledge it needed to make the leap into the mysterious ocean of faith.

You get the idea. I won't go any further because I know you want to get to the part about what Kevin from *The Office* ordered for lunch, but I do want to discuss a couple of things that struck me as I came back to faith.

In reexploring the beliefs of my childhood I came upon a central tenet that I had not explored before. One of the principal teachings of the Baha'i Faith is *THE INDIVIDUAL INVESTIGATION OF TRUTH*. That is to say, it is the OBLIGATION of every human being to find the truth for themselves. This is not a suggestion; it's mandatory on our life's journey. But so liberating! We not only should not simply take on the truth from our parents or our families, but we should also not inherit the truth from our surrounding culture and media. This teaching was absolutely incendiary and revolutionary when it was revealed in the mid-1800s in Persia (perhaps the place on earth where the LEAST amount of self-searching goes on, both now and a hundred and fifty years ago). We get inundated with so many messages about belief, about what is true and what is not, from both our families and our culture, and it's crucial that every single one of us come to our *own* well-excavated understanding. That's not to say we might not eventually share the same beliefs as our parents or the prevailing culture, but as Thoreau and Socrates (and all the great spiritual teachers) implore: "The unexamined life is not worth living."

Looking back on those years I realized that *the individual investigation of truth* is exactly what I had undertaken in my own way. By discarding the faith of my parents and diving into the religion of art and the theater, I was finding my own peculiar path. By getting lost in "self" and unhappiness and then going on a spiritual search, I had been fulfilling my personal obligation to find the truth for myself.

(Fortunately for me, I came out of my misadventures with drugs and alcohol with my life, health, and soul pretty much intact. I know many who didn't. It's not harmless. I've lost many friends to that way of life. Some have died. Some have simply fried their hard drives for the rest of time or live in a perpetual chemical fog. I'm betting not one of them would say, "It was worth it.")

The other thing about my faith that I discovered is that the dichotomy I was experiencing around art and faith wasn't a dichotomy at all. In the Baha'i Faith there were many writings I uncovered that connected the arts with the divine or spiritual. As I explored, I unearthed a quote that blew my mind.

'Abdu'l-Baha, the son of Baha'u'llah and the leader of the Faith from 1892 until his death in 1921, once said in a letter to a believer, a young artist:

I rejoice to hear that thou takest pains with thine art, for in this wonderful new age, art is worship. The more thou strivest to perfect it, the closer wilt thou come to God. What bestowal could be greater than this, that one's art should be even as the act of worshipping the Lord? That is to say, when thy fingers grasp the paint brush, it is as if thou wert at prayer in the Temple.

Remarkable. For the head of a religion with tens or hundreds of thousands of adherents at the turn of the century to say, in essence, that art is the same as worship was, again, truly revolutionary. And to me, in my search, the most inspiring thing I could hear.

The way I see it, when you *create* something you are emulating THE CREATOR. God has many titles in the many faith traditions, and one of them is "the Fashioner." There used to be nothing and then there was the universe. God made it in his spare time, I suppose. Like *Minecraft*.

There was a blank piece of paper and then there was a poem or a story or a screenplay or a beautiful picture created by an artist. What greater testament can an artist make than to emulate the Great Artist upstairs? And when you add the altruistic component to art, that you're making something true and beautiful and relevant as a SERVICE to others, that's when the spiritual aspect of art truly soars. We seek to transcend, we monkey people, through love, service, art, prayer, and faith in something outside of ourselves.

Art and worship are two sides of that profound human coin that separate us from the orangutan, chimpanzee, 49ers fan, or any other creature known for flinging its feces. That longing to connect with something beautiful outside of ourselves from our hearts. To uplift, entertain, beautify, and express the profound is a mysterious spiritual act.

Perhaps *that* was what I was striving for in my various experimental artistic exploits—my zeal and fervor for opening people's minds and hearts through doing weird little plays in tiny theaters for dozens of viewers.

And then, having had these profound, heart-opening revelations, I went and did something spiritually questionable and maybe even flat-out ludicrous. I became a celebrity.

Chapter 13

WELCOME TO LOS ANGELES

—

C LOWNS AT HOME. A SLACKER VAUDEVILLE."
   With those few words a remarkable and demented theater piece was born. An event that would bring me to Los Angeles, launch my career in television and film, and change the entire course of my life.

Some younger friends at NYU, David Costabile, Kevin Isola, and Michael Dahlen, had approached me to direct them during their "Free Play," a three-week session of one's third-year training where you could do whatever the hell you wanted. People would do improv, stage a preexisting play, write something new, or do performance art using the facilities and resources of the school.

The guys wanted to do something involving clowning. I had always loved the art form and had studied it with several other teachers after graduating from NYU.*

---

* Note: The kind of clowning we're talking about here has nothing to do with circus clowns, big shoes, and face paint. It's theatrical clowning: a cross between the zany characters that pop out in Cirque du Soleil, Pee-wee Herman, Borat,

We got together for dinner at a Ukrainian restaurant (the borscht was excellent but the pierogies a bit doughy), and I pitched them the idea: "A day in the life of a trio of clowns. Clowns at home. A slacker vaudeville." Whatever the hell that meant. I didn't really have a clue, just an instinct about the way some scenes could build and intertwine to create the most basic of story arcs.

"What should we call this thing, whatever it is we're doing?" one of the would-be clowns asked.

Our Ukrainian waitress dropped off our check. Her name tag read BOZENA.

"Excuse me," another clown asked the waitress. "Bo-zeena? Is that your name?"

The waitress huffed disdainfully. "It's pronounced 'Bo-shjenah.'"

And with that, *The New Bozena* was born. (We still insisted on pronouncing it "Bozeena.")

We worked in a little rehearsal room creating the *New Bozena* characters using many devices and exercises that I had learned from Gates McFadden, Jim Calder, and other clown teachers. David became Ramón, the innocent, sweet-faced tuxedoed clown with an indeterminate accent and a brain of flan. Kevin transformed himself into Revhanavaan Sahaanahanadaan, a horned creature in a unitard who always carried a suitcase with a ham in it. And Michael was Spiv Westenberg, a slack-jawed hipster in a vintage suit with drumsticks and an Afro (a description that applies to about half of the graduates of the Tisch School of the Arts).

We imagined the clowns waking up, cooking breakfast (Jell-O sandwiches, of course), going to their various workplaces (a restau-

---

Inspector Clouseau, and Harpo Marx. Larger-than-life but strangely real characters that operate by their own bizarre theatrical rules. In a lot of ways Dwight was just such a clown: physically bold, truthful, pathetic, and bizarre.

rant, an operating room, and an office filled with pencils), and then auditioning for and eventually performing in a community theater production of the Albanian masterpiece *Winter Is the Coldest Season* (in the original Albanian language). I played the offstage voice of the arrogant theater director putting them through their paces in the audition process on a "god mic." There were also interstitial sketches about giant talking birds, Doug and Eric, one of whom began a love affair with their roommate, a human boy, played by Kevin.

It was a strange mélange of angst-ridden existential clowning, absurd dance routines, and sketch comedy, and it absolutely killed. The audiences at NYU went nuts for the piece in ways I'd never seen in the theater before. The students and their friends were literally cheering, shouting, and jumping up and down in their seats like it was a WWE wrestling match, admittedly a slightly less homoerotic one.

We knew we were onto something.

Some folks from a now-defunct Off-Off-Broadway theater had seen the play and invited us to be a part of their season that summer. We improved on the show and put it up again with the same result. Crazed audiences and a clamor for more *Bozena*.

Onward and upward. After securing some financing and collaborating with producer extraordinaire Michael Winter, we put on an expanded, brighter, and slicker version of our show Off-Broadway at the Cherry Lane Theatre in the West Village.

This is when the reality of New York theater hit us like the 6 train. In order to make money you need to charge a ton for tickets. The weekly "nut"—that is to say, the amount you spend each week on union dues, newspaper ads, cast and crew salaries, equipment, and theater rental—is pretty darn high. To make a PROFIT, you have to get butts in seats. Butts that can afford seats. Week after week after week. Our key audience of young folks, students, downtown artists, and wackadoodle nut jobs had perfectly acceptable butts—very nice butts, in some cases—but butts that couldn't afford the show. And the richer folks over fifty (with their saggy butts), who really didn't respond to demented clowns juggling Jell-O and head-butting hams, were just not buying those tickets.

Then the *New York Times* came to town. We got rave reviews literally everywhere else, including *Time* magazine, *The New Yorker*, and *The Wall Street Journal*, but because we got a mediocre review in the "Gray Lady," we were sunk. That's the only paper folks in NYC read. They didn't care if the *Daily News*, the *Post*, and the Newark *Star-Ledger* loved our show. Audiences only listen to the (extremely conservative and occasionally snobby and Anglophilic) *Times* for some reason. Probably because ticket prices are so high, they want to have insurance that the show they're investing so heavily in will be worth their very expensive evening. I hope all those audience members enjoyed Dennis Franz in *Rutherford B. Hayes: A One-Man Show* or whatever the *Times* recommended instead of us.

Anyhoo. We closed after three amazing but difficult months.

But to go from a rehearsal room in NYU to rave reviews Off-Broadway was a miracle. We made a great piece of daring theater that people who saw it still talk about to this day. That's worth something.

Plus, making audiences laugh and gasp night after night in ridiculous ways was one of the greatest experiences of my life. Especially doing it with some of my bestest friends.

And it was *The New Bozena* that brought us to Los Angeles.

Our producer, Michael Winter, moved to California a few years after the show closed and kept coaxing us to come. His plan? To have us perform it in LA and try to find a way to turn all that clowny insanity into a TV show. We had some money to do this from our investors and finally the timing became perfect.

Holiday and I were bought out of our incredible Brooklyn apartment, as I mentioned before. We packed up an old SUV with most of our books and knickknacks and a wok and a cow's skull, as well as our pit bulls, Edison and Harper Lee, and we drove across the USA to make a new home for ourselves in Los Angeles. All thanks to some "clowns at home."

Los Angeles lay before us like a sparkly tortilla baked in the cinnamon farts of starlets.

The various clowns plus Holiday and our pit bulls all moved into a grotesque abomination of an apartment building in Koreatown that smelled like cat pee, chlorine, and kimchi. It was peopled with the lowest dregs of show business: broke actors in town for pilot season, unemployed writers, and exiled Korean grandparents. (In all fairness, the Korean grandparents did have a first-look deal with CBS.)

We began rehearsals to put a slightly stripped-down version of our show up at the Hudson Guild theater in Hollywood.

Hollywood, for the seven of you who don't know, is not anything like you think it is from the association with that famous, grandiose name. There's nothing tinselly or fabulous or razzle-dazzle-y about the place. This was especially true in 1999. Busy and yet somehow completely destitute, it was populated with drug addicts, strippers, schizophrenics, and Scientologists. Besides a wax museum, some sickly palm trees, an occasional confused Dutch tourist, and the stars on Hollywood Boulevard, there was nothing there to let you know that there was a show-business industry in its history or in the vicinity. But if you wanted marijuana, wigs, or a taco, it was definitely the place to be.

As we were getting ready to launch the show I had a crazy show-biz misadventure that points out both the absurdity of the entertainment business and the mystery of the great universal ebb and flow of life.

After a lovely year being a signed client with a bicoastal, midsize talent agency in New York, I kept trying to connect with its LA office.

No one would return my call. Literally. Silence. I kept pestering my New York contacts to try to get me in to see or even speak to the agency where I WAS A SIGNED CLIENT. It was impossible. I was, after all, hoping to audition for some of those things called TV SHOWS that they supposedly had so many of in Los Angeles.

The New Bozena was opening, so I called yet again to reach the agent who was supposed to be representing me and finally got him on the phone. He promised repeatedly that he would come to our small LA premiere.

The night of the big opening. Huge success. Afterward, I looked all over the crowded lobby for someone who looked like they might be an agent. Nothing. Then a slight twenty-two-year-old dweeby guy came up to me and said: "Hi. My name is Michael. Robby the agent couldn't make it tonight. He sends his apologies and I'm his assistant and he sent me instead! It was a great show! I brought my friend Vanessa!"

I was stunned and pissed.

Then little Vanessa, standing by his side, piped up. "Hey, I'm assisting some producers on a pilot over at NBC called *The Expendables* and you guys were all so funny I'm going to call and get you all in for auditions!"

I was politely dismissive. "Okay, great. Thanks, Vanessa. Yeah, yeah, sounds amazing. Thanks so much for coming, you guys." I was secretly fuming.

Sure enough, the next day I FINALLY got a call from my LA agent, who told me in a chain-smokery voice, "We got you an audition for this pilot on NBC. I'll fax you the pages and the information." I bit my tongue about the fact that it was actually little Vanessa from the lobby of the Hudson Guild who got me the audition, not any agent.

All of us clowns auditioned that same week. We all got called back several times and eventually the producers wanted to "test"* me for the pilot.

After five auditions, I booked my first lead television part in what is perhaps the most gloriously awful half-hour "comedy" pilot ever made. Apparently America was not ready for a not-funny, single-camera comedy featuring television-obsessed indestructible androids who spend most of their time fighting crime naked.

It was a great experience, I earned my Screen Actors Guild card, and finally my agents started returning my calls.

Soon thereafter I got a call to meet one of the most talented and nicest human beings on the planet, Cameron Crowe. I had put an audition on tape in New York a few months before moving to LA. I had never been to an audition before where the director ushered me to a chair in his office and then promptly sat cross-legged on the floor in front of me as I prepared to read.

In the original script of the "Untitled Cameron Crowe Project" (aka *Almost Famous*), the small part I would end up playing, Dave Felton, a real boss of Cameron's at *Rolling Stone* in the seventies, tracks down the young hero, William Miller, to the airport and gives him a wise and valuable lecture on the meaning of art and life. This scene was eventually, heartbreakingly, cut before we started shooting. I know this because after I was cast I was allowed to come into the office's conference room, sign a nondisclosure agreement, and read the full script, which was almost two hundred pages long.

---

* A test is where an actor's weekly salary has been predetermined and you pre-sign a seven-year contract. The five or six actors for each part gather and audition for the executives at the television studio, contracts in hand. If you then get the part, you have your deal points already in place. If you don't, you try not to let the door hit you in the ass on the way out. Because Hollywood doors are notoriously heavy, with well-oiled hinges, and the impact can cause serious ass damage.

I had never read anything like it before or since. Perhaps the greatest work of screenwriting ever. It was gorgeous and funny and complicated. Bursting with emotion and, of course, music. The final movie is a classic of the cinema, but the script was an even more incredible work of art that stands on its own.

Immediately after getting cast in *Almost Famous* I got an audition for and was cast in *Galaxy Quest*, another classic comedy of that year. The alien I played, Lahnk, was supposed to be a much larger part, but because NBC was still deciding whether or not to pick up that piece of TV doo-doo *The Expendables*, I was only able to be in a handful of scenes.

That movie provided me with a tormented initiation into the world of Hollywood.

In a now-deleted scene, my weird little Thermian character gives Tony Shalhoub a tour of the beryllium sphere in the engine room. The dialogue I had was chock-full of techno-speak, and try as I might I simply could not get the language to stick in my head. It didn't help that I was nervous as hell and sweating up a storm in my tinfoil alien unitard. On various breaks, I called Holiday to interrupt her writing and have her run the endless nonsensical lines with me over the phone as my breathing got shallower and shallower and my head spun more and more.

Then it was time. We started to shoot. Standing right behind me were Alan Rickman, Tim Allen, Sigourney Weaver, and Sam Rockwell. Sweat started to roll down my face and head. My knees were shaking. Take after take after take, the technobabble monologue just would not come out right. It was an actor's nightmare come to life; I was stuttering and floundering and sweating my way through an impossible little monologue with half of my acting heroes behind me.

Finally, on the fifth take, I was able to get through the lines. Although when you look at the deleted scene you can see the tense struggle to remember lines behind my beady, panicked alien eyes. My only solace is the thought that someone, somewhere, has done a "Lahnk the Alien from *Galaxy Quest*" cosplay at a nerd convention.

Suddenly I thought I had this whole LA thing figured out. I had rolled into town and gotten a pilot and a couple of film roles without a single hitch. We set up *The New Bozena* at Fox to do a pilot presentation, and I had made more money in a couple of months than in all the previous years combined. I was "in" and feeling like a made man. Holiday and I decided to really settle down in LA and make a go of it; she would finish her book of short stories and I would be an actor who could actually pay his bills.

Then, within a few months, *The New Bozena* got rejected by Fox and I was unemployed for a full year. Showbiz!

Eventually, after doing *House of 1000 Corpses* for Rob Zombie, I started getting some momentum as a journeyman actor in Hollywood. That job was one of the most fun things ever and I had an absolute blast doing it. It's every actor's dream to get clubbed in the mud by a scarecrow who has come to life, then get sawed in half and have your lower torso attached to a giant fish's tail, and then be placed still-life style on a table surrounded by a cornucopia of fruit, and then be revealed to your bound and gagged girlfriend with a sheet being pulled off of you and the words "BEHOLD! FISHBOY!" and then be sketched by the crazed, homicidal villain as she screams horrifically. I guess dreams really do come true! Now whenever someone passes me on the street and calls me Fishboy, I smile politely and think, That's an extremely sick person.

I did the movie *America's Sweethearts*, *CSI*, *Law and Order*, and a couple of pilots, commercials, and canceled shows that no one ever heard of to pay the bills and continue building my career and résumé.

As with most actors there were many close calls on projects that would have sent my life spiraling in an entirely different direction. I was one of the final three actors up for Gob in *Arrested Development*. I remember reading that pilot script and it was as if a golden glow emanated from the pages; it was so funny and original.

After several auditions I was once again being tested for the project. There were two final scenes that we Gobs would be doing alongside the rest of the family, who had already been cast. In one scene there were one or two lines and in the other scene there were a couple of pages of really funny dialogue and a great chance to show off what you could do with the character. We all filed in, one at a time, to show the head of Fox the first, short scene. Then the other Gobs went in to do the second, bigger scene. I waited, nervously going over my lines and bits in preparation. And waited. And waited. I was sitting all alone in the waiting room and after ten or fifteen minutes or so I wandered out into the hallway. Everyone had left. I mean everyone. Actors, casting agents, Fox executives, janitors, everyone. I finally saw a casting assistant cleaning up in a corner and asked what was going on. "I guess they saw all they needed to from you," she chirped merrily, and I slunk away embarrassed and miserable, having only auditioned with two lines for the best comic role I had ever read.

Apparently they fell in love with Will Arnett right away, and in this case they absolutely made the right choice for Gob. He turned out to be hysterical in a star-making performance. The universe had other things in store for me.

The story of how I got the role of Arthur on *Six Feet Under* is a doozy. That role is what eventually landed me *The Office* and many other great jobs. It was the catalyst that put me on the radar of folks in the entertainment biz and truly launched the second half of my career.

I had auditioned for the terrific casting directors Junie Lowry-Johnson and Libby Goldstein on a couple of projects. Having done well at the auditions, they started calling me in for whatever they were working on.

They started casting *Six Feet Under*. I really loved the show and wanted desperately to get on it. In any capacity. Even if it was just a costar role with a handful of lines. Anything.

They kept calling me in for various parts. A priest. A dead guy. Several members of the gay chorus that Michael C. Hall's character was singing with. And I kept *not* getting cast. Not even close. It was eating me up. I was exasperated beyond measure as I really wanted to be on the show.

One day I was going in to audition for them again as another one of the gay choir members, and on a table in the waiting room I saw the description for the character of Arthur. He was described as an innocent but strange Chauncey Gardiner type and was going to be doing several episodes in a character arc. I knew that he was right in my wheelhouse. So I went to Libby after my audition for the other role and bravely asked if I could try out for it. She consulted with the producer and said yes, giving me the several pages of scenes to work on. I spent about half an hour preparing in the waiting room, but I couldn't wait to get in and show them. Some roles you play you need to work on very hard. Research. Explore. Excavate. And some roles you just instinctively know how to perform. Arthur, like Dwight, a character I will later describe in some detail, was in my bones. I knew his heart. I knew exactly how he should be played and I couldn't wait to show everyone involved with the program exactly who this person was.

Sure enough, even though I'd only had a short time, the audition went great. The next week I was called in to read with the incredible Frances Conroy, my eventual love interest, and I got the part. It helped, I suppose, that I knew both Michael C. Hall and Peter Krause from NYU and I had them put in a good word for me to Alan Ball.

I'll never forget getting that phone call from my agent and manager. I was driving with Holiday to see one of those ridiculous Cirque du Soleil–esque shows, only with horses and unitards, *Equinosity* or

Horse Majeure or something. I said to my great manager, Mark Schul-man (who had been with me since the days of *The New Bozena*), "This is pretty big, right?"

And he simply said, "You have no idea. Your whole life is about to change."

Holiday and I pulled over to the side of the freeway, put our fore-heads together, and screamed with excitement.

What he said may sound a little pretentious, but it's important to remember that at that point in time HBO was the bee's knees. EVERY-ONE was watching *The Sopranos*. *The Wire* was in its heyday. *Sex and the City* was making women coo and boyfriends nauseated on a weekly basis. *Curb Your Enthusiasm* and *Entourage* were just getting going. It was the beginning of the whole "Golden Age of Television" that every-one talks about. And *Six Feet Under*, although it had a small audience, was one of the most influential projects going.

Had I been cast in one of the other extremely small roles I audi-tioned for, I never would have booked Arthur and then subsequently Dwight (Greg Daniels, the creator of *The Office*, had watched every single episode of *Six Feet Under*) and all the other great roles I got to do after 2004. As frustrated as I was at the time that I didn't get cast as Tommy, gay choir member number three, I now couldn't be more grateful.

You never know what the cosmos has in store for you, and some-times repeated rejection is simply the *All-Encompassing Creative Life Force*™ preparing you for something greater, a different and grander plan.

For me, that plan led to the defining role of my career, Dwight Kurt Schrute. I was about to receive the worst haircut of my entire life.

ADVENTURES IN FILM
AND TELEVISION

―――

ONE LIFE TO LIVE

Dear Diary, I got my first television job, you guys, right here in 1997!
It's playing Casey Keegan, a homicidal stand-up comic on the soap
opera *One Life to Live*. I'm doing five episodes shot over three days and
I get $750 an episode. (Minus the $1,200 I have to pay to join AFTRA,
the union.) I'm set for life!

The first day went pretty well. The actor who played the hunky
Santiago thought we were rehearsing a scene when, in fact, they were
shooting it and the director wanted to move on after just one take.
Santiago went ballistic, kicking over furniture and swearing at the
producers. They shut down production for a couple of hours, he
calmed down, and then we proceeded. I guess that's how TV stars
act. . . . Maybe one day I'll be a TV star and do the exact same thing!

Day two: tons of action! I tried to poison Santiago at the comedy
club I was working at, but he wouldn't drink from the concoction I
made for him (probably because it turned green and started smoking).
So the mob guy who wanted me to kill him slipped me a gun. The

camera lingered on my gigantic, terrified face, staring at my "piece," as they went to a commercial break. I got tingles!

After lunch break I did a set of real stand-up comedy in character at the fictional Comedy Club. The monologue was written by the amazing joke writers on the staff of *One Life to Live*. My favorite? Easy. "What's the difference between an Irish wedding and an Irish wake? One less drunk!" The seven extras seemed to really eat it up.

Day three, I tried to kill Santiago (with my gun!), but his stupid girlfriend was a cop and pinned me to the roof in an incredible stunt worthy of a *Mission Impossible* film. They interrogated me in a comfy chair and ultimately let me go because I tearfully pleaded with them so successfully!

Later that week I got my first fan letter! The developmentally disabled girl who wrote me said, and I quote, "Dear Casey Keegan, I think you are good actress."

And later still, when the episodes aired, I actually got RECOGNIZED as an actor! For the VERY FIRST TIME!!! Folks would stop me on the subway and say, "Hey, you that guy who tried to kill my man Santiago? You do not f*#* with Santiago!"

And that's a wrap, folks. Probably the last TV I'll ever do, but I had a blast!

CHARMED

Believe it or not the worst acting I ever did in my life was not on *One Life to Live* but on the TV show *Charmed* in 2001. I was cast as Kierkan the demon alchemist who created a beautiful woman/demon in his demon lab.

I was crazy nervous about doing a big guest-star role on a hit TV show. I was also unsure how to play this larger-than-life supernatural weirdo who spent the episode running around in his purple gossamer robes, chasing Terra, the demon seductress who had escaped his lab. I remember I had terrible BO from my nerves and the heavy polyester robes and kept hoping that Alyssa Milano, Shannen Doherty, and that other one wouldn't get too close and notice. My acting was so forced, stilted, and unnatural, I'm sure the telegenic witches wanted nothing to do with me.

One memory: that the leads would shoot a scene and then beg to "move on" after one take. This differed from *The Office* in the sense that it was the *exact opposite*. We'd always beg for more takes.

FULL FRONTAL

Getting cut out of a movie is one of the worst things that can happen to an actor. Getting cut out of a movie when the director is Steven Soderbergh and you're at the premiere and don't know you've been cut out is the absolute worst.

Very early on in my Hollywood career I got cast in a small but terrific part opposite Catherine Keener in *Full Frontal*. The original script was entitled *How to Survive a Hotel Room Fire* and was a fascinating, experimental narrative exploration of the underbelly of American commerce. I had a lot of fun shooting my scene and everyone was very nice.

I was invited to the small premiere and said hello to everyone, and people treated me very awkwardly, recoiling oddly. My wife and I watched the movie and when it came to the scene, the scene I was so excited to see, my first scene in a *STEVEN SODERBERGH MOVIE*, all you saw was the back of my enormous round head as the camera stayed on Catherine Keener for the entire twelve seconds of what had been originally a three-page scene.

(FYI, the entire movie had obviously been all improvised on the fly and was one of the worst, lamest pieces of experimental film poo that had ever been excreted onto a screen.)

My heart sank into my chest. We slunk out through the party in the lobby with all the people slapping each other on the back and laughing, went out to my 1993 Volvo clunker, and drove up to the Griffith Observatory, traumatized. I sat devastated in the car as Holiday put her arm around me and we gazed at the stars over the City of Angels.

(Note to directors and producers: If you cut someone out of a movie, that's totally cool. Just give them a call and let them know ahead of time. Takes about thirty seconds.)

SLICE O' LIFE

One of the oddest acting jobs I've ever had is one that never happened.

I was on my way to a table read for a new ABC single-camera comedy pilot, called *Slice o' Life*, with Janeane Garofalo, when I first heard about the "American *Office*." I ran into a guy I knew at Universal Television in the parking lot and he told me they had just secured the rights. I had recently been watching the original BBC episodes and had been captivated. (More on that later.) I remember getting super bummed out, because although I was enthused to be doing a funny pilot with the great Janeane Garofalo, I would have MUCH rather been doing the pilot for *The Office* as that was my absolute dream TV job.

It was a terrific cast for *Slice o' Life*, including Bob Odenkirk and Marc Maron. We were excited as we gathered to read the script aloud. We were all packed, had our plane tickets to leave that night, and the set was all built and ready in Vancouver, British Columbia.

For those of you who don't know, "table reads" are this very peculiar, particular Hollywood television phenomenon. The cast gathers at a long table with their scripts and all the executives file into the audience of the enormous rehearsal room, stoic and impeccably dressed. These are nerve-wracking events at which actors occasionally get fired due to the weakness of their "read."*

This table read was happening in the period not long after 9/11 during which Janeane Garofalo, who was a very vocal spokesperson for the political left in the media, had become quite unpopular with the Fox News set. She was a polarizing figure, to say the least.

Anyhoo, we did the table read and it SUCKED. Janeane seemed quite nervous, we didn't get any laughs, and the phalanx of ABC execs marched out of the room in a huff. (It certainly didn't help her case with the network that she wore torn black jeans, tons of punk jewelry, and a cut-off Black Flag T-shirt that showed all her tattoos.) Within the hour, the plug was pulled, our plane tickets canceled, and the project killed.

Many speculated that it was Janeane's anti-American politics that got the show canceled. Some said it was her likability issues for an ABC sitcom. Others, the script. I say it's the incredibly artificial, awkward, and bizarre tradition of judging the worth of a project by having actors nervously read a script (that's meant to be filmed on camera) in a huge rehearsal hall filled with inscrutable executives.

Needless to say, I was secretly psyched that I would soon get an audition for *The Office* now that *Slice o' Life* was officially *Slice o' Death*.

---

* Television development executives are a hysterical bunch. They all have steno pads and appear to be very wise and take lots of notes all the time, but for the most part they really have no idea what they're doing. Most of them have not actually made shows or movies or comedy, but rather started as interns, assistants, and script readers at the network level. They've never been artists or craftsmen, only corporate workers. Plus, the way television studios are structured there's usually one person at the top who makes ALL the decisions and whose opinion is the only one that really matters. So all the underlings are simply lackey yes-men who are trying to look busy and important, all the while merely trying to please their boss and guess at their whims and tastes.

For instance, the head of a network or studio might say offhandedly at a

SAHARA

Somewhere between *Six Feet Under* and *The Office*, I got cast in *Sahara*, the lawsuit-addled McConaughey action extravaganza known as the biggest independent film bomb in cinema history. Due to the discovery on the lawsuit by Clive Cussler against the film, my salary on *Sahara*, 45K, the SAG minimum, was there for all the world to see. I literally was paid less on that film than Matthew McConaughey's stunt double. I did, however, have an absolute and total blast. A month in Morocco and two weeks in Barcelona—what's not to like?

There are so many great memories of this bloated, ridiculous (and really fun) film, I can't even list them all. Actually, I can.

- Bargaining like a madman for rugs with merchants over mint tea in the middle of the desert with the cast of the film.
- Wandering the back alleys of Marrakech with my pregnant wife, Holiday, looking for tribal antiques. (We once stumbled accidentally down an alley and into a wall of violent stench, the remote area of the city where they slaughtered all the chickens, and she passed out and vomited into her hand.) We held hands through

---

meeting, "I used to love *FRIENDS!*" All of a sudden, the word goes out like wildfire through the development departments, agencies, and management companies throughout LA: "Bobby Sternboss *LOVES* Friends-like shows. Bring us shows with ensembles filled with attractive roomates, ASAP!"

The entire TV industry gets into high gear and all of a sudden hundreds of *Friends*–esque pitches are coming through the development offices. Fourteen different pilots, all with variations on the same premise, are shot, and Bobby Sternboss sees them and goes, "Why are all these stupid pilots exactly the same?" and fires his development executive. The second-in-command is promoted and the entire process is repeated.

outlandish bazaars, wanting to share the sights and sounds of Morocco with our beautiful little fetus.

- Playing *Tiger Woods PGA Tour* in Steve Zahn's trailer during a literal plague of locusts.
- Spending day upon day on a speedboat (for all the rip-roaring water chase scenes) on a beautiful alpine lake in the mountains. We would get there crazy early every morning and get to watch the sun rise over the Atlas Mountains. Gorgeous.
- Getting lost in the medieval maze of the city of Fez while being hounded by a gang of scraggly Moroccan kids all saying, "Meester! Meester! *Americain?* Hellooo. How are YOOOO?"
- A camel ride in the dunes where *The Mummy* and *Star Wars* were filmed. The road literally ends, sloping down into the sands of the Sahara at Erfoud, and there's an arrow-shaped sign that says TIMBUKTU 52 JOURS pointing out into the vastness. And the crazy thing? Dudes are riding donkeys and camels and motorcycles out into that vastness, loaded up with wares from the market. People actually live out there!
- My four-months-pregnant wife getting McDonald's cravings and us eating McNuggets and milkshakes at the Marrakech McDonald's. EVERY. SINGLE. NIGHT.
- Visiting monkeys that live in remote passes of the Atlas Mountains with my driver, Zaid, when he counseled me that I needed to get a second, more "dutiful" wife once our child was born, as mine was far too challenging and independent.
- Marveling at the exquisite, chiseled, bronze manliness of Matthew McConaughey and the exquisite, chiseled, bronze womanliness of Penélope Cruz as they circled each other like Aphrodite and Apollo and began their ill-fated, gossip-rag-fodder relationship. I imagine that they never actually made love, they just looked

at each other incredulously and said, "You're sooooo beautiful," "No, *you're* so beautiful." Over and over and over again.

THE ROCKER

When the comet of my Dwight fame was at its zenith, I got to star in a comedy movie for Fox called *The Rocker*. I played Robert "Fish" Fishman, a former heavy metal drummer for the fictional band Vesuvius, who had been kicked out right before they made it big. A loser at forty, he's enlisted to play again for his high school–age nephew's rock band and goes on the road, finally getting to live his rock-and-roll dream. Hilarity ensues.

I was completely unproven as a lead in films, so it was a huge risk for Fox to green-light this picture. They weren't going to give the film the go-ahead until our producers, Shawn Levy and Tom McNulty, went into the office of the big cheese at Fox, Tom Rothman, with a plan. When Tom posited his many reservations about the project to them, they were ready. One of his main issues, apparently, aside from the fact that I was completely untested as a movie star, was his concern that I wasn't "rock and roll" enough. He thought Dwight was a funny character, but I didn't, as an actor, have that "rock vibe" that the character of Fish needed. As if on cue, Shawn and Tom opened a laptop, where they had a scene from *The Office* cued up. It was Michael and I on the roof, from the episode entitled "Safety Training." Dwight was doing air guitar and singing a heavy metal riff to celebrate. "Kiss the sun!" I sang in ridiculous metalhead full voice. They stopped the clip. There was a pause. "Okay, go ahead and do the movie," Tom Rothman said. And with that twenty-second clip, the film was green-lit for fourteen million dollars and we were off and running.

We managed to gather together one of the best comedic ensembles of all time for the film, including Christina Applegate, Jason Sudeikis, Emma Stone, Bradley Cooper, Will Arnett, Fred Armisen, Jeff Garlin, Jane Lynch, Demetri Martin, and Josh Gad. Our director, Peter Cattaneo (*The Full Monty*), brought a ton of warmth and humor to the shoot.

It was a brutal, low-budget filming experience, with long hours, little luxury, and TONS of sweaty locations and night shoots. All the while I had to learn the drums to be believable as a great rock drummer. Not only did I need to learn the basics of drumming, but I also had to specifically learn each song that was composed for the film, as they rolled in from the composer, in order to play along believably in the film. I had a drum coach and a little drum kit in my tiny half trailer that I would bang away on during breaks.

Then came the editing and the long wait before the release. After moving the premiere date four different times, Fox essentially dumped it in a bunch of theaters over Labor Day weekend in the summer of 2008, even though the movie tested quite well with audiences. It bombed. And how. In fact, *The Rocker* was one of the biggest bombs in movie history. The per-screen average was one of the very lowest of all time. The film went out on over twenty-five hundred screens (on one of the worst weekends for movies of the year, in one of the most crowded comedy summers ever—*Tropic Thunder* and *Step Brothers* had just come out a few weeks before), and it only sold an average of $259 per showing. We came in twelfth on the opening weekend for a total of $2.8 million and the film only made $6.8 million in total at the box office. Which sucks. Big-time. That essentially translates to: NOBODY WANTED TO SEE RAINN WILSON STARRING IN A MOVIE AS A NAKED DRUMMER. America had spoken with their pocketbooks. I was done for as a "movie star."

This was one of the most painful experiences of my life. I had poured my heart and soul into the film as well as into its promotion. I genuinely believed (and still believe) that it's a terrific family film, with great music and a ton of heart. I was devastated.

It's the Tuesday morning after the *Rockalypse*, five thirty a.m. I'm driving to work in my Prius down the desolate 101 freeway, absolutely spent and miserable. Kevin and Bean from KROQ are on the radio. They start yappin' like puppies on helium about the weekend movies and the top-ten box-office list. "Wait a minute," one of them says, "what about that Rainn Wilson comedy? I don't even see it on the list." "OOOOOOH NOOOOOO!" the other DJ says. "Look here. It opened all the way down at number twelve!" "Oooooooh, ouch! That's gotta sting! Poor Rainn, the guy must be hurting right now. Ooooooooh, poor guy. *It BOMBED!*" Their voices ring with pity and concern throughout the crappy interior of my Prius.

I started to cry, tears sliding down my cheeks, driving down the pitch-black, predawn 101 to my job at *The Office*, where, fortunately, the cast and crew cheerily and diplomatically didn't mention the film or ask how it performed. Thank God I had a pretty good day job.

SUPER

Super, written and directed by James Gunn (*Guardians of the Galaxy*), was perhaps the greatest film I'll ever be a part of. Jenna Fischer of *The Office* used to be married to James and one day said to him, "You know who would be perfect for that old screenplay you wrote? Rainn!"

James was intrigued. Later, I was hanging out with Jenna at her receptionist desk, chomping on the candy in the little clear plastic candy dispenser, when she told me of her conversation with him.

"Send it over!" I said. By the time I got back to my trailer, James had sent it to my inbox and I started to read.

By the time I got to the part where the lead character, Frank, was having a two-page prayer monologue and then had his head cut open and his brain touched by the finger of God, I knew that this was one of the greatest things of all time.

I called James half an hour later, only halfway through the script.

I said, "I have to play this part. I love it. This script is incredible. Let's do it."

We hit the pavement, James and I, trying to raise the money to make the film during the depths of the recession in 2008. It was tough. We must have visited a dozen production companies. Eventually, with Miranda Bailey and Ted Hope on board as producers, we were able to gather our dream cast—Ellen Page, Liv Tyler, Kevin Bacon, Michael Rooker, and Nathan Fillion. And the rest is history. (If you can call it "history" when you make a great indie film that no one watches until years later when it's on Netflix.)

The movie is tragic, funny, dark, silly, thrilling, and grotesquely violent all at the exact same time. It's a work I will always be insanely proud of. If you haven't seen it yet, put down this stupid book and go watch it already.

BACKSTROM

Let's skip ahead to the spring of 2013. *The Office* is just ending and my agents call about a script I should read. A movie script, I ask? No. Television, they reply. You're kidding me, I say. You realize you're calling me as I'm finishing my two hundredth episode of a TV show. The LAST thing I want in my life right now is another TV show. "Wait wait wait," they say. "Just read it. Trust us. It's an amazing script. The best of the whole of pilot season. Just read it."

And so I did. The author was Hart Hanson, creator of the hit "crimedy" *Bones*. It truly was expertly written and mesmerizing. The character of Backstrom was funny, sad, infuriating, and filled with many increasing levels of complexity. I had never read an antihero like him before. And best of all? It was written specifically for a large, ungainly, offbeat, tortured actor like myself. I got Holiday and other friends to read it, and after a few truly difficult days of hemming and hawing, I decide to do the pilot.

After a half-day session with the great acting coach Larry Moss, I'm up in Vancouver two weeks after wrapping *The Office*, starting a new TV show. Cray cray.

Everyone had warned me about playing the single lead of a single-camera one-hour show, but *Backstrom* was beyond hard. In fact, I've never worked so hard in my life. Thirteen- to fourteen-hour days on little sleep and seven or eight pages to memorize a day. But I loved it. The cast and crew were exceptional and I was happy to be filming in the great Pacific Northwest again.

After getting passed on at CBS due to financial wrangling between them and 20th Century Fox Studios, we ended up finding a home at the Foxy Network. The next year we shot twelve more episodes and were on the air in the winter of 2015.

And then, a few months later (a few short weeks before I'm writing this), we were canceled. Just like that.

There were so many things I could blame our show's failure on, but ultimately we just didn't find an audience. Sure, we were given one of the toughest time slots in the history of television to try to establish a foothold, opposite the runaway hits *Scandal*, *The Blacklist*, and the final season of *Two and a Half Boob Jokes*. And our ad campaign, featuring me chomping on a cigar with the words *TOTAL DICK* above my head, while punchy and attention grabbing, didn't really make viewers feel like cuddling up for a nice character-driven crime story with a bowl of pretzels and a glass of Chianti. I also think that the tone of the show was somewhere betwixt and between cable and network—generally too dark and edgy for prime-time TV and yet too warm and accessible and predicable for, say, *Breaking Bad* fans.

I will always wonder what that disturbed and difficult character I birthed is up to. Probably brilliantly solving crimes, drinking himself into oblivion, and flying lonely kites while longing for some human connection to break through the thick scar tissue of his cynicism. I can relate.

Chapter 14

DWIGHT K. SCHRUTE, ASSISTANT (TO THE) REGIONAL MANAGER

———

(Note: I'm going to be talking about working on the television show *The Office* for a couple chapters now. If you are not interested in *The Office* and purchased this book because you are a big fan of *Charmed*, SoulPancake, or double-reed instruments, I suggest you either skip ahead or cut these chapters out of the book with a pair of cuticle scissors.)

I WAS THE VERY FIRST PERSON TO AUDITION FOR *THE OFFICE*. Literally.

Our incredible casting director Allison Jones (who casts all of Judd Apatow and Paul Feig's movies as well as *Veep* and myriad other brilliant comedies) had recently gotten to know me as an actor, and I was starting to get some notice because of my role on *Six Feet Under*.

She called me in to audition for both Michael and Dwight, and I was excited beyond words as I loved the project so much. I sat in the waiting room, clutching my pages, literally more eager for this audition than any of the hundreds I had been on in the past.

My friends Sam and Julie had somehow found some early epi-

229

sodes of the British *Office* on BBC America. They had recorded them and Sam called me one day to tell me about it.

"You have to see this TV show. It's unbelievable. It's comedy and tragedy and documentary all rolled into one! Come over for dinner and we'll watch the first three." Something like that.

Holiday and I watched, astounded. I had never seen anything quite like it. If a young Anton Chekhov and a young Woody Allen were making a TV show together, *The Office* on the BBC would be it.

What was so transcendent about it? Too many things to list. But I'll try.

THE DOCUMENTARY STYLE

The documentary/reality style where the lo-fi cameras awkwardly became characters in the world of Wernham Hogg was the foundation of the show. One of the central comedic ideas is the self-conscious relationship the characters have with the cameras and the film crew working around them. Some, like Gareth, are completely unaware of their own boobery and see the camera as a drinking buddy. Others, like Tim and Dawn, use the camera as an ally as they double-check their own sanity in a workplace gone mad. "Are you seeing what I'm seeing? Can you *BELIEVE* this person?" they say in a subtle arch of an eyebrow.

And for the David Brent character, of course, the cameras provide the chance to showboat and preen for a captive audience. A demented star is born.

And all the wonderful things you could do with those cameras! Run alongside characters, push focus deep and capture a moment in the background, whip back and forth capturing a conversation, and, best of all, sneak "spy shots" through venetian blinds and discover those poor souls who don't know they're being filmed, sharing heartbreaking or ridiculous moments in imagined private.

And don't get me started about the "talking head." A brilliant element of direct address to the camera and crew that the creators, Ricky Gervais and Stephen Merchant, perfectly lifted from documentaries and reality shows and then twisted to their own comedic ends. In a handful of lines, a character could 1) move the plot forward, 2) reveal something hidden about them as a character, and 3) deliver a perfectly crafted, personality-laden joke.

THE AWKWARD PAUSE

Cringe humor has actually been around for a very long time. Many a sitcom and movie have used the uncomfortable pause for comedic effect, from Chekhov to Bob Newhart to Albert Brooks to Steve Coogan, but no one has wrung as much embarrassment, humiliation, and train-wreckishness from a moment as Ricky Gervais and Stephen Merchant, the ringmasters of discomfort.

After a cringe-inducing debacle by David Brent, there is usually a delicious pause in which the characters swing in the breeze, too uncomfortable to talk, move, or even speak. This was the glorious comedic bread and butter of the original *Office*.

HEART

There was a real, living, beating heart under the British *Office*. The love story between Tim and Dawn was simply heart-wrenching. We've all had some kind of experience with unrequited love, and the longing looks and doubt-filled moments were perfectly executed. Every character has their hopes and dreams living under their pasty skin, if you just look hard enough. David Brent, as much of a colossal ass as he is, is a sad, failed man who is simply looking to be loved. This subcurrent of despair, longing, and vulnerability made the show and its bleak landscape riveting.

Our version (all two hundred episodes) was able to delve even deeper into the emotional underbelly of the characters, and our show-runners, thank God, were not afraid to allow true emotion to occasionally shine through the awkwardness and silliness.

GARETH

Gareth, the British Dwight-prototype character, was a revelation. I was in awe of Mackenzie Crook's performance. Nobody had ever seen a character like that before. He was singular. You couldn't put your finger on what exactly Gareth was. Was he a toady ass-kisser? A nerd? A bully? A reactionary? An annoying idiot? A nut job? All of the above?

After so many years of auditioning for oddball characters in terrible TV pilots and movies, I was used to the one-dimensionality of the typical comedic sidekick. There was the stock nerd with the plastic pocket protector and adenoidal voice. (Hey! Someone should make a whole show about them! Oh wait, they did.)

Sidekick tropes: There is the uptight, know-it-all lackey. The coarse, back-slapping, wingman, women-hating slobby guy. The arrogant but actually dumb guy. The innocent, slow dumb guy. The wacky, scheming eccentric neighbor. You know the types. You've seen them portrayed sometimes brilliantly, most times stereotypically and grotesquely. But Gareth contained various elements of most of those characters rolled into one skinny, unpredictable, and completely real human being.

I will be forever grateful. Mackenzie (and Gareth), I salute you.

THE LANDSCAPE

Sad, drawn, pasty, forlorn faces of lost souls under fluorescent lights. Why had nobody ever made a show about them before? Dressed up in wool/poly blends that can be found in any local Sears or JCPenney. Bad hair. Bad teeth. Deep sighs.

Real conference rooms and microwaves and gray mottled carpeting. Cubicles. Cluttered desks. Venetian blinds. Phones and faxes echoing in the distant soundscape. Not a Hollywood set built on a soundstage, but a real, actual office just like the ones we've all slogged around and toiled in before.

The English *Office* created a distinct world that WAS our world. A world ripe for mocking and cherishing.

When people visited our set they would wander around amazed at the minutiae and detail. The Scranton take-out menus, stuck to the refrigerator with ridiculous local magnets. The cupboards filled with office supplies, the kitchen filled with actual food. The motivational posters adorning walls covered in finger smudges. The family photos intricately lining each character's desk. The fake plants. Every room was filled with the tiny details of everyday life, bursting with personality and ennui.

THOUGHTS ON BBC *OFFICE* FANS

Fans of the BBC *Office* were passionate, vocal, vitriolic, and, yes, snobby as hell. Throughout my time on *The Office* I would constantly hear or read two related refrains (sometimes directly to my face, other times online or in articles):

1. "Why would they even make an American *Office*? Hollywood is so out of ideas. Why don't they just show the British *Office*! I won't

even watch, I don't want to see how they'll ruin it. Ugh! Nothing can ever be better than the original BBC *Office*."

2. "I wasn't going to watch the US *Office* because I loved the British *Office* so much. I was put off by the idea. After a few years I saw an episode and was really surprised at how good it was and now I watch it all the time!"

These two statements indicate a cultural problem of vast proportions with deep, grotesque implications for the future of humanity.

Let's examine these statements a little bit.

First of all, let's try to shine a little light on the differences between British and American television. In England, for some inexplicable reason, they are able to do "series" that have a very small number of episodes. Like six. Seriously. The original *Office* had thirteen episodes. Total. Thirteen. Over two and a half years. That's how many episodes we would make in a three-month span. That's nothing.

The BBC is a government-funded television organization for news and programming. They do not run commercials. This means that half-hour shows that run on the BBC can be literally twenty-eight minutes long. Half-hour television shows in the United States are 21:20 or so. The brilliant idea of "Why don't they just show the original episodes in the US?" is impossible. You would need to cut more than a quarter out of each episode. And what would need to come out? All the uncomfortable pauses. Then the show just wouldn't be funny anymore.

Not to mention the fact that most prime-time TV watchers in Kansas and Michigan don't really understand English accents and lingo. All that talk of "the boot of your lorry," "cheers, mate," "bloody 'ell," and "bollocks" goes completely over the heads of most corpulent mid-Americans who have grown up watching *The Brady Bunch*, *Dr. Phil*, and *Sabrina, the Teenage Witch*.

The American television model, unless you are working for PBS, is entirely different. A prime-time show is only profitable if it reaches enough episodes to achieve syndication—eighty-eight or more, give or take. So our television business model is not to make thirteen episodes that are half an hour long but to make over a hundred episodes that are basically twenty-one minutes long.

Both shows were entirely successful in their respective countries, fulfilling the business requirements that they needed to. The BBC *Office* format was also re-created in other cultures for other markets, such as French Quebec, Israel, Chile, Germany (which tried to rip it off until the BBC threatened to sue), and France. Some were successful, some not. We ended up making 202 twenty-one-minute episodes of television. One of the longest, most successful runs of a TV show in history. (But you probably knew that.)

The strange snobbery that was elicited toward our show by (mostly) Brits and some snooty Americans is absolutely mystifying to me, and if you really examine the tendency, nauseating.

Let's examine the underlying issues of all this television outrage. What the hypothetical TV snob is emphatically saying is:

1. "There are thirteen episodes of a brilliant TV show that I love and is SO GOOD that no one should ever do another version of it, EVER. Aaaaahhhhh!!!!!"
2. "All the BBC episodes will somehow disappear from existence if the Americans, French, or Germans make their own versions! DVDs will melt and all record of the beloved show will disappear and we'll never be able to watch the British *Office* again if it's remade in America. AAAAAAAHHHHHHH!!!!!!"
3. "The world will be a worse place if stupid Hollywood messes up this gem like they have so many other transplants from across the pond. This will cause me such psychic and artistic pain that

I will be personally adversely affected and our entire culture will
be degraded by this potentially heinous act."

4. Some said: "The pilot of the American *Office* was literally ripped
off from the BBC *Office*! It was exactly the same! They don't have
an original idea in their heads! How dare they?!"

5. Others said: "The other episodes of the *Office* are *different* from
the BBC *Office*! Why don't they use the plots and ideas from the
original *Office*? How dare they?!"

My response:

This hypothetical person we're talking about is a TV snob. Television, in and of itself, is really not something to have snobbery about.
We're not talking about a television remake of *A Portrait of the Artist
as a Young Man*, *The Waste Land*, or *Guernica* here. We're talking
about THIRTEEN EPISODES OF A TELEVISION SHOW, IDIOTS!

There are so many things to be upset about in the world. Hunger,
education, the environment, all those needless stickers on fruit. But
this hypothetical BBC TV snob is wasting amazing, huge amounts of
time and energy being upset by something SO incredibly minor.

There are so many things to be loyal to in this world: one's faith,
the cause of social justice, a spouse or family, the idea of furthering
progress. But fervid loyalty to a television miniseries is exceptionally
misguided.

You get the idea.

And, as for statement number two, when your loyalty to a handful of
episodes of a brilliant TV show actually prevents you disdainfully
from watching another version, something is wrong with you. Just
check it out. Give it a gander. It's not gonna hurt you. You're not going
to lose hipster street cred by saying, "Yeah, I checked out the NBC
remake of *The Office* and I liked it/didn't like it." Back in 2004, when

our show premiered, this was in the cultural groundwater. Back then, saying you would never watch the American *Office* was the equivalent of saying today, "I don't own a TV" or "I don't have a Facebook." It was a badge of ridiculous pride.

There was an ancillary form of TV snobbery/idiocy that ran as a strain throughout this whole BBC vs. US *Office* debate that raged in the first few years of our show. This was: "Hollywood doesn't have any original ideas of its own and needs to constantly pilfer and raid other people's great ideas in order to provide content."

This is ridiculous. There is SO much to complain about with Hollywood and what it stands for. BUT I will say this: It is an IDEA FACTORY.

Let's look at the television business. There are four or so major networks that develop lots of scripted content each year (never mind the *countless* cable outlets). Let's examine them for a second.

Many of you probably know this, but every year each network develops approximately eighty to one hundred pilot scripts each for what is known as "pilot season." Of those scripts, twenty or more will "go to pilot" and be shot. Of those, only a small handful will be "picked up to series" and only a small percentage of them will actually last on the air. So that's four major networks shooting around eighty television pilots EVERY YEAR.

Yes, many of the shows are crappy rehashes of old, worn-out ideas: unlikely roommates, fat guy/hot wife, sexy doctors hooking up, lone detective who just can't play by the rules (guilty!), etc. . . . But many if not most are also completely original ideas, like *Lost, House, Seinfeld, 24, Freaks and Geeks, 30 Rock*, etc. . . . *Some*, but a very small percentage, are remakes or reimaginings of movies or shows from other countries or other formats from other places. Some of these shows end up working quite well, like *Ugly Betty, All in the Family*, and *Sanford and Son*. Many don't, like *Coupling, Kath & Kim*, and *American Idol* (jk).

So, to posit that Hollywood is devoid of original ideas and needs to steal all the great ideas that come from other lands is a truly silly thing to say.

But back to the audition.

The sign-in sheet for the first day of auditions for *The Office*. Some GREAT names on this list, including Adam Scott, Mary Lynn Rajskub, Hamish Linklater, and, of course, Jenna Fischer.

I gave the world's lamest audition for Michael Scott. (Allison Jones has it on tape somewhere or other.) I simply did a very bad Ricky Gervais imitation with a lot of tugging on my tie and eye rolling. In the back of my mind, I knew the best was yet to come.

Occasionally—you can ask any actor—there comes along a part

that you just instinctively know EXACTLY how to play. I knew that Dwight was the role for me. I knew in my bones that no other actor in Hollywood had that combination of absurd intensity, white trashiness, and total goofball nerd in them the way I did. I knew the part was mine from the get-go. Most of the time I fumble my way through awkward attempts at roles during auditions and am filled with doubt, so when a role comes along that I feel such a deep inspiration from and affinity toward, I am truly grateful.

(Later, after I was cast, I sat down to lunch with the writers and brought in pictures of my family—my achingly odd, offbeat, working-class weirdo family. I also brought in pictures of my achingly gawky teen self. I told them tales of my suburban Seattle upbringing, raspberry picking, heavy metal, chess, the bassoon, and muscle cars. I told stories to them of Chris Cole, my self-serious Dungeons & Dragons pal who wore actual *Battlestar Galactica*-brand glasses and later would study fencing and become a coronet player in the Marines. [Chris was a great inspiration for Dwight in many ways. He was skinny as a whippet, but his D&D characters were always immensely muscled barbarians who looked like Vin Diesel with Fabio hair. He had that amazing balance of nerd and bully as well as a ridiculous haircut. If you're reading this, Chris, thank you. And I'm sorry. Both in equal portions.] I like to think that this glimpse into my odd past influenced the way the writers thought of Dwight and his background and allowed them to help make him as complex, bizarre, and indefinable as he ultimately was.)

I absolutely killed the Dwight audition in front of Greg Daniels as well as producers Howard Klein and Teri Weinberg and waited for the phone to ring telling me I got the part. I was so excited and wanted the part just immediately handed to me.

And then the phone didn't ring. For months. I was totally freaked as I heard they were auditioning every living and breathing comedy actor in the Western Hemisphere. I believe my first audition was in November, but I wouldn't get a call back for a "network test" until January.

Normally screen-testing for lead roles on network television shows involves traipsing into a conference room filled with ADHD television executives who are furiously thumbing away at their phones, doing a couple of short scenes in the most nerve-wracking environment known to man, and then waiting an hour or two to hear if you got the part or not.

Greg Daniels, our exceptionally bright creator/show-runner, did things completely differently. The pilot for *The Office* was to be shot on a soundstage but in reverse. We would shoot the scenes in the upstairs production offices and prepare for the shooting down in the giant soundstages below. This had never been done before in the history of Hollywood, I believe.

It was up in those drab offices above the enormous stages, over the course of a weekend, that Greg, our keen director Ken Kwapis, and the other producers held the final auditions for the finalists. It was there that I would first work with Jenna Fischer, John Krasinski, and Steve Carell.

There were five or six people testing for each of the major roles. The producers mixed and matched all of us over the course of a weekend in scripted scenes as well as improvised ones.

There were some really interesting and talented actors, but the only scenes I really remember doing were with Jenna and John, who were absolutely adorable and hysterical in the roles. I remember thinking that they WERE Jim and Pam. They WERE the characters, effortless and charming as all get-out.

The other actresses were kind of nervous and flustered in the waiting room, but Jenna just sat there, reading *Wired*, a John Belushi biography. I remember asking her about the book and her offhandedly saying something about how it was a book Pam would probably be reading.

John was SUPER young back then (seventeen? twelve?) and had a fun, exuberant energy that was really positive and infectious. The funny thing was that the NBC New York casting agent told his manager that John was only right for the character of Dwight and insisted that he would only bring him in for that role. John rightfully refused to go in for Dwight and kept trying to get an audition for Jim. Eventually, of course, they relented and allowed John to try out for Jim Halpert, and the rest is history. We did some mix-and-match, scripted audition scenes, and then came the fun part: the improvisations.

I remember doing an improv with Jenna where Greg instructed me to let her know that if she was breaking up with Roy, I was available to date.

I was off to the races. I knelt in REALLY close to her (too close, creepy) and started telling her about my girlfriend, Regina, who was stationed in Kuwait City, and how much I missed her. I went on and on in a really hushed, conspiratorial way, and Jenna just sat there with an impossibly pained expression on her blank, lovely face. I let her know that I was a good sympathetic shoulder to lean on if she ever wanted to talk about her problems with Roy and with men in general, and that we should go out sometime and get a smoothie.

Here was the most brilliant thing about this improvisation: not my silly prattling on, but the fact that *Jenna said almost nothing.* Many actors when improvising believe that talking more is the key to being more interesting and/or funny. The very best improvisers have the ability to use silence and understand that less is more. Most actors in her situation would probably have started babbling and trying to get some jokes in. Not Jenna. She bravely just sat there looking disgusted, polite, sweet, and constipated all at the same time. I knew that she was going to be Pam.

For YEARS afterward the writers talked about giving Dwight a former girlfriend who had been stationed in Kuwait City and would come back to town and butt up against Angela. I begged them to cast Katee Sackhoff from *Battlestar Galactica* in the potential role. It never quite happened. But the card with the idea written on it, based off of the improvisation from my audition, hung on the wall in the writers' room for years and years.

During this endless and incredibly fun audition process, I got to do a number of improvs with John Krasinski. It was a blast and we had amazing combative chemistry right from the start. We did a scene where he had to ask me to mind his phone while he went to the bathroom (I refused, of course, infuriating him). And another where he generously gave me a glass of water (which I was terrified of and paranoid about to an impossible degree). Our characters butted heads in a visceral, exciting way from the very beginning of our coming together at that now-famous desk clump.

(To the very end there was no one I had better chemistry with than John. As different as we are as people, there was a strange, almost psychic rapport we had while acting. We would often know exactly what the other was going to do and say, and play off of it. I also really appreciated the working relationship in that we could direct each other without any ego. We would often give each other lines to try out and little comic bits to play. Some of Dwight's funniest moments came actually from the fantastic brain of John Krasinski.)

All I remember about working with Steve at the audition was an improvisation where he was taking me to task for borrowing his coffee cup and leaving it dirty on his desk. I denied it, of course, and that's when he told me with disgust and venom that he had found OVAL-TINE in the cup! I started laughing and I couldn't stop. They had to end the scene right then and there.

Later I found out that I was the only person the producers submitted to the network for approval for the role. Soon thereafter I was cast as Dwight and my life was transformed.

In one of the oddest meetings of my life, Greg Daniels called me and took me out for coffee. He had a very strange acting note. He told me in a very diplomatic way that he loved my acting during the improvs and he liked my acting much less in the scripted scenes. I was a bit puzzled by this. Then I got a bit panicked. Could I lose the role because I improvised well but seemed less interesting while acting scripted lines? I tried to act cool and called our great producer Howard Klein and asked to see the audition tapes. I went into his office and furiously studied my scenes, both improvised and scripted, searching for what Greg might have been talking about. And there it was, right on the crummy video. In the improvised scenes my focus was on the scenes themselves and on the actor I was working with and not on the lines, while in the scripted scenes occasionally there were times when the scenes *seemed* scripted, where the lines *felt* acted, a bit forced, a bit purposeful. I learned a very interesting and valuable lesson in this process. This documentary that was filming the characters at Dunder Mifflin was simply capturing the behavior of the workers there. This is how the acting needed to feel. Not deliberate or planned in any way at all. The lines, as scripted, needed to feel completely UN-scripted, natural, off-the-cuff, as if the characters were in fact making them up on the spot.

The greatest compliment we ever got as a cast—and we got it all the time—was in the form of a question: "How many of the lines are improvised?" Or "It feels like the whole show is improvised at times." This is a testament to the cast's acting ability. No matter what the venue—film, theater, or TV—good acting should really feel improvised all the time, so that you don't notice the lines are prewritten. This is also a tremendous compliment to our writers, who wrote such natural-sounding lines that resonated with tremendous absurdity at the same time.

(Note: The *answer* to the above question is that once we got the lines as scripted we would improvise our way through scenes, trying out different "alt" lines and seeing where else we could try to mine some comedy. Many cast members never improvised, but most of us would, especially Steve, the grand master of ad-libbing. I would say in the end, in the final cut, the show ended up being about 75 percent scripted. Remember, the writers were also the producers on the show and oversaw the editing process, fighting all the way for the lines they had written to stay in the edit. Had the actors been overseeing the editing process the show might have been 50 percent scripted and the rest improvised.)

After we were all cast on the show, me, Steve, John, and Jenna went out for lunch at a nondescript little sandwich place down the street from the studio. We had a conversation that, grandiose as it may sound, is etched into all of our minds. We giddily discussed the very real possibility that this show could go on for eight years and that it would change the course of our lives and how these parts we were about to undertake would most likely be our most defining roles. "Just think about what we're getting into; the journey we're about to go on could be AMAZING," I remember saying. I remember Steve, who was just coming off of doing *Anchorman* and *The 40-Year-Old Virgin*, saying, "Of all the roles I'll end up doing and all the films I may shoot, I believe that Michael Scott may be the role I'll always be most known for." It was one of those moments when our destiny was seen with complete clarity, like a country road from a hot-air balloon. And all while eating a tuna sandwich.

Chapter 15

ALMOST FAMOUS 2

———

IT WAS EIGHT A.M. ON THE FIRST DAY OF SHOOTING AND THE entire cast of *The Office* assembled in the "bull pen," the main work area of Dunder Mifflin. Ken and Greg had the idea to create a real workplace on our set. We all showed up for work in character, cameras capturing our every move. We then improvised our work lives: sold paper, made phone calls, sent faxes, did desk work. Ken wanted to create the relentless banality of work in an office like Dunder Mifflin. We would do this routine for about half an hour every single morning while filming the pilot, and the "B roll" we shot during those times was used in the title sequence and throughout the course of the show. This helped ground us all in the early days in the fact that this was a REAL work space and not the set of a television sitcom.

Shooting the pilot was a real pleasure. It was relaxed and collaborative, much like the rest of *The Office* would end up being. We knew we had something really unique and special on our hands. Then the trouble started.

After we did the pilot we didn't hear anything from NBC for a long, long while. When the network announced what shows it was picking up, ours was not on the list. This was terrifying and depressing. All that work. All that waiting. The part I had coveted so passionately, gone. That amazing cast that Greg had assembled. We were devastated.

Then, at the very last minute, Kevin Reilly, the head of NBC at the time (now the head of TBS and TNT), called Greg Daniels and told him that they were going to pick up five additional episodes. (Most television shows are picked up for thirteen.)

At the last second we were rescued from the dustbin of television non-history. Excited, a bunch of us flew to New York the next day for the "upfronts," the big television conference with the advertisers where networks splashily announce their fall shows.

Jeff Zucker, the head of all of NBC Universal at the time (now the head of CNN), was never a fan of our show. He just didn't get the humor and didn't think it would find an audience. In fact, at one point in the development process he decided *The Office* should be a multicamera sitcom (like *Friends* or, better comparison, *NewsRadio*). Greg Daniels immediately said that he would quit the project if that were the case and the show was back on track to be a single-camera mockumentary. Kevin Reilly and the other NBC execs who believed in us had an uphill battle to fight to try to get us on the air.

It also didn't help that we were one of the lowest-testing pilots in NBC history. Right down there with *Seinfeld*. The test audiences HATED us.

(For those of you who don't know, TV pilots are screened for a test audience, who are given these funny little dials. They can turn the dials up when they're enjoying something and turn them D O W N when they don't like something. Then they're interviewed and give the shows a rating. The television networks and studios say they don't, but they actually put a great deal of importance on the numbers that come out of testing, and a show that tests badly stands a much poorer chance of getting picked up to series.)

Our show got picked up for five additional episodes in the spring of 2004, but we didn't air until the spring of 2005. And then when we did, we tanked.

Everybody hated us. Our reviews were awful.* People either didn't understand the show or HATED the fact that we had done a pilot that was 90 percent similar to the lionized British *Office*. I know this because I sat in front of my computer for hours reading all the online comments with a sad, long, diarrhea face. (I now know better than to do this.) I was called "over-the-top," "annoying," and "pig-like" on countless online message boards. The show was reviled as an ugly-looking, unfunny train wreck by some, and a blatant, pathetic, unfunny rip-off of the classic BBC gem by others. "Unfunny" was the common ground that both camps could agree on, apparently.

The reason we did essentially the same script as the BBC *Office* was a very simple, practical one. When you do a pilot for a television studio and network, they are notorious for meddling with the material. They give notes on every aspect of the script and shoot. They want control of the casting. They want the set design to be brighter

---

* A note about reviews: Pretty much everything I have ever done, other than *Juno*, has gotten slammed in the reviews. I have been eviscerated by hundreds of film and TV critics for over a decade. I believe it is much easier to write a negative, snarky, contemptuous review than to write an evenhanded one. It also gets more reads. But the thing that gets me the most is comparisons. *The Office* was compared (unfavorably) to the British *Office*. *The Rocker* was compared (unfavorably) to *School of Rock*. *Super* was compared (unfavorably) to *Kick-Ass*. *Backstrom* was compared (unfavorably) to *House M.D.*

See a pattern here? There are a limited number of stories on the planet. Shakespeare told most of them. And *The Sopranos* and *The Simpsons* the rest. The easiest, laziest thing for a reviewer to do is to compare something to another work

and more "fun." They want the story to have clarity, meaning, and heart. They water down the jokes out of fear of offending and do their darnedest to try to make all the characters "relatable" and "likable." Occasionally a network can help a show. Most of the time, however, it degrades the original idea of how the show was conceived and makes it blander, more palatable, boring, and more like other shows already on the air.

This philosophy doesn't really work for a show like *The Office*. The two main characters are purposefully not relatable and likable but annoying and difficult. The lighting, set, and haircuts are meant to be an eyesore. The jokes are awkward. The story isn't really a story at all but a slight, realistic framework to allow the characters to live, breathe, and thrive. It's purposefully unflashy and off-putting, two qualities networks and audiences don't usually gravitate toward.

So, what Greg Daniels did was rely on a proven entity. He told NBC, "Hey, the BBC *Office* was pretty perfect so we really should just stick with what works, right? I mean, why change it if it's such a classic?" The network had no argument for that and we stuck close to the original pilot. Greg didn't want what was fresh, original, and odd about the great British show to be lost in an American translation. He

---

that is a classic and has some similarities. It's a gross misuse of critical power and a disgusting waste of ink and time. Take *The Rocker*. There are similarities to the flawless classic *School of Rock* in that there is an older character who loves rock and roll and he's interacting about said music form with younger people. But that's where the comparison ends. One is a movie about an unemployed rocker who gets a job teaching at a prep school and charmingly and chaotically coaches his twelve-year-olds in a battle of the bands. The other film is about an old former metal drummer who accidentally becomes a YouTube sensation and goes out on the road with his eighteen-year-old nephew's band. Yes, there is an older rocker character and younger characters, but past that the comparison just doesn't hold

also knew that in upcoming episodes we would have a chance to find our own voice. Which we soon did.

Our pilot episode got decent enough ratings, but we went WAY down after that even though the following episodes were some of the best we'd ever do.

"Hot Girl," "Health Care," "The Alliance," "Basketball," and especially "Diversity Day" were the episodes no one watched when they originally aired but some of the ones our fans would later consider classics.

We started as this big family of dweeby television basement dwellers, excited by the possibility of our show, and gradually, gratefully, our dreams would end up unfolding and coming true in front of us. I realize, looking back, that in this family we had a stable of the most incredible writers ever assembled. These writers would eventually pen dozens of our very best episodes.

First was Mike Schur, cocreator of *Parks and Recreation* and *Brooklyn Nine-Nine*. He had just come off of being the head writer on *SNL*'s "Weekend Update" for several years. He was obsessed with baseball and politics. And comedy. One of the finest men you'll ever

---

water. And yet, every single review of *The Rocker* said it was trying to be *School of Rock* and wasn't as good.

As for *Backstrom*, is every single show that has an antisocial, destructive, and brilliant lead character going to be compared to *House* until the end of time? When does that stop? Is it not a viable setup for a television show? The differences between *Backstrom* and *House* FAR outweigh the few similarities. (Not to mention the fact that the entire conceit of *Backstrom* is based on a series of Swedish books. Do the reviewers believe that the crime novelist Leif G. W. Persson based his books on the American TV show *House*?)

Now, is an occasional comparison warranted in a review? Yes. *Occasionally.* But for the most part it's a lazy, easy, obvious way to review work. But let's face

meet. Writer of "The Alliance" in season one, "Office Olympics," "Valentine's Day," and the Christmas episode of season two (all seminal, crucial, classic episodes). And eventually, he would become an actor, playing a cousin of Dwight, the mentally challenged Amish creepster Mose Schrute.

(Funny story: Our show was starting at the same time the TV megahit *Survivor* was launching and Mike broke the story of "The Alliance" when the writers jokingly suggested in the writers' room, "What would Dwight say if Jim came up to him and said, 'Will you form an alliance with me?'" "'Absolutely I will,'" was Mike's immediate response in the room, and they knew the episode HAD to be written. Those two lines have proven to be perhaps the most evocative couplet of dialogue in the entire series.)

B. J. Novak was an incredibly young stand-up comic out of Harvard when Greg Daniels discovered him. I've never met anyone with a sharper, darker wit. He's got lasers in his brain. He wrote "Diversity Day," the episode that made everyone (eventually) sit up and take notice of what our show was capable of comedically. Besides writing and directing so many other classic episodes, he memorably created shallow Ryan the temp, whose rags-to-riches-to-rags journey over the course of eight seasons was one of my favorite stories of the entire show.

Mindy Kaling is a horrible person. She doesn't deserve a paragraph in this iconic pantheon of writers. (B.J. writes most of her stuff anyway.) She's an insufferable flibbertigibbet who is obsessed with fashion, shopping, Beyoncé, and cutting off the penises of the men she's slept with and putting them under her mattress. She also owes

---

it, for the most part reviewers have never created or made anything. They righteously pass judgment from their laptops on other people's work and have simply never laid out their hearts and minds and souls to an audience attempting to entertain, uplift, and challenge. So suck it, critics.

me two hundred fifty bucks, a soy latte, and a guest-star role on her dumb new show. She makes me sick. I need to stop writing about her now.

Paul Lieberstein was the quiet genius behind the show. Besides playing boring, lovable, pitiful Toby, he eventually became our show-runner, leading us creatively in many of the later seasons. So many of *The Office*'s most memorable scenes and moments came from Paul's twisted brain: crentist, Dwight's speech, the Holly/Michael romance, the Michael Scott Paper Company, Prison Mike, Dwight's B&B, "Abraham Lincoln said I will attack you with the North," and many, many more iconic events.

Other early writers who helped shape the show were Larry Wilmore, who played Mr. Brown in "Diversity Day" and eventually would become an incredible *Daily Show* correspondent, and the amazing and incredibly bighearted Lester Lewis. (He passed away recently and is terribly missed by everyone he ever worked with. Rest in peace, Lester. Thanks for the laughter.)

Later we would be joined by even more writing and directing talent, like Jen Celotta, Brent Forrester, Danny Chun, Justin Spitzer, and the team of Gene Stupnitsky and Lee Eisenberg,

Paul Feig, the great, dapper director of *Bridesmaids* and *The Heat*, was a director on staff and did many (fourteen!) of our very best episodes in those first couple of years, including "Halloween" and "Office Olympics."

A lot of press and attention was given to the fact that so many writers on the show were also actors in the cast. This was another simple stroke of brilliance by Greg Daniels that once again filled a very practical need. We required bodies. It was an office we were creating, after all. Besides the five lead actors, we had six or so supporting cast members in that first season. Later these amazing players (Angela, Kevin, Stanley, et al. . . . .) would become series regulars and their characters would become further fleshed out and absolutely integral to the show. But an office has a lot more people in it than ten! Greg knew he could get interesting writers with a natural penchant for acting and since he had them under contract in the writers' room, he could send them over to the set and have them add memorably to the population and life of Dunder Mifflin. Like many great innovations, this was undertaken as a way to save money and fill a very practical requirement of a workplace mockumentary.

Again, the future of *The Office* was a rough road. After the traumatic birth of our son, Walter, during the "Hot Girl" episode, the stakes were quite high for Holiday and me as we had a baby mouth to feed and the future was a complete unknown. After not hearing anything for several more months, all of us being sure because of our low ratings and scathing reviews that the show would be canceled, we were shocked when again at the last minute NBC picked up another partial order of six more episodes for the fall. Our second season!

The chairman of General Electric, Bob Wright, had a teenage son who LOVED *The Office*. GE owned NBC at the time and the Wright family apparently watched all the pilots and shows. Bob became very interested in us after his kid told him how much he and his friends loved us. This literally may have been the deciding factor that pushed NBC away from canceling us after that failed first batch of episodes. Our hero, the Wright family teenager: tastemaker, game changer, *Office* fan, and bazillionaire.

We went back to work in August 2005, eventually making some of *The Office*'s very best episodes, including "The Dundies," "Halloween," "Booze Cruise," and, perhaps the greatest of all episodes, "The Injury," written by She-Who-Will-Not-Be-Named.

Every week the episodes aired we would check the ratings the next day with actual bated breath. Our first several episodes seemed to be doing all right, with much higher viewership than our brief first season but lower than many other comedies in the same time period. But we still weren't getting a full pickup of shows from NBC. We were terrified of cancellation. We shot each week with great passion as well as pins and needles. I was certain that we would have a fate similar to some of my other favorite shows, *Arrested Development* and *Freaks and Geeks*—do a couple of handfuls of shows and be well regarded and cherished over time on DVD and in cable reruns.

Suddenly NBC called at the last minute again and ordered two more episodes just as we were finishing up our first batch. Our ratings continued to inch up very slowly. It was excruciating. Then they ordered two *more* episodes from us. Then one more. Then three more. And then?

We exploded.

Several important things were happening all at the same time. *My Name Is Earl* was a big hit right out of the gate and we rode on its coattails for quite some time. Our shows matched up well together and, along with *Scrubs* (and later *30 Rock* and *Parks and Rec*), NBC started making some great inroads with single-camera comedies.

Young audiences, tired of all the hackneyed, broad, unrealistic multicamera sitcoms, were turning toward single-camera shows for a different kind of comedy experience. And this was the strangest thing about our audience: THEY WERE SO GOSH-DARNED YOUNG! Now, don't get me wrong, we loved that fact (and so did the advertisers), but we were all a bit surprised. We were doing a show about an average American workplace, after all. We expected an audience of people who had interacted with a similar environment or experience at some point in their lives. Perhaps even people who didn't work in an actual office but had to deal with crazy bosses and workmates. But junior high and high school students? That just didn't make sense. To this day I meet preteens who are devouring the show and older fans who started watching it as a young adolescent. Many teens grew up watching the show, starting in high school and finishing the series by the time they were graduating from college. Our show had ushered them into adulthood. They grew up with us.

One of the things I'm most grateful for is that families could and would watch *The Office* together. Kids and teens and parents. I can't tell you how many times I would hear from fans who would say something to the effect of "The only time all week our family would sit down with one another and laugh together was on Thursday nights when *The Office* was on." This is both an incredible compliment and a terrible indictment of the modern American family. But I'm grateful nonetheless.

And then there was iTunes. Apple started—get this—to sell television shows on a music website! Then they started selling iPods with a SCREEN on them that would PLAY VIDEOS! Remember those?! The first batch of video iPods went on the market in October of that year and, true story, the top-of-the-line ones were preloaded with *The Office*'s "Christmas Party" episode on them. That meant that all the rich kids of America who got a video iPod for Christmas in 2005 had an immediate hookup to our show. They would pass their iPods around, listen to a little Kelly Clarkson and Rob Thomas, and then watch the episode with their little rich-kid friends. Our show started to spread throughout high schools like a mild STD.

In those first years of *The Office* episodes' being available on the iTunes store, very often our show would take up five of the top ten positions on the sales chart. Young folks who were downloading shows were watching *The Office* more than any other program.

I remember staring at those iTunes charts in complete joyous disbelief. We were POPULAR! A show I was a LEAD on was actually SUCCESSFUL!

Then, all of a sudden, NBC put a giant billboard of us in front of their Burbank offices. Someone on the crew had taken a photo of that billboard while driving past and I, John, Jenna, and Steve huddled around looking at it, laughing ecstatically. After about a hundred elated high fives we settled back down to do the scene at hand, giggling secretly. A photo of that billboard was hung on the wall just outside of our set and stayed there for the duration of our show. We knew then we were going to be on the air for a long, long time.

We were off and running. There's nothing like the energy that fills a cast and crew when you know you're on a hit show. For Holiday and myself, who had struggled financially for decades, this was an incredible relief. I immediately traded in my dilapidated Volvo for an expensive luxury racing car that had just hit the market, the Toyota Prius.

The moment I knew that our show was entering "beloved cultural landmark" status, I was in the Detroit airport and an overweight old baggage handler came running up to me with his out-of-date flip phone. I was a little scared. What did this enormous Michiganian want from me? Did he want a photo? Did he want me to fix or bless his phone? He said, "Dwight, Dwight, look!"

On the phone, in flip-phone-style text, were the words: "I can and DO cut my own hair."

He goes, "It's from my daughter! We text each other Dwight lines back and forth!"

He was as excited as a schoolboy.

Our show's legacy was later secured when we were surprise winners of the 2006 Emmy Award for Outstanding Comedy Series and when Steve Carell won the Golden Globe that same season.

DIARY OF AN EMMY LOSER

Eventually I was nominated for three Emmy Awards in a row (for seasons three through six) but never won squat. I was beat out by Jeremy Piven (twice) and Jon Cryer (once). I would always somehow run into Neil Patrick Harris in the Emmy bathrooms for some reason, and we'd shake hands (after washing) and wish for one of the two of us to win in a secretive whisper. We never did win. He's a nice fellow. But we're both big-time Emmy losers.

There is really no more nerve-wracking experience than waiting in a big-ass theater in your tux with your spouse to see if your name will be called and you will need to bound to the stage and give a witty, heartfelt, off-the-cuff talk in front of twelve hundred judgmental industry leaders and twelve million people watching at home. Live.

There you are in the Kodak or Shrine theater or whatever, dressed in your finest duds, trying not to look sick. Suddenly, they announce: "After this commercial break, the nominees for BEST SUPPORTING ACTOR IN A COMEDY!" and a bunch of cheesy music starts playing. Your heart starts thumping in your tux like a bongo drum being played by a stoned Matthew McConaughey. Sweat starts to pour down your armpits and your temples. Your mouth gets dry. You grasp your spouse's hand and coat it in your musky, desperate sweat. They look at you with compassion, empathy, and a little bit of queasy disgust at all the clammy sweat you're oozing onto their hand.

AND WE'RE BACK!

A jocular, telegenic host comes out and introduces the award. A video montage of all the nominees begins to play. Your throat is dry and your blood pressure is boiling like water in a teakettle. Your spouse's hands are completely coated in your briny perspiration and you can see the worried look of concern and pity on their face.

A giant TV camera comes up the aisle and is pointed directly at your face to watch you if you win and to watch you if someone else wins. The camera reminds you: "Look humble! Look grateful! Look placid! Look calm! Look upbeat! Look supportive! Twelve million people are watching your big, weird face! You could really stand to lose a few! Nobody likes you! Smile!"

What are you going to say if you win? You panic and completely lose track of whatever clever little bits of dialogue you were going to lead off with. DON'T FORGET TO THANK YOUR SPOUSE, you say to yourself. PLEASE LET IT BE ME, you say to yourself. PLEASE LET IT BE SOMEONE ELSE, you say to yourself. WHAT IF I FORGET HOW TO TALK? And WHAT IF MY HEART EXPLODES THROUGH MY THROAT AND A FOUNTAIN OF CLAMMY BLOOD ERUPTS THROUGH MY ESOPHAGUS ONTO KIEFER SUTHERLAND AND SHONDA RHIMES?

And the envelope is torn open by the jocular, telegenic MC. TIIIIIMMMME. SLOOOOWWWSSS. WAAAAAYYYY. DOOOOW-WWWN. (McConaughey is doing a frantic, voodoo-intensity bongo solo that echoes in the blood behind your ears.)

And the name is called . . .

JJJJJERRREEEMMMMYYYY PIIIIVVVVVEEEEEENNNNN!

And all of a sudden it all stops. Boom.

Time moves in a regular fashion again. You hear things normally. The bongos and the blood stop. Your pulse slows back down. You hear applause everywhere and remember that it's not for you. You remember the camera pointed at your face and you try to master that perfect expression of "Aw, I'm kind of disappointed but I'm REALLY excited for this very talented other actor who did win."

You feel both relieved and pissed. Like a bully chose not to beat you up but only to punch you in the stomach and knock the wind out of you.

You look to your spouse and they smile a sad, supportive smile. You squeeze their waterlogged hand.

"Next year," you say to them in a whisper.

The next day you go back to work.

RANDOM *OFFICE* MEMORIES

———

- Before the pilot was shot, John Krasinski and a bunch of his buddies decided to go to Scranton to do some research. They brought a crappy little video recorder and interviewed people who worked at actual paper companies in the Scranton area. This tape would greatly influence the set design and decoration. As they drove around the city they literally shot out the window at some passing Scranton landmarks. These shots would eventually find their way into our opening credits and would stay there through the entirety of our show. Thanks, Kras!

- There was an interesting process to decide on our theme song. Many songs were being considered seriously, including "Better Things" by the Kinks and "Float On" by Modest Mouse. Greg graciously sent out a list of songs and links to them as well for the cast to weigh in on. The one we all wanted most of all was "Mr. Blue Sky" by Electric Light Orchestra. It's a sensational song and its jubilant, upbeat refrain would have fit perfectly over the drab video of the opening credits. Then we found out another show, the doomed and dismally conceived *LAX*, used the song. (Yes, this was a television show that was about the day-to-day operations of A GIANT CRAPPY AIRPORT starring Heather Locklear. THINK ABOUT HOW STUPID AN IDEA THAT IS! Besides prison and a dentist's office, what place do we want to avoid more than any other? Long lines, missed flights, shootings, pushy crowds, metal detectors, overpriced food. Just the kinds of things you want to curl up on a couch with a bag of yogurt raisins and watch more about week after week, no?)

- The theme we eventually ended up with was a beaut. Composed by former seventies rock/pop star Jay Ferguson, it was fun and catchy with just a hint of melancholy. It perfectly set the tone for the show. I've written pretend lyrics to it on many occasions. Perhaps I'll sing them to you one day if you're nice.

- This lovely but relatively unknown actress named Amy Adams came in to play the "purse girl" in Mindy Kaling's first episode, "Hot Girl." The various men of Dunder Mifflin pursued her and competed for her affections with great abandon. Little did any of us suspect that the actress playing that little role would eventually become a ginormous movie star, an Oscar nominee, and a secret ginger sex concubine of Kim Jong-un.

- Our camera operators Randall Einhorn and Matt Sohn were brought over from *Survivor* to work on our show. Greg wanted experienced documentary/reality camera guys who could find details and shared moments and make the action of scenes feel organically captured as in a documentary. These two great talents would end up directing many of our episodes and were instrumental in creating the look of the show as well as finding creative and unique ways to discover the visual comedy of the

Office world. Also, they'd eaten bugs with Richard Hatch, *Survivor* supervillain from season one.

- Mindy and B.J. were always apparently dating, breaking up, and getting back together throughout seasons three through six, approximately. I don't know this for a fact, but I heard it from those nosy-ass writers. I would occasionally see Mindy in tears and B.J. frantically gesticulating to her the way tempestuous lovers often do in various corners of the set. Their offscreen shenanigans were great inspiration and fodder for the eventual Ryan/Kelly "on again, off again" relationship. Now they're best friends, finish each other's sentences, and talk about me behind my back constantly.

- It takes a brave and confident show-runner to allow lines that the actors make up on the fly to remain in the show. I have friends on very successful shows where they are not allowed to change ONE SINGLE WORD. To most comedy actors that is a strange form of hell. Here are some of my favorite improvised lines that actually made it into the show.

> When I was in the sixth grade I was a finalist in our school spelling bee. It was me against Raj Patel. I misspelled, in front of the entire school, the word "failure."

> "And just as you have planted your seed in the ground, I am going to plant my seed, in you." (And B.J., the writer of the episode, effortlessly replied: "I don't think you know what you're saying.")

> I have hunted werewolves. I shot one once, but by the time I got to it, it had turned back into my neighbor's dog.

Have you ever seen a burn victim, Phyllis?!

Hot dog fingers.

I thought your vagina was removed during your hysterectomy.

Another improvisation that stayed in the writers' imagination was an early talking head where I said off-the-cuff: "My name is Dwight Schrute. My father's name? Dwight Schrute. His father's name? . . . Dwide Schrood. Amish." This eventually DID make it into the show and it's one of my proudest creative moments as it eventually spawned Dwight's Amish past as well as Mose and eventually the beet farm.

• One of the more challenging things about working on *The Office* was that the way the show was filmed, documentary style, we always had to be in the background of each other's shots. For instance, if you were shooting a scene in Michael's office, there would always be the possibility of the camera peeking over someone's shoulder and catching the rest of the cast out in the bull pen of the main office. This meant that we would sometimes spend COUNTLESS hours pretending to work at our desks while scenes were going on in other rooms or other areas of the main office. (In the first season we didn't have working Internet and those hours were especially grueling. We DEMANDED working Internet in a show of diva-like solidarity.) There were many days of production in which I did no acting whatsoever but merely sat for twelve hours at my desk using my actual Internet to read the news, play online chess, and text-chat with my castmates. I would sometimes remind the producers that I was the best-paid background actor in all of Hollywood. It was excruciating, but I would remind myself that it was a hell of a lot better than working at that New

York insurance broker's. I made a deal with our assistant director Kelly that if the cameras ever caught anything I was reading on my computer screen I would donate $100 to Meals on Wheels. Let's just say a lot of sick shut-ins got fed because of Dwight and his computer screen. You're welcome, sick shut-ins.

• The best use of our desktop Internet? Easy. Fantasy football. We had a league for six of the nine seasons of *The Office*. Myself, Brian Baumgartner, and John Krasinski were all avid participants, as were many crew members and writers. Trades were going down like on the floor of the stock exchange. Research was being done and strategies for benching and starting players were being constantly hatched. I know what you're asking. Once. I won once. Thanks, LaDainian Tomlinson!

• Oscar Nuñez had the only computer with a functional speaker attached. He would spend the entirety of his days on the set doing background work in other people's scenes while watching the most ridiculous YouTube videos you've ever seen. He loved watching random fistfights, karate competitions, judo matches, and MMA highlights. He also loved to watch endless videos of people falling down, running into things, "wracking their balls," and generally wounding themselves.

• Dwight's blog. For the first several years of *The Office* I wrote a blog in Dwight's voice. Blogs were just becoming a "thing" in 2004. This began in season one, when we had no working Internet and were pretending to do actual work on spreadsheets and Word docs. I, in character, started writing some imaginary blog entries for Dwight. I showed them to the producers and they called NBC, who started running them on their website. I believe I was the very first actor to write a blog as his character. It was a lot of fun, and writing as him helped me understand Dwight's voice.

• Steve Carell has some very active and serious sweat glands. When the temperature would get hot or he would get nervous, he would erupt like Vesuvius and there would be a flash flood of sweat down his face. (There was a famous early Jimmy Kimmel appearance where Steve was so nervous that sweat just started POURING down his face in sheets. They joked about it and there was a funny bit later where he appeared in nothing but a towel, having just taken a shower to rinse off from his flop-sweat attack.)

To counteract this absurd physiological abnormality, the temperature on the set was situated at a ridiculously cold 64 degrees. This temperature issue was a constant struggle and source of great pain in the cast, especially for Jenna Fischer, who wore skirts and thin blouses all day long, and for Angela Kinsey, who has no discernible body fat and is the size of a baby sandpiper. Over the years, as the show got more and more luxurious, eventually the women of *The Office* got space heaters, which were surreptitiously placed under their desks to help with the arctic acting conditions.

• Things I was known for on the set: coffee breath and hurting people.

I have literally wounded pretty much everyone in the cast. I have hit John Krasinski in the eye and enormous nose with an icy snowball and various other desktop objects. I have accidentally punched Phyllis and Brian Baumgartner multiple times. In a football scene I tackled to the ground Creed (who is ninety-seven), who then knocked over Leslie David Baker (Stanley), who then fell on top of Angela. I have thrown Angela on top of desks and car hoods and spanked her randomly (far too hard), leaving severe and debilitating bruises every single time. (Truth be told, she bruises like a tiny, overly ripe, albino nectarine.) I once stupidly threw a five-pound dumbbell in Darryl's office up in the air for no reason and it came down on Craig Robinson's head, leaving a lump the size of a hard-boiled egg. In the "Beach Games" episode I accidentally kicked sand into Leslie David Baker's eyes and he had to be rushed to the hospital and have his enormous eyeball washed out and treated for a scratched cornea. This is my chance to apologize to the entire cast. I'm sorry. It's a wonder that I was never sued. (I wonder when the statute of limitations runs out?)

• People always ask, "How do you say all those lines with such a straight face?" The fact is we never did. We "broke" and laughed ALL the time. Just watch the bloopers (which are all over You-Tube). In fact we often had to hold the filming so that the laughter could die down enough to shoot. The worst culprit? Easy. Brian Baumgartner. You could sneeze wrong or say a silly word like *rumpus* or *porcupine* and he'd start to lose it.

The longest inappropriate laughter was during the episode "Lecture Circuit," when Dwight and Jim are put in charge of the Party Planning Committee and Dwight hangs tiny brown and gray balloons and a banner that reads IT IS YOUR BIRTHDAY. John and I literally could not stop laughing. We laughed until we cried. Production needed to be shut down for a twenty-minute break while we gathered ourselves and returned to film the scene.

Chapter 16

SOUL PANCAKES

———

SOME FRIENDS OF MINE AND I NEEDED A NAME FOR OUR NEW website venture. We got out some four-by-six note cards and started writing words we loved for the potential name on them and taping them all over the walls of singer/songwriter Andy Grammer's crappy West Hollywood apartment in 2007. (He was still a street musician on the Third Street Promenade at this point and not the international pop sensation of "Honey, I'm Good" and "Keep Your Head Up.") We sat on a recycled couch and stared up at the words in front of us. We needed something really special.

We had been talking for some time about a website that would explore "Life's Big Questions," that would dive into philosophy, creativity, and spirituality, attempting to make conversations about those topics cool again.

Then began the very bizarre quest to find an available domain name that worked for our idea. We knew we wanted a food item of some kind, something to "chew" on, something to "cook up." My original idea, Metaphysical Milkshake, was, *like me*, clunky, pretentious, and full of dairy.

We tried a number of different domain names with the word *spirit* at the top. Our first choice? *SpiritStew*. It was taken (damn!), so we tried *SpiritSouffle* (also taken), *SpiritSandwich* (an existing food blog), and *SpiritWaffle* (a hippie restaurant). (Note: *SpiritHákarl* was available, but *hákarl* is an Icelandic dish made of rotten shark meat. That's why the name was available.)

We tried leading off with *Profound*, but that didn't really resonate. Same with *Mystical* and *Holy*.

Then we moved on to the word *Soul* as a header. Somehow, some way, soul-crushingly, our top choice, *SoulTaco*, was also taken. This devastated us. I mean, who the HELL would have bought the domain name SoulTaco.com?!?!

Taped onto Andy's tacky textured, cream wall sat the word *Soul* on a card and *Pancake* on another, not far away. My eyes connected the dots. It was a delicious combination. Fun and accessible, it had an irreverent tone that referenced spirituality but didn't seem precious or overly serious. It was chewy and buttery and, most of all, the name stuck in your head. Like one of Andy Grammer's songs. (Which he insisted on practicing over and over again in his thin-walled bedroom down the hall while we were trying to pick our URL name.)

Miraculously, the domain was available and SoulPancake.com was born.

You see, in 2007 or thereabouts the Internet was a pretty sad place. There were far fewer positive options than there are these days. Whether it was degrading porn, cruel gossip, crass trolls, or meaningless materialism, the Web was a place to explore the very worst that humanity had to offer. It was like Caligula's Rome instead of Augustus's Pax Romana—filled with sadism, mindless debauchery, and pop-up ads for Viagra and credit scores. (Although the banner ad for cheap car insurance with a little Obama dancing the Cabbage Patch was pretty fun.)

A year earlier, when *The Office* was starting to take off, I knew I had a delectable opportunity. There were going to be resources available to do something really cool on the Web. I wanted to create something good and interesting and beautiful in that otherwise Hieronymus Bosch–esque landscape.

After some long consultations and soul searching with some spiritual-philosopher friends of mine, cofounders Joshua Homnick and Devon Gundry, we decided to create a destination on the Web for people interested in exploring big ideas through the portals of philosophy, creativity, and spirituality. We wanted our endeavor to be a successful business venture and not a nonprofit, because we felt there was a large, young audience out there that was longing for positive content. We wanted to try to make a beautiful Web destination with lots of eye-popping art, thought-provoking articles, inspiring videos, and discussion boards where people of different belief systems could come together and share their hearts and minds. A place to explore what it means to be a human being. Having myself been on a dramatic spiritual roller coaster earlier on in my life, and being fascinated by the mystical journeys that we all take on our short, eighty-year rides around the sun, I wanted to create a place where it would be safe to talk about the soul and faith as well as other big philosophical ideas.

The term *spirituality* had become so misused that people had a tremendously adverse reaction to the actual word itself. Similar to *moist, phlegm,* and *Bieber.* As I mentioned earlier, people seemed to associate the word *spirituality* with either 1) church or some kind of known religious institution, usually fundamentalist, or 2) a kind of hippie-dippy, airy-fairy, vague notion of a mystical pursuit that involved precious, tearful connections regarding auras, crystals, and yoga pants.

Would it be possible to take the word back in some way? we wondered. What could we do to make it the teensiest bit "cool" to talk about our hearts and minds and souls?

I had been wrestling with the word myself for quite some time and had come up with a peculiar spin on it. *Spirituality*, the way I had come to see it over the years, really referred to any expression of our higher self.

Example: We share a number of behaviors in common with monkeys. Both species like to poop and fornicate and fight and eat mangoes and groom themselves a great deal. We both have hierarchies, revere status and power, and hoard shiny things.

There are also a number of things we do that monkeys don't. We like to ponder our death and our fate as well as meditate and marvel on/at the beauty of the universe. We pray to a Creator and find meaning and devote altruistic acts of selfless service to one another. We long for purpose, share gratitude, and seek to connect hearts on ever deeper levels. We make artistic works of incredible mystery and vivid beauty. We make music. We dance. We weep and laugh. We love with a searing intensity.

It's those things, the things we *don't* have in common with the monkey, that, in my mind, are spirituality. The *life of the spirit* part of ourselves that is beyond the material, the animal, the base. It was those things we wanted to explore with SoulPancake. And we wanted to kick ass and have a great sense of humor while doing it.

The lens that we all settled on to view these disparate topics through came down to the phrase "CHEW ON LIFE'S BIG QUESTIONS." We at SoulPancake didn't have any answers or agenda. We wanted to make a playground for our users to search through these issues by themselves and find their own truth, just as I had done in my youth. We were really creating a tool that I might have used when I was a confused twenty-eight-year-old.

Humans have been chewing on the big questions of life since we were dancing by firelight in ancient caves and placing our handprints on the walls, drawing the spirits of the animals we hunted, and telling stories of ancient gods and the mysteries of existence. The ancient Greeks were awfully good at discussing and dissecting these most basic of human issues: free will, beauty, meaning, morality and ethics, and metaphysics. The Greeks themselves (especially Plato) were greatly inspired by the Jewish and Zoroastrian philosophies and the more mystical teachings of the Torah and the Pentateuch. Humanity continued these crucial conversations into the following centuries in the debates of Muslim poets and philosophers, the monasteries of the Middle Ages, and the bistros of Paris and Prague. The conversations continued, from the dorm rooms and coffee shops of twentieth-century universities all the way through to the message boards of the "question collective" on SoulPancake.com.

First we designed a website and brought on board our incredible creative team of Shabnam Mogharabi and Golriz Lucina, who have led our vision and aesthetic from the very beginning and continue to do so today. Golriz was a marketing and design genius from New Zealand and Nashville who has given our brand a vital, creative look and feel. Shabnam, our incredibly effective CEO, did her thesis at Northwestern's journalism school about a magazine that could make spirituality cool and relevant again for a young audience. When she heard about my plans through an early interview I did, she tracked me down and begged to be a part of it. And thank God she did, because her journalistic expertise was crucial to our launch and her business acumen has greatly aided our company.

We launched with a piece or two of content every day on our website, which was a tremendous amount of work. But most important, it was the Question Collective, where people could post and respond to each other's Life's Big Questions, where the site really took off. It was a dream come true to watch thousands of people diving into HUGE questions of life, philosophy, and humanity with creative gusto and open hearts. And the best thing? Pretty much troll free. All right, there was one guy who did call me "Lame" Wilson. And that one still stings a little bit. Full disclosure.

Probably the thing that helped us the most was a woman you might have heard of before called OPRAH FRIGGIN' WINFREY! Right as we were launching, I did a podcast with Oprah in Chicago for her *Soul Series* radio show. It was supposed to be a fifteen-minute conversation and we ended up talking for almost an hour. We discussed the ideas behind SoulPancake, the Baha'i Faith, and my life's journey, getting along famously all the while. Later, we would begin our foray into video production by creating what Oprah would call "little pieces of light" for her new channel, OWN. That set us down the path of doing more video production work for television and the Web. (And we're forever grateful, Ms. O!)

Things were buzzing along. Our mission was getting clearer.

I remember once on the set of *The Office*, Ed Helms asked me, "What's this SoulPancake thing I've been hearing about?" I told Ed that it was a website where people could explore creativity and spirituality.

Ed responded quizzically, "Aren't those things kind of mutually exclusive?"

I think Mr. Helms addressed a very sad fact in our contemporary culture. Art and spirituality, as I mentioned before, are simply different branches of the same expression of human transcendence. It's pretty pathetic that being creative, expressing one's soul, and creating things of beauty should be so separate in our society from the expression of the divine, the sacred, devotion, and faith. This is a new and not healthy thing, I believe. Throughout history, humanity has linked the expression and sacredness of the divine and the creation of art. Only today are they so compartmentalized. From Navajo rugs to the Sistine Chapel, from the whirling dervishes of Sufism to the statues of the Buddha, from the stories of the Mahabharata to Handel's *Messiah*, art and devotion have always been inexorably connected.

The founding team wrote a cool art/think book called *SoulPancake: Chew On Life's Big Questions*, and it became a *New York Times* bestseller. We made an iPhone app and moved deeper into television production, eventually doing a special for OWN, a documentary for MTV, and a music special for VH1, among other projects.

But it was on YouTube that SoulPancake found its voice and its purpose. We became a funded YouTube channel and entered a great relationship with Google, providing daily video content that sought to uplift and challenge our viewers and "Make Stuff That Matters."™

It was an exciting time, finding talent to collaborate with on our mini-network. We started shows like *Live a Little* with Candace Carrizales (Hunan Penguin), *The FlipSide* with Ben Shelton, and *SubCultures* with Erin Cantelo. We had shows featuring cutting-edge artists and man-on-the-street interviews. We profiled the homeless and staged gigantic street art installations. Our subscribers grew and grew. But it was two shows that we green-lit at the end of our first season that really put our channel on the map.

When we started brainstorming content, one of the topics I insisted we explore was the big D. No, not Deflategate. *DEATH!* I knew we had an opportunity to tackle this tremendously difficult universal human issue head-on, and our curious and brave audience would be up for the ride.

We started working with the talented filmmaker and actor (and fellow Baha'i) Justin Baldoni (*Jane the Virgin*), who approached us with a great idea. *My Last Days* was an exploration of what it means to experience life as related by people with terminal illnesses. No one knows better the intense gratitude, passion, and deep-hearted experience of living life to its fullest than those who are face-to-face with their own mortality on a daily basis.

What Justin and SoulPancake created was breathtaking. Heartwrenchingly life-filled stories brought to us by noble souls at the tipping point of death. Instead of maudlin, tear-jerking videos that leave you depressed, what Justin created were inspiring stories that filled the viewer with light, hope, and purpose. They were videos that could literally change your outlook on life as they moved you to your core. I would run into people who would tell me that they watched a *My Last Days* video every single day to remind them what a precious gift life is.

The show truly made its most profound impact when we profiled the late, great Zach Sobiech, who was diagnosed with osteosarcoma when he was fourteen. Zach was an angel. He glowed with love, wisdom, kindness, and life. He loved music and recorded several of his songs before he passed away. His gorgeous melody "Clouds" was made into a star-studded music video that went viral right before his passing.

When Zach died at age eighteen, "Clouds" went to number one on the iTunes chart and all proceeds (through Rock the Cause) went to the Zach Sobiech Osteosarcoma Fund, which is connected to the Children's Cancer Research Fund, raising over $1.2 million for research into a cure for this devastating children's cancer. That amount, doctors at the fund related, was potentially sufficient to be a catalyst for a research project for an effective treatment. In other words, Zach's courage, passion, talent, and sacrifice might someday lead to a cure for the cancer that ended his life far too soon.

We were honored to be a part of it and help tell Zach's story.

During our first year producing videos for the SoulPancake YouTube channel we had a very important discussion. Devon Gundry brought up the fact that our channel needed more "joy," and that the bringing of joy to our viewers was part of the service that SoulPancake needed to provide. It was our mission to break through the dark cynicism of the Internet with pure unadulterated upliftment (is that even a word?).

Bobby Miller, our resident Internet savant/YouTube channel manager, pointed out a couple of low-rent videos by an outrageous personality in rural Tennessee, "Kid President." Robby Novak was a nine-year-old boy in Henderson, Tennessee, who, along with his brother-in-law, the outrageously talented writer and director Brad Montague, had started to make some very charming videos with an outrageous persona. Their first video, in which Robby played the part of Kid President in his cardboard Oval Office, had only a few hundred views. We invited them to join SoulPancake, and a few months later, we produced his infamous "Pep Talk" video, which spread like wild-fire across a myriad of Facebook pages and has gained over thirty-five million views to date. An Internet star was born. One who has gained almost one hundred million video views, cowritten a bestselling book, and acted in ten episodes of his own TV show. His inspirational videos for moms, graduates, teachers, and kids are brilliantly set up as silly State of the Union addresses with stop-motion animation, non sequitur humor, and heartfelt messages woven in. He's met and in-terviewed President Obama and Beyoncé, as well as dozens of top film and music stars. He's helped the homeless by collecting over fifty thousand clean socks with the "Socktober" campaign and (with

ConAgra) helped donate two million meals to food banks across the country. Most important, Kid President's messages of hope and inspiration have touched millions of hearts and created millions of smiles. All this coming from a joyous young star who has suffered more than anyone can possibly imagine.

You see, by age eleven young Robby Novak had broken more bones than you AND everyone you know put together. The radiant little boy with that gigantic heart and contagious laugh tragically suffers from what is known as brittle bone disease and has had over *seventy broken bones* in his short life. I find it incredibly touching and beautiful that someone whose life's goal was to make the world more awesome has suffered so much pain. Ah, life.

My Favorite Kid President Quotes

- "Create something that will make the world more awesome."
- "Treat everybody like it's their birthday."
- "If you can't think of anything nice to say, you're not thinking hard enough."
- "Be somebody who makes everybody feel like a somebody."
- "Give the world a reason to dance!"
- "Us humans are capable of war and sadness and other terrible stuff. But also CUPCAKES!"
- "Love changes everything so fill the world with it!"
- "Grown-ups who dream are the best kinds of grown-ups."
- "Don't be IN a party. BE a party."

And my personal favorite,

- "Mail someone a corn dog."

I finally revived the name Metaphysical Milkshake and used the title for a philosophical talk show in the back of my 1976 Dodge van with such incredibly diverse and brilliant guests as Mindy Kaling (blech), Russell Brand, Deepak Chopra, Elon Musk, Joseph Gordon-Levitt, and Olivia Wilde. All these guests were so articulate and insightful (except for Kaling, who just kept checking her phone the whole time). There have been many other SoulPancake hit digital shows along the way, such as *Impress Me, The Science of Happiness,* and *Have a Little Faith,* and our little media company with a heart of gold keeps plugging along.

What we do touches people's hearts. There's nothing better in this world. I remember running into a young, excruciatingly shy SoulPancake fan at an unnamed conglomerate coffee chain who, halting and embarrassed, told me that he had suffered from depression his whole life, but one thing that helped him get through the day was watching a SoulPancake video every single morning for the past two years. That was one of the most satisfying conversations I've ever had in my life. But I still made him buy me a five-dollar decaf soy latte with nonfat vanilla. I gotta be me.

It's a difficult tightrope to walk, being a mission-driven company, balancing profit and heart. All difficulties aside, however, being able to connect the dots between creativity and devotion in an intimate way on SoulPancake has been richly personally satisfying. The concept of the "individual investigation of truth," which was so crucial for me in my own spiritual and artistic journey in my twenties, had now perfectly culminated in what we created on the Web. It felt humbling and gratifying to bring to life an actual tool that could aid young people on their own life's journey toward finding what was true for them. Perhaps they won't have to go down as many painful detours, with substances and self-imposed hurt, as I did at their age.

But there's another event that deepened these two aspects of my life to an even greater degree.

Like many other actors before me, I suppose, when I was starting to get well-known for my work, I was suddenly approached by dozens of nonprofits. Physicians for Social Responsibility, UNICEF, Libertarians for Somalia, Kitten Cancer League, Tree Huggers Who Hug Other Tree Huggers, Save the Grubworm, Kill the Grubworm, Sex Toys for Tots, the Union of Lisping Cyborgs, you name it. They wanted me to be a spokesperson, a board member, to speak at an event or MC a gala dinner or to just plain pony up some money.

I didn't want to blithely just say yes or no to all of these amazing and worthwhile causes without serious consideration. I wanted to deeply reflect on what role I could play as a minor television celebrity in relation to charity work and how I could best "give back."

When I reflect on my life and how much selfish career obsession I wallowed in during my youth, I wish that I had begun working in service to others at a much earlier stage. I mean, you don't need to be on television to start helping people. What a disgusting thought. I did occasionally volunteer or teach at inner-city schools, but it was piecemeal at best. There was a lot I could and should have given in my twenties and thirties. I think this happens a lot in our culture. People often think: If I can make X amount of money a year, once I have a family and a career, THEN I can give to others, but right now I'm focusing on my career and social life. This way of thinking, which I stupidly followed for years, is utter nonsense. Anyone at any time can participate in making Earth and humanity better by giving of themselves and their time.

But back to the moment at hand. Where did I want to put my time, energy, and resources? There was a tremendous opportunity for me to lend my voice to a cause. But what cause specifically? And why? It all felt a bit overwhelming.

That's when I heard from the Mona Foundation. Mona supported education internationally and its founder, Mahnaz Javid, knew my dad back in Seattle in the eighties. I was intrigued and started to dig in deeper. I read through its website and dug into its annual reports. What I found truly resonated with me and Holiday.

I realized that education was everything. Personally, it had obviously impacted my life to an incredible degree, but the more research and soul searching I did, the more connected to that fact I became. If one wants change in the world, education is the key. If you want to help with the environment, poverty, water issues, nutrition, global warming, hunger, women's issues, or discrimination, it is only through *education* that real change can be effected.

Also, education isn't "charity." I've come to despise that word. *Charity* implies *giving out* something to people who are less fortunate. It implies "we have" and "you don't have." There's a sense of pity attached to doling out to the poor. Education empowers. It uplifts. It allows the student to learn to give to themselves and their family, country, and community with self-respect and self-determination. Charity makes people dependent. Education makes them independent.

What was fascinating about the Mona Foundation was its commitment to *grassroots* education. It would find locally inspired educational initiatives that were *already working* and help those schools to grow over the years through long-term partnerships. The Mona schools had a commitment to the education of women and girls, a commitment to local sustainability, and, most important, a commitment to service in the community.

As opposed to the American model of education charities in developing countries, which was to plunk down in the middle of a poor place, build a fancy school, and try to get the students into top Western universities, the Mona model was to locate and assist preexisting schools that were already successfully serving their localities, run by a local board and having a commitment to uplifting both the country and their surrounding neighborhoods.

After doing many fund-raisers and interviews in support of Mona, Holiday and I got the chance to go down to Haiti to visit several of the Mona schools in late 2009. We were blown away.

The poverty was like none I'd ever seen before. I'd traveled a great deal in Central America. Been to Morocco and the Middle East as well. I'd seen much poverty in my travels but not anything *close* to what I saw in rural Haiti. It was like a chunk of the poorest Africa was dropped down on the end of a Caribbean island. Garbage was everywhere. Everything seemed broken. There was rampant unemployment and the most basic hygiene was impossible to maintain. It was a devastating experience to witness. And yet an inspiring one.

Holiday and I were instantly enamored of and taken with the Haitian people. Through the tremendous difficulties there, the Haitians rose tall. They had a vibrant culture, a beautiful language, and a fierce nobility and independence. We fell in love with Haitian arts and the indomitable spirit of the people. They were tough, bighearted, and funny as hell. We knew we wanted to be a part of Haiti in some way, shape, or form. It's a magical place, and people who visit fall in love with it.

Then came the *Goudou-Goudou*, the newly minted Creole word that onomatopoeia-dically symbolized the rolling shake of the great earthquake. On January 12, 2010, over the course of forty-five seconds, approximately two hundred thousand people died, three hundred thousand were injured, and more than a million were displaced. The hotel we had recently stayed at in Port-au-Prince was completely demolished, everyone inside crushed.

The world sat up and took notice of the disaster in a really positive way, and out of that unspeakable devastation some change and help seemed to be on its way to Haiti.

You all know the story of Sean Penn and his work in Haiti after the quake. It's indescribable what that man was able to do. Love him or hate him, the facts are that Sean formed J/P Haitian Relief Organization (J/P HRO) and saved thousands of lives, built tens of thousands of shelters, cleared hundreds of tons of rubble, and distributed medicine and hope throughout the country. Even now, the organization continues its amazing work and has single-handedly transformed a huge segment of the capital.

Six months after the quake, Holiday was invited to J/P HRO to do arts workshops with adolescent girls in the tent camps as part of a program sponsored by the United Nations and Full-Circle Learning. I was allowed to tag along and teach, but I was quietly skeptical. Why would adolescent girls without jobs, shoes, roofs, or food benefit from doing drama, photography, creative writing, and visual arts? They needed job training and pants and fresh water, not theater games, poetry, and pretty pictures.

Boy, was I wrong. The girls came in shy, insecure, timid, and filled with fear. Teenage boys from the surrounding tents gathered around the "community center" that had been built for us (a twenty-foot-by-twenty-foot mud patch surrounded by a wood fence and a straw roof, with chickens, pigs, and naked babies running around under our feet) and jealously jeered as the girls filed in to do the work.

One of the most eye-opening experiences was when we asked the girls some personal questions about themselves in a simple getting-to-know-you exercise. One of the questions was "What is your favorite color?" With the boys leaning in over the fence, the girls were shame-faced and quiet. As they attempted to answer we had a powerful realization. NO ONE HAD EVER ASKED THEM WHAT THEIR FAVORITE COLOR WAS BEFORE!!!

You see, in Haiti, as in many other lower-income countries, women for the most part are treated as work animals. Starting around age nine or ten they do all the cooking and cleaning, child rearing, water fetching, and selling in the market. Women and girls are the lowest priority to get an education in a family and often are doing the difficult work in the fields while the men and boys sit around and talk or play soccer with an old tennis ball. More than a third of Haitian girls are victims of sexual abuse and violence, and they are often pregnant by the time they're in their early teens.

Because of the cultural station of women, very rarely are girls asked even their most basic opinions or feelings or what they might care about. The educational system in Haiti is exactly the same as it was about a hundred years ago, with a lot of repetition and rote exercises that don't foster creativity.

So when we spent an intensive two weeks teaching the arts, creativity, and individual expression to forty brilliant young Haitian women, they truly bloomed with the work and the attention. By the final day, when they invited their families to view their artwork and photos, hear their stories and poems, and watch their theater presentation, the girls had truly transformed. They proudly disregarded the catcalling boys at the fence. The frail, insecure girls who had filed in two weeks earlier were now standing tall, sharing their work with a newfound confidence and power. And beaming faces. We knew we were onto something.

After getting many of them scholarships for furthering their schooling or vocational training, we discussed continuing the work on a greater scale along with our friend Dr. Kathryn Adams. Holiday is an insightful creative writing teacher who really knows how to coax out the genius in adolescent girls, and with my experience teaching acting, improv, and theater games, we knew we had something to offer. The idea of using the arts as a tool to empower adolescent girls, teach literacy, and help them begin their educational journey was the inspiration behind the foundation we created in 2013, Lidè.

Lidè currently serves almost five hundred at-risk girls in rural Haiti with a staff of thirteen Haitian teachers. (It should be noted that almost all girls in rural Haiti are "at risk.") We partner with local grassroots educational initiatives and offer our program as a way to help adolescent girls find their voice through the arts as well as provide scholarships, tutoring, and support for their future education.

There have been numerous studies suggesting that one of the most effective ways to reduce poverty is through the education of women and girls. It's one of the best returns on investment in the developing world, but sixty-six million girls worldwide are not enrolled in school. Educated women spread what they've learned to their families and villages and children. Educated girls get pregnant later, have fewer children, and have a far lower infant mortality rate. Educated women and girls have greater power to determine their own fate; earn more; live a rich, fulfilled life; and give back to their communities at a greater level.

I can't express the deep gratitude Holiday and I feel around being able to share the arts in a way that might be helpful to the incredible young women of Lidè. It puts everything in deep perspective.

For an even greater perspective, let's check out this poem by Esther Lajoie, who is fifteen years old, works on a farm, and is a student at Lidè. The students were asked by my wife as a writing prompt to compose a poem from the perspective of the sky.

I See the Sky

Yes.
I see the sky.
I see that sky looking at me

I see the sky as a great river
I see the sky as a giant tree
that sways with the wind as a rain falls

I see the sky
Yes, I see the sky
*I see the sky as the poto mitan**
I see the sky as the branches of the mango tree
that lets its mango fall

I talk to the sky
Yes, I talk to the sky
I tell him,
"Look at me to not make a mistake.
Look at me to not be afraid."

I talk to the Sky
Yes I talk to the sky.
I tell him,
"Never see just my surface. See me."

There's always been this strange kind of disconnect between playing oddball, mostly comedic characters and being a person who views himself as on a spiritual and artistic journey through life. As time goes

---

* A *poto mitan* is the pillar/central post that holds up a traditional Haitian round-house. Women in Haiti are called the *poto mitan*.

on I am finding new ways to greater link these two seemingly disparate sides of myself. It was through the creation of SoulPancake and Lidè that so many of my personal passions have been pulled together: comedy and spirituality, entertainment and big ideas, the arts and service to humanity. I've been blessed with these two great outlets in my life. With SoulPancake I've been able to combine creativity, humor, and service in a tangible, impactful way, and with Lidè, I've been able to use the arts to help heal, educate, and transform.

Actually, I should say, *three* great outlets. Because when I need to get a little crazy, just throw out all the rules, and vent the wild, untamed part of me, I break out my old bassoon. AND. I. ROCK. To quote Jim Morrison: "I am the Bassoon King! I can do ANYTHING!"*

---

* I may have gotten this quote wrong.

TEN THINGS I
KNOW FOR SURE

ONCE UPON A TIME, IN THE MAGICAL KINGDOM OF CHICAGO, the late great film critic Gene Siskel asked Oprah Winfrey, "What do you know for sure?" The question stumped her, inspired her, and the rest is history. She spent fourteen years giving an answer every week to that question on her website. The result became a bestselling book and a vehicle to distill the wisdom she gleaned in interviews with the world's greatest thinkers, writers, mystics, and artists over the past decades.

It's a great exercise. "What do you know for sure?" It's a question that reaches for the depths of any person's experience and wisdom.

Here I give it my best try at the tender age of forty-nine. (When I try this list again at ninety-nine, I'm sure it will look very, very different. It will probably have a lot more complaints about the government, technology, and "kids these days.")

Dear reader, I ask you to try the same thing! Take the "TEN THINGS I KNOW FOR SURE" CHALLENGE! Let's compare lists! What do you say?

1. THE DEEPEST HAPPINESS COMES FROM SERVICE TO OTHERS

I've written a good amount about happiness in this book, but I want to come back to one central idea. We often think that the best way to become happy is to focus more on ourselves, to take better care of ourselves and put our attention on the things that make us happy. While this is important, I've found that it often doesn't work.

There's kind of a strange paradox in happiness. The more we seek it for ourselves, the harder it often is to find.

But when we give service to others, uplift them, make them feel better, and sacrifice our own comfort to give them help and solace, we often feel joy. I know that I get a nice warm glow in my heart when I've helped a friend or someone in need. The same kind of glow you get when you watch that video on YouTube where that cat hugs that baby goat. (There's actually two cat and baby goat videos; one ends violently. Don't watch that one.)

One of my favorite quotes from the Baha'i Faith, attributed to 'Abdu'l-Baha, sums it up nicely.

> Be not the slave of your moods, but their master. But if you are so angry, so depressed and so sore that your spirit cannot find deliverance and peace even in prayer, then quickly go and give some pleasure to someone lowly or sorrowful, or to a guilty or innocent sufferer! Sacrifice yourself, your talent, your time, your rest to another, to one who has to bear a heavier load than you—and your unhappy mood will dissolve into a blessed, contented submission to God.

Try it at home, kids! Let me know how it works.

2. IF YOU THINK YOU'RE BEING FUNNY, YOU'RE NOT BEING FUNNY

My least-favorite kind of comedy acting is the kind where the performers know they're just being hysterical. Anytime I see that twinkle in an actor's eye where they're just certain that they're being cute, charming, and inventive, I want to throw up in my mouth. That little know-it-all wink and smirk that many actors bring to their characters completely takes me out of any belief or enjoyment.

The most lasting and riveting comedy performances are the ones where the actors are as deeply invested in their emotions and stakes as if they were in a Shakespearean tragedy. Personally? I want to see *real* characters in comedy, dealing with the essential things we all struggle with but on a grander and more absurd scale. That's the essence of "clowning," I believe, and allows comedy to transcend and explode.

Some great examples:

a. Chris Farley's motivational speaker
b. Buster Keaton
c. Nicolas Cage in *Adaptation*
d. Peter Sellers as Inspector Clouseau
e. Fox News

The only exception:

a. Jerry Seinfeld

3. GRATITUDE CHANGES EVERYTHING

When I'm feeling sorry for myself, negative, or depressed, I try to go to gratitude. There's always something to feel grateful for. Even a person who has nothing but a chicken and a shiny pebble can be thankful for the health of their nice chicken and the luster of their pebble. It's really a matter of focus.

Try making a list of ten things you're grateful for every day for a week. Send that list to a good friend. You'll find that your week will greatly improve.

Even when I've been at my lowest I'll try to put my attention toward a tiny handful of things I feel grateful about and find a subtle but much-needed shift in my mood and outlook.

I'm so grateful that you've read this far in my book!

4. ROME IS THE GREATEST CITY ON EARTH

If you put the Eiffel Tower on the banks of the Tiber, no one would ever go to Paris again. Rome kicks Paris's butt. First of all, Italian is such a cool language! It's the real language of love. It's also the language of Marcello Mastroianni, da Vinci, and the cast of *Jersey Shore*.

The food is incredible. The ancient ruins spill out onto the Roman streets, which are filled with buzzing, Day-Glo Vespas. The art is exquisite and spans the centuries. There are fountains everywhere.

Also, get this. Paris was founded by a Roman! And Rome itself? Founded by two guys who were NURSED BY A WOLF! Take that, Paris.

Also, pear gelato.

5. THE OPINIONS OF OTHER PEOPLE ARE NOT SOMETHING TO WORRY ABOUT

I once heard this awesome quote from a friend of mine:

"What other people think of you is none of your business; what you think of other people is ALL of your business."

I have spent so much of my time over the course of my life wondering, worrying, and fretting about what other people think of me. It's such a colossal drag. When I can occasionally remember this quote, I retain my balance and find my center again.

I also can quite easily slip into judgment and resentment about other people. When I'm able to remember the second part of this quote, it brings me back down to earth in a gentle way.

My job, I believe, is to stay the hell out of other people's heads and just focus on what's going on in my own big, weird head.

6. *GAME OF THRONES* IS OUR GREATEST TEACHER

A few things I've learned from the greatest TV show in the history of everything:

  a. Get a wolf
  b. Get a dragon
  c. Women should rule the world (unless it's Cersei Lannister)
  d. Politics are a waste of breath and time

I was truly struck by this amazing quote from Ygritte, the wildling lover of the bastard Jon Snow: "All men must die, Jon Snow, but first we'll *live!*"

That pretty much sums it all up, doesn't it? We are all going to die, but let's live to the fullest before we kick it. It doesn't matter if you live in Westeros or on planet Earth. Whether it's checking out the slave fights in the Great Pit of Daznak in Meereen or canoeing the Colorado River, whether it's exploring the lands north of the Wall or dancing the samba in Rio, we all need to LIVE before we die.

The other lesson that can be learned from *Game of Thrones* regards its famous refrain: "Winter is coming." In the books by George R. R. Martin, seasons last for decades, and as the story is kicking in, the long summer and fall are ending and freezing storm clouds are massing in the north along with the terrible White Walkers and their vast undead army.

So basically, unavoidable chaos is coming and winter will destroy the whole kingdom of Westeros. And what do the folks of Westeros do when their very existence is at stake? They battle and intrigue and gossip and infight and drink buckets and buckets of wine.

And us? We spend most of our time talking about Kardashians, partisan politics, the next iPhone, and offensive tweets by professional athletes instead of climate change and global warming, which could very well be the greatest challenge for survival humanity has ever faced.

Basically, I'd like to see Hillary Clinton on a dragon.

7. SUSHI IS ABOUT THE FISH, IDIOTS

Sushi is raw fish. Fresh, oily, fatty, delicate, slightly cool, thinly sliced or expertly cubed sections of the delicious nectar of the sea. That's the whole point of sushi.

When you eat rolls slathered with cream cheese, fried onions, flavored mayonnaise, syrup, tempura shrimp poppers, mango chutney, and deep-fried marshmallows, you are missing the entire point of sushi and should just go eat at Applebee's™. (Especially on "Wings 'n' Waffles Wednesdays.")

When you roll your piece of sushi in a pool of salty soy sauce, stack a pile of ginger on top of your fish, or wipe the entire surface of the sushi with wasabi, you are committing a crime against fish, the ocean, and even the great Poseidon himself.

Eat a delicious raw piece of fish, wrapped in a tiny belt of seaweed on a small bed of fluffy rice. Stir a little bit of wasabi into the soy sauce and let a small amount graze the fish itself (without using your rice as a soy sauce sponge). Enjoy the piece in one single bite, and savor the glorious explosion of seafood goodness. You're welcome, America. And Japan.

8. MY SON IS MY SENSEI

Walter has an open heart, a ridiculous sense of humor, and an ability to always be curious, making every moment an inspirational adventure.

Also, he sings and dances unprompted at any occasion.

Every problem, issue, anxiety, fear, and stressor that I have can be solved by watching my son explore the woods, the beach, or even the backyard and by singing and dancing as he does, spontaneous and unself-conscious.

9. STORIES MAKE THE WORLD GO ROUND

The greatest thing ever in the history of the world and all of human endeavor from time immemorial is *stories*. Think about it. Where would we be without them? From shamans dancing around a fire to the Bible. From Norse myths to Greek drama, from West African griots to ghost stories, from fairy tales to *Star Wars*. Stories not only entertain us but tell us who and why we are, and what we believe collectively and individually.

My wife has taught me so much about stories as she writes them, ponders them, spins them, and as we read them aloud in our home. We work with at-risk, traumatized girls of rural Haiti to tell their stories in their unique voices.

When you are able to tell your own story, you heal yourself. Therapists work with victims of trauma to tell the story of their life, to help them *own* their story, warts and all, and in so doing to find their voice, spirit, and healing.

Children from every culture and era on Earth have listened with rapt attention to stories. All you need is a hero; a beginning, middle, and end; some kind of surprising twist, and you've got a story. You've just read mine. What's yours?

10. I DON'T KNOW ANYTHING

Addendum

THE BAHA'I FAITH

An Introduction

(Because People Keep Bugging Me for One)

I'm going to attempt to summarize the newest, the second-most widespread, and one of the fastest growing of the world religions, the Baha'i Faith. It's a bit tricky to try to capsulize in a few short pages a global faith that has six million adherents, hundreds of prayers, thousands of pages of holy writings, and a rich, complex, dramatic history. A faith that is filled with numerous mystical teachings, practical guidelines for the betterment of both oneself and the world, and simple, profound truths to help the human heart find peace and meaning. But if I *HAD* to sum it up—like, say, into the length of a tweet—I would say, "Awesome religion that acknowledges the awesomeness of all the other religions too." However, that would be an extremely limited definition. (Which is why Twitter may not actually be the ideal vehicle for complex philosophical and geopolitical discussions.)

So, to paint a fuller picture of what it is to be a Baha'i, let's start at the very beginning. With God. Always a good starting point.

GOD

To every discerning and illuminated heart it is evident that God, the unknowable Essence, the Divine Being, is immensely exalted beyond every human attribute, such as corporeal existence, ascent and descent, egress and regress. Far be it from His glory that human tongue should adequately recount His praise, or that human heart comprehend His fathomless mystery.

—Baha'u'llah

In the Baha'i cosmology, there is one God. This might not be a God like you've ever conceived of before. This God is an all-knowing, all-loving, creative force whose presence is felt everywhere and yet whose essence is unknowable. This is not some anthropomorphic deity—a judgmental old man with a beard in a cloud-studded landscape, scowling down on us, keeping tabs, and deciding who is naughty and nice. That would be Santa. (If you worship Santa, no offense; that's actually pretty cool and I'd love to hear about it!)

This is the omniscient, eternal, infinite Creator of light, nature, science, and love. This God knows our hearts better than we do and is a better friend to us than we are to ourselves. This is the God who ignited the big bang and fills our world with beauty, mystery, and science. The Lord of not just this physical universe, but of myriad other universes and planes of existence as well. The Great Mystery.

I have breathed within thee a breath of My own Spirit, that thou mayest be My lover.

—Baha'u'llah

What's great about what Baha'is believe is that there are *not* lots of different gods in the world. There is only *one*. Allah, Jehovah, Ra, Brahman, Wakan Tanka, Elohim, Ahura Mazda, the Great Spirit, the Prime Mover, the Big Guy Upstairs. Call Him/It/She what you like, there is only one all-seeing Creator.

GOD'S MANIFESTATIONS

This Divine Mystery wants what is best for us all, both individually and collectively. So what does He do? He sends us great spiritual teachers every five hundred or thousand years or so to help our species move forward. I'm sure you've heard of most of these prophets (in no particular order): Jesus, Muhammad, the Buddha, Abraham, Zoroaster, Krishna, Adam, Moses, and now, most recently, the divine messenger and central figure of the Baha'i Faith, Baha'u'llah, a man who lived in nineteenth-century Persia.

These "divine physicians" diagnose what humanity most needs and bring a remedy, focusing their spiritual cure on the specific time, place, and culture where they appear. Just as humanity needs to progress materially and scientifically, we need to progress *spiritually* as well. It is these special "messengers" of God who bring the revelation and teachings from our Creator that aid us in progressing morally, emotionally, and ethically, and give our warlike, selfish, animalistic species wisdom and peace. These prophets of God (or, as Baha'is refer to them, "Manifestations of God") rekindle the flame of the eternal faith of God in the land in which they appear. This concept is called "progressive revelation."

You see, according to the Baha'i Faith, there is really only one religion. One God. One faith. Baha'u'llah calls it "the changeless Faith of God, eternal in the past, eternal in the future."

Every religion is eventually corrupted by its fallible clergy and the slow, inevitable drift toward hollow ritual and empty ceremony. Every faith gradually moves away from the spark of sacred divine light that was at the center of its creation toward hollow superstition. The differences in the world's religions aren't to be found in the essential teachings of these divine manifestations but in the dogmas and creeds that were developed over long periods of time by their followers, administrators, and clergy.

That's why religion needs refreshing every millennium or so. (Like Spider-Man, Congress, or *The View*. Sorry, couldn't resist.)

WHAT BAHA'U'LLAH TAUGHT

Every faith on earth has a mythology contained in it of a "promised one." The return of the spirit of Truth that will guide us unto all truth. That is who Baha'is believe Baha'u'llah is: the promised one. The Prince of Peace. The new messiah.

Baha'u'llah teaches that it is time for humanity to heal itself, to mature, to seek love and unite.

He says: "O ye children of men! The fundamental purpose animating the Faith of God and His Religion is to safeguard the interests and promote the unity of the human race, and to foster the spirit of love and fellowship amongst men."

He brings the word of God for today, Baha'is believe. And what is that word? That all prejudice, of race and class and every other stripe, be eliminated because we really are one human family. That women have a station equal to that of men and that their rights need to be upheld until gender equality and justice have been achieved. Baha'u'llah taught that science and religion are like two wings of the bird of humanity and need to be in harmony in order for humankind to thrive. Science without religion is materialism and religion without science is mere superstition. Baha'u'llah professed that universal education is an essential component of the maturation of humanity and a crucial force for the elimination of the terrible radical extremes of wealth and poverty that plague our planet today. He encouraged Baha'is to promote social justice but stay away from the dead-end bickering and financial corruption of partisan politics.

The need for a clergy is now over, Baha'u'llah taught. Humanity can interpret the word of God for itself and doesn't need any kind of intermediary who holds a special divine station. So the Baha'i Faith has no priests or mullahs or rabbis or gurus. Instead, the administrative affairs are governed by various democratically elected "Assemblies" that function on a local, national, and international level.

Baha'u'llah revealed moral laws to protect us, such as abstaining from drugs, alcohol, and gambling as well as backbiting and gossip. These rules are not a mere "code of laws" but are there for the benefit of our souls, to help us as we develop them in this material world. It is our spiritual qualities that we take with us when we move on to the next world (there is no hell or eternal damnation or any of that nonsense), and it is virtues like compassion, honesty, kindness, humility, and the like that we need to nurture and grow during this short life we're given.

The metaphor that's often used in the Baha'i Faith is the comparison of the growth of our souls on Earth to the growth of a baby in the womb. The baby has no idea why it's growing its fingers and legs and eyelids and toes while hanging around in utero. Those things are pretty useless for it in the womb but absolutely crucial when it emerges into this world. In the same way, we're growing spiritual fingers and eyelids and toes right here and now that we'll need when we leave this plane of existence. Those qualities of God, the virtues perfectly manifested by Jesus and the Buddha and Baha'u'llah, like wisdom, service, and love, will be our spiritual arms and legs before too long. That's why we need moral laws to protect us and why walking the spiritual path is crucial to our ultimate development and our deepest individual and collective flourishing.

Unfortunately, as all the great religious teachers tell us, it's through tests and difficulties that our souls grow the most. The Buddha tells us, "Life is suffering." He and Baha'u'llah both teach that it is our ego and our attachment to the material world that bring us the most distress. As our trials in this world release us from these attachments, ever reminding us that love, connection, service, and unity are what truly matter, we grow closer to God and more spiritually mature.

BAHA'I HISTORY

Baha'u'llah (Mirza Hussein-'Ali), who was born in 1817 in what is today Iran, was tortured terribly and banished from country to country. He was a follower of a man called "The Bab" or "The Gate" (Siyyid 'Ali-Mohammad). The Bab, Baha'is believe, is also a divine teacher, one who was sent, like John the Baptist for Christ, to prepare the way for Baha'u'llah. To claim to be a prophet from God, or to follow someone who made that claim, was considered blasphemy by the Islamic clergy, punishable by death. Tens of thousands of followers of the Bab and early Baha'is were killed and tortured in the first decades of the Faith, their property confiscated, their holy sites desecrated. (In fact, still to this day, Baha'is are the largest religious minority in Iran and are brutally persecuted in all sorts of overt and covert ways.)

Baha'u'llah received his revelation from God while incarcerated in a legendary dungeon in Tehran, a former underground water cistern used to hold prisoners on death row called the Black Pit. There he was visited by an angelic presence. He says:

> I was but a man like others, asleep upon My couch, when lo, the breezes of the All-Glorious were wafted over Me, and taught Me the knowledge of all that hath been. This thing is not from Me, but from One Who is Almighty and All-Knowing. And He bade Me lift up My voice between earth and heaven . . .

It was in 1863, in Baghdad, after his property was confiscated and he was booted from Tehran and Persia, that Baha'u'llah proclaimed his "Mission." He had been on a walkabout of sorts, spending two years living as a mystic and a hermit in the mountains of Kurdistan, and a while after he returned he stood before a small group of followers and proclaimed what had been revealed to him, that he was the Manifestation of God for this modern age. He was then banished to Constantinople and then to Adrianople by the Ottoman government, and he and his family finally ended up in the prison city of Acre (Akko) in Palestine (near Haifa, Israel, today). It was in and around that miserable prison that Baha'u'llah spent the rest of his days. It is there where he is buried, where the Baha'is have their Holy Land. On and around Mount Carmel lie several Baha'i holy shrines as well as the Baha'i international administrative offices.

Baha'u'llah wrote tablets to all the kings and rulers of the earth, announcing himself as the Promised One of the Ages, the mouthpiece of God for this day. Every one of those kings and emperors ignored the letters (except for Queen Victoria) and every single one who did, as predicted by Baha'u'llah, was overthrown or fell from power shortly thereafter.

'ABDU'L-BAHÁ

After Baha'u'llah passed away, his son Abbás Effendí, who called himself 'Abdu'l-Bahá (the Servant of Glory), was appointed to take the reins of the budding faith by his father. He is considered the perfect exemplar of the teachings of his father; he wrote countless letters and tablets and in 1912, having been released from imprisonment, he traveled all around America, proclaiming universal love and brotherhood and the beauty of the faith of his father.

One of 'Abdu'l-Bahá's most compelling teachings has to do with the spiritual destiny of the United States. He has said:

> The American continent gives signs and evidences of very great advancement; its future is even more promising, for its influence and illumination are far-reaching, and it will lead all nations spiritually. The flag of freedom and banner of liberty have been unfurled here, but the prosperity and advancement of a city, the happiness and greatness of a country depend upon its hearing and obeying the call of God.

ADDENDUM: THE BAHA'I FAITH

WHAT DO BAHA'IS DO?

At this time, the Baha'i Faith is the second-most widespread of the world's religions and there are many areas of the planet where the Faith is especially flourishing and spreading, transforming lives and communities—places as far-flung as India, Mongolia, the Pacific Islands, Congo, Colombia, and Cambodia. There are also many areas in the United States where the Baha'i Faith is quite strong and growing in a lively fashion.

So, what do Baha'is do, exactly? (Other than play nerdy office workers and alcoholic detectives on network television, of course.) They pray and meditate every day. They meet every nineteen days for what is called a Baha'i Feast, where there is music, prayer, and food, and where the administrative affairs of the community are discussed. Baha'is fast by not eating or drinking for nineteen days in the spring from sunrise to sunset in a similar fashion to Ramadan.

But most important, Baha'is believe that we have a twofold moral purpose. We need to work on making ourselves better human beings, one day at a time, working on our character defects and our spiritual qualities. The other moral purpose we must undertake is to make the world a better, more just and unified place.

Everywhere you go, you will find Baha'is involved in their communities, volunteering and promoting education. They hold devotional gatherings for people of all faiths as well as neighborhood children's classes that stress positive virtues and character traits. There are study circles that are held in homes, where many aspects of the Faith are explored, and what are called Junior Youth Spiritual Empowerment Programs, where teens of all faiths mentor and train preteens in an effort to promote service to the community.

There are many ways to positively affect the world: political advocacy, nonprofits, environmental movements, faith-based initiatives, therapeutic and new age classes, economic plans, etc. . . . But Baha'is believe that lasting, significant change can only be brought about through the fundamental spiritual transformation of humanity. Until all seven billion of us individually, collectively, and politically truly know in our hearts that it is through loving harmony and the pursuit of true collaboration that we can heal the problems of the world, nothing will be attained. The issues facing our race are vast and the needs of the hour are imperative. Baha'is believe that Baha'u'llah's profound message of peace and unity is crucial in facilitating this transformation.

I hope that summed things up well enough. There are hundreds of other ways to find out more detailed information. I'll leave that for you to find. Bahai.org is a good enough place to start.

I will end with one of my favorite quotes by Baha'u'llah. Here he describes something incredible to strive for, as difficult as it may seem.

Be generous in prosperity, and thankful in adversity. Be worthy of the trust of thy neighbor, and look upon him with a bright and friendly face. Be a treasure to the poor, an admonisher to the rich, an answerer to the cry of the needy, a preserver of the sanctity of thy pledge. . . . Be a home for the stranger, a balm to the suffering, a tower of strength for the fugitive. Be eyes to the blind, and a guiding light unto the feet of the erring. Be . . . a dew to the soil of the human heart, an ark on the ocean of knowledge, a sun in the heaven of bounty, a gem on the diadem of wisdom, a shining light in the firmament of thy generation, a fruit upon the tree of humility.

A "fruit upon the tree of humility"? Obviously, I've got some work to do.

ABOUT THE FONT

This book was printed in Augstaben, a font created by Augustus Rookenstabën, a printer and punch cutter from Trier, Germany, who attempted unsuccessfully to create a typesetting machine that would be suitable for use by the undead. In 1714 his body was repeatedly run through his printing press by an angry mob until, it was rumored, his blood trickled out in tiny, perfect Augstaben. Rookenstabën died penniless, driven to madness by the greater success of his estranged wife, Helen Vetica.

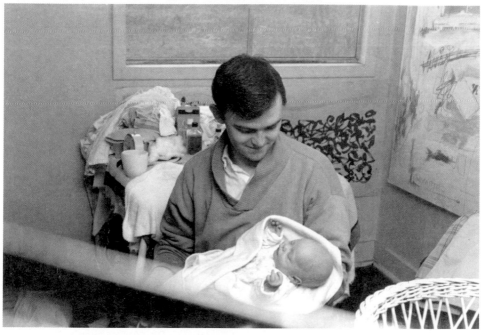

My dad holding Baby Fathead in 1966

Shay holding Baby Fathead in 1966

Mom-less kid (circa 1967/68)

Stepmom Kristin and me in Mexico. Right before Nicaragua.

Flying a kite on the streets of Bluefields, Nicaragua

My dad and me on a Nicaraguan beach

Bowl-cut Seahawks fan (circa 1978)

My dad and Oscar with his $1,000 check for the publication of *Tentacles of Dawn*. I'm wearing a terry cloth shirt.

A prescient yearbook entry by one Brian Highberger. Dear Brian, my name has two n's; and guess what, my show WAS CANCELED!

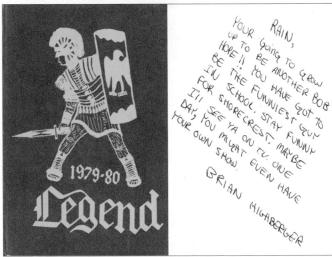

RAIN,
YOUR GOING TO GROW UP TO BE ANOTHER BOB HOPE !! YOU HAVE GOT TO BE THE FUNNIEST GUY IN THE SCHOOL. STAY FUNNY FOR SHORECREST. MAYBE I'LL SEE YA ON TV. ONE DAY, YOU MIGHT EVEN HAVE YOUR OWN SHOW.
BRIAN HIGHBERGER

CHESS CLUB/SKI CLUB

Chess Club

LEFT: Chess Club did very well this year. The group had four wins, one loss to Blanchet, and one forfeit to West Seattle. The group took second place at the Shoreline Invitional and did very well at State. Members, shown left, are: Advisor-John Tracy, BACK ROW: Tony Matosich, Jeff Schuh, Todd Born, Blake Kremer. ROW 1: Carolyn Gross, Mike Wenzel, Terry Hsu, Rainn Wilson.

WE ARE THE CHAMPIONS! (I cut out the ski club. Idiots.)

So excited about my shiny new bassoon!

Me playing Alfred
Doolittle in *Pygmalion*
at New Trier High
School, 1983. That night
I improvised putting
candy in my pocket.
(With Peter Leondedis,
Jim True-Frost, and
Terri Kapsalis)

Trying to be "New Wave." Notice the Jam poster, the cassette deck, and the sci-fi books.

My very first actor's head shot, in 1985

Holiday and me when we first got together in 1990. The hair! (This photo was later altered to show young Dwight and Jim at Dunder Mifflin.)

IRENE HAUPT

With Jeffrey Guyton in the Acting
Company's 1990–91 production of *The
Two Gentlemen of Verona*

Man with a van (circa 1994)

True love with
crooked paintings

Backstage for the show *Venus*. Getting ready to put a penis on my face.

Long Day's Journey into Night (with the late, great Tana Hicken) at Arena Stage

JOAN MARCUS

Our incredible volcano wedding

London Assurance,
Roundabout Theatre
(with Kathryn Meisle)

CAROL ROSEGG

The New Bozena: Ramon (David Costabile), Revhanavaan Sahaanahanadaan (Kevin Isola), and Spiv Westenberg (Michael Dahlen)

On the set of *Almost Famous*

One of these things is not like the others (*Sahara*)

Coming back from
the hospital, miracle
baby intact!

Me and baby Walter

Halloweird

Behind the scenes at *The Rocker*: Fish and son

Weird-ass crime fighters (*Super*)

The baby whisperer

My hot wife

Emmy reject

Three dirty girls

Behind the scenes at the Sesame
Avenue Daycare Center for
Infants and Toddlers with Mose
Schrute (Michael Schur)

Camaro love

Final night of shooting our show

Bobbleheaded. (At *The Office* parade and concert in Scranton where 10,000 people came to bid us farewell. One of the funnest days of my life.)

Holiday and me teaching theater games for Lidè in Haiti

Our extended family, including Riba, the miniature horse, and Derek, the zonkey